SELF PUBLISHING BLUEPRINTS

MAKE YOUR BOOK A SUCCESS

Albert Griesmayr

Copyright note:

Disclaimer:

While every effort has been made to accurately represent how to successfully market books and how to increase sales revenue and readership from books, there's no guarantee that you'll earn any money. Examples and income projections in this book shouldn't be interpreted as a promise or guarantee of earnings. Also, keep in mind that digital publishing is changing fast; as a result, examples or projections might be different at your specific time of reading. Earning potential is entirely subjective and dependent on the person utilizing the strategies, tools, and resources contained herein.

Disclaimer [Thumbnails & External Sources]:

This publication uses thumbnails (or small screenshots), compressed preview images of originals with links to external sources, to illustrate teachings and to help students and readers understand the concepts and materials. For most thumbnails and sources used, the original creators and sources have been contacted in order to receive permission to use photographed material. However, in some cases, this might not have been possible. In case you are featured in this publication in some form (source, screenshots, thumbnails) and you do not want that, please contact us via hello@scribando.com. We will investigate your request and remove copyrighted or otherwise restricted material related to your personal or business rights within a reasonable timeframe. Thank you.

CLAIM YOUR SURPRISE GIFT

Thank you for purchasing this book.
To show my appreciation, I've prepared a special gift for you that will help you to sell more books.
Access it by visiting:
www.albertgriesmayr.com/thank-you

TABLE OF CONTENTS

ABOUT THE AUTHOR

Albert Griesmayr (MBA) is founder & CEO of the book publishing startup Scribando | Novelify. It has proudly helped more than 10,000 authors to create successful book projects since 2013. He personally has consulted for more than 100 authors, among them bestselling- and award-winning authors, such as BC Schiller, Patrick McKeown, and Garret Kramer, with combined sales of more than 2 million copies. His company Scribando | Novelify was selected as a 2013 participant of the Go Silicon Valley initiative of the Austrian Chamber of Commerce.

In addition, he is the innovative creator of the book marketing initiatives "Lean Book Publishing" and "Who-Wrote-It". He shares his latest book marketing insights on scribando.com and albertgriesmayr.com, and is a frequent speaker at global book marketing events.

INTRODUCTION

Dear author,

When I look at my most successful client projects over the last few years, I see one thing they always have in common: they are built on the foundation of a brilliant book.

A book so brilliant that you can plug it in to proven marketing processes and know that it will take off from there.

A book so brilliant that once it reaches the tipping point of marketing, it will sustain itself.

If you have that foundation – a truly brilliant book – and combine it with the proven book launching tactics in this book, you'll find success. That's my promise from the start.

On the other hand, you might ask yourself, "If it's that simple, why do I need to read this trilogy and learn more about book marketing?"

The challenge here is developing a deeper understanding, as well as following through with excellent execution.

Newbies in any given industry or sport don't have a chance at their game simply by understanding what is required on a higher level. Rather, a newbie needs to dive deeper, learning the many facets that go into their chosen area. And it's the same with finding success with your book – if you're a newbie, you need to learn how to create a truly outstanding book, as well as the intricacies of marketing. In the end, once you develop that understanding, it still requires a substantial amount of willpower and persistence to execute the launch in a way that works.

That's where the need for powerful knowledge comes in. Powerful knowledge of proven techniques and insights that have helped the hundreds of authors and publishers that I've worked with over the years. Powerful knowledge that has catapulted them into true excellence, enabling them to outsmart their competition. With this trilogy, I'm inviting you to look behind the curtain – to really understand what is needed for success in self-publishing.

This trilogy is designed to be used in this way:

- ☑ First, read Book Marketing Secrets to equip yourself with timeless, fundamental marketing insights for successful book publishing
- ☑ Second, read Bestseller, which contains the Perennial Bestseller Blueprint, my recommended approach to the core process that creates a book that is successful in the long-term and brings in constant passive income
- ☑ Third, read Book Sales Explosion, which shows you the thirty best tactics for selling books and growing book sales over time – plus some bonus tricks and tips

The powerful knowledge in this book has helped dozens of award-winning, best-selling authors that I've worked with, such as Patrick McKeown (The Oxygen Advantage), Harvey Mackay (Swim with the Sharks) and James Kahn (Melrose Place, Star Wars), to find success with their books.

The main competitive advantage for today and the future is wrapped up in the attitude of excellence. Competition increases year by year, with more books being released every day. Book marketing technology, especially as used by the big-name retailers, is becoming more and more sophisticated. Amazon already calculates conversion rates based on specific search terms, position on bestseller lists, and other placement data. It will continue to use its own data in order to decide which books to promote and which to ignore.

The good news is that, once you've achieved "excellence," success will become easier.

The bad news is that getting to that point is getting harder every day.

That's why you need to be prepared. That's why this trilogy might be one of the most important reads in your career as an author.

Before I invite you to start reading Book Marketing Secrets, I'd like to tell you the following story. During the Tokyo Olympics in 2021 there was an Equestrian competition in which a female German athlete, who was far ahead of the competition before the last run, basically only needed to walk through the final round on her horse to win the gold medal. Everyone thought that all was settled. Destiny, though, had prepared a different outcome. Just before the run, the horse decided to refuse to walk and jump, causing the athlete to aggressively force the horse into movement. Not only did it cause something of a scandal, it cost the athlete her dreams of an Olympic medal. As sad as it was to watch the scene, it's a powerful reminder of an important lesson.

I watched this scene live on TV and felt deeply sorry – first of all for the horse, which was treated badly and should have been immediately removed from the competition for its own well-being. Secondly, I felt bad for the competitor. Not only did she lose her dream of winning gold, but she also lost her reputation due to treating the horse badly. For her, it all changed in just a matter of seconds. Later on, I thought over the event and realized three things I could learn that related to book publishing.

1) It takes a lifetime to build up a reputation, but only seconds to destroy it. Don't take shortcuts in critical areas, such as citing and referencing correctly. Be careful and ethical with the information you publish. Make sure to use correct data, don't blatantly offend people, and act according to values and shared principles.
2) You can be the best in the world in what you do, but you still need the elements to align in order to win and succeed. In book publishing, most importantly, you need a fantastic book for your foundation.
3) Listen to the universe. You might want to reach your publishing goals so badly that you take risky shortcuts, dismiss concerns, and ignore negative feedback. Sometimes, though, it's important to stand still and listen. Listen to your readers, to the voice of the universe, and to your own best self. Take the time to stand still and listen often, reflecting on

what you've done and what you plan to do, to make sure that it feels right.

Over the next 400 pages, you will learn all you need to have outstanding book success, and I am glad that I am able to help you along your journey.

Albert Griesmayr
Vienna, August 25, 2021

BOOK 1

BOOK MARKETING SECRETS

The 10 fundamental secrets for selling more books and creating a successful book publishing career

X- NOTE FROM THE AUTHOR

Hello author,

It's great getting to know you. First of all, I want to extend my gratitude to you for purchasing my book. This book contains my most valuable and timeless secrets for making your book successful. This is knowledge that I've proactively acquired by helping more than 10,000 authors to market their books successfully through my book publishing platforms over the last 10 years. It embodies lots of timeless knowledge, tactics and strategies that, applied correctly, would have made your book successful not only in 2019, but earlier as well. My goal is that it'll also make your book successful in 2020, 2025, and hopefully even in 2030 and later. I will certainly update the book over time, and make sure it stays on top to deliver you and your book the cutting edge you need to succeed in the changing book publishing landscape.

Before jumping right into the 10 book marketing secrets, I want to use this chance to quickly introduce myself and to share with you why this book is so important to me.

So who am I? My name is Albert Griesmayr, and I'm the founder of the book publishing startup Scribando

| Novelify which focuses on helping writers to sell more books. Besides this, I'm the creator of Lean Book Publishing [leanbookpublishing.com], Who-Wrote-It [who-wrote-it.com], and the Modern IQ [modern-iq.com].

Over the last 10 years, I have been fortunate enough to work personally with more than a hundred authors and publishers from around the world. I have helped them to create winning book marketing strategies and shared my insights with them along their publishing journeys. Helping authors and working with them is immensely rewarding to me.

There is one thing, though, that keeps hurting me. And this is seeing authors with great book ideas and everything necessary to make it big, failing because they did not know about the fundamentals and underlying secrets behind successful book publishing before they embarked on their journey.

That's why I decided to write this book. With this book, I want to offer you as an author a comprehensive guide that helps you to master the fundamentals of successful book publishing and book marketing.

I hope this book will offer you immense value. The information here has certainly facilitated my role as a book marketing consultant. Not only do I know all these secrets by heart, but I also apply them in my daily practices while working with authors. I'm confident that if you follow the advice in this book, you'll not only sell more books, but also become a better author as well. Book marketing is unique, and yet fundamentally similar to any product marketing. That's why you will find insights in this book that apply to marketing other products as well, and which are beneficial for other areas of business. I wish you the best for your continuing career as an author! Make sure to take a look at scribando.com and albertgriesmayr.com, where I deliver the latest strategies about how to succeed in the quick-changing book publishing landscape. And don't hesitate to send me an email sharing your questions or feedback with me.

Best wishes,

Albert Griesmayr
Founder & CEO of Scribando | Novelify
Vienna, Austria, January 1, 2020

FOREWORD

It was 2008. A windy, chilly morning. I was tired, but felt fulfilled. I had made it. I had finished my novel, 180 pages of the story that I had always wanted to write, in only 3 months, but with full focus. I had spent long days and nights alone, working and writing more than 18 hours a day, often staying up until 4 in the morning. I had been completely immersed in my story for 90 days. Having finished the book felt like an enormous victory to me. And it was. It felt good. And more than 10 years later I realize that writing my novel was one of the most fulfilling experiences I have ever encountered.

To keep the story short: the book never became a major success. It maybe sold 300 copies, was featured in a student newspaper, and filled my mom with pride. But it did not become the major bestseller which first time authors normally dream about. Unfortunately.

However, I learned two important lessons that would prove priceless for the upcoming years to follow:

1) How wonderful the immense feeling of fulfillment which comes from writing your own story is.
2) How hard it is to market a book successfully without any prior experience.

It was the early days of self-publishing. Not only was it clear that marketing was changing rapidly, but even more that authors were looking for help to navigate the landscape.

What followed was that I decided to focus my business career on book publishing, with the goal of helping authors. I founded my startup, Scribando, to help authors to find more success launching their books. My company quickly found clients and was selected by the Austrian government in 2013 as a participating startup at Go Silicon Valley.

I also founded initiatives like Lean Book Publishing, which aimed to bring the Lean Startup Movement to books.

Going forward almost 8 years, the book publishing landscape has changed dramatically. Amazon has become a giant of book e-commerce and self-publishing has become a serious alternative, even for the most respected authors and business professionals.

Writers are a lot more educated when it comes to book marketing and understanding the business of book publishing. However, there is still a lot of space for helping authors to succeed.

What I do with Scribando is make sure that authors are up-to-date on the market. However, with this book, I want to cover the fundamentals. These fundamentals are often timeless and very critical for the success of a book. Basically, it comes down to understanding the secrets of product marketing and combining that knowledge with profound experience in book marketing.

These fundamentals are about acknowledging that book publishing is as much a business nowadays as it is about being an artist. Marketing and publishing go hand-in-hand and cannot be seen as isolated from each other. Great book marketing results are mostly the result of process thinking, applying lean practices, good planning from the start, and lots of persistence when it comes to marketing and improving books over the years after launch.

Writers, if you have just launched your book, that was just the beginning.

I am happy to be able to accompany you on your journey. I hope this book is of as much value to you as it is to me in my daily practice of helping authors from around the world sell more books and achieve more success with their book projects.

1

THE BOOK IS THE STAR

*B*ook Marketing Secret #1 is to understand that the book is the star. Always and always. It always comes down to the book. It is the groundwork that you lay for everything to come. Keep Secret #1 in mind at all times and you will be rewarded. Create a fantastic book that you are proud of. Your readers will thank you and reward you. True perennial bestsellers are great books. There is no exception to the rule.

But let's take a closer look at what "the book is the star" means. First of all, it means that the product you are selling is the book that you have. If I take your book away, you will have nothing to sell. You will stand naked. Understanding this automatically shifts your focus towards your book, which is the second important aspect. "The book is the star" also refers to a mindset of focusing on your book, instead of activities around it, like advertising campaigns, PR, book funnels, readings, etc.

From my experience working personally with more than a hundred authors from around the world, most books fall short when I see them the first time for a consulting session. And it's not because I expect too much! Most of the time, the authors I talk to are also not entirely convinced about the books they have created. After the initial call, on average only 1 out of 5 books need just a little polishing. Most books undergo deeper optimization, such as a new cover and improved first 10 pages. And improving the book is the best thing an author and publisher can do for success.

Your book is the most powerful weapon you have for making your book successful. It sounds obvious, but just visit Amazon.com and open some random niche and you will see what I mean. Publishers and authors still make too many shortcuts in this respect.

But I am not here to blame. We all have busy lives and many priorities. Just the ability to finish a book is a big victory that many people who want to never achieve. It's logical to try to get books on the market, so when the writer feels they are good enough, they move forward. But the point I want to make is that true book publishing experts know that every shortcut you make with your book will hurt you later.

When doing paid advertising, you will have to pay a higher CPC, your reviews will have lower ratings, you might have to correct issues with typos or the layout, try harder to convince a journalist to cover your story, and the list goes on and on. Too often, book projects fail because the initial launch does not bring the satisfaction an author wants. He moves on, leaving behind a book which has far more potential, but which never got the attention it would need to truly shine. Or, on the other hand, a neglected book needs a costly makeover and re-launch years later in order to fix what was an obvious problem right from the beginning, just because it wasn't taken seriously enough.

So in my role as a book marketing consultant, whenever a client comes to me, the book is the first thing I look at. I look at the 7 book marketing keys, which you will discover in Chapter 2, and the manuscript itself. That's where my work begins. I help the publisher or author to improve the book so that it shines. Because that profoundly affects everything that follows.

One of my favorite sayings in coaching calls is, "Every dollar spent in the book is worth more than the same dollar spent in advertising." And this is true in almost all cases.

> *"Every dollar spent in the book is worth more than the same dollar spent in advertising."*

So if the quality of the book is so important, the question arises whether it is at all possible to become successful with an average or even a bad book. Well, the honest answer is yes. At least, in the short run it is possible. However, it requires a good advertising budget, an experienced publishing house, a celebrity endorsement, or book marketing pros to achieve success with mediocre books.

And what's more: a good book will always pay off more. Because it will create word-of-mouth, positive reviews, lower CPCs, and happier stakeholders on all sides. The best long-term investment in your publishing career you can make today is to tackle any known issues with your book and to make your book fantastic.

To further illustrate the power of a great book, I want to give insights into two popular books you're probably familiar with, which only found their way to success because of their true inner strength.

The first book I want to talk about is J.K. Rowling's *Harry Potter*, the best-selling book series in history. At this time of writing (October 30, 2019), it has sold more than 500 million copies worldwide.

You might think that the success is due to the fact that there's no way a book like that could possibly be overlooked by experienced publishing houses. But that couldn't be further from the truth.

Did you know that the book was turned down by 12 publishers before being accepted?[1] That J.K. Rowling received rejection notes advising her to take a writing course? That even the small British publisher Bloomsbury which eventually accepted *Harry Potter* was skeptical of its commercial potential in the beginning?

It was not until the chairman of the publishing house gave the first chapter to his then eight-year-old daughter, who then demanded to read more and more, that the book was accepted and the commercial potential seen.

Once *Harry Potter* was in the hands of its target audience, everything changed and the rest is history. *Harry Potter* is a great example of "the book is the star". Not only does it show that a great story can quickly find acceptance once in the hands of its true target audience, but it also demonstrates how great writing can turn a new book, by an unknown author, into a bestseller in just a few weeks, largely by word of mouth.

---

1 Source: https://riseupeight.org/jk-rowling-harry-potter-books/

The second book I want to talk about is *Chicken Soup For The Soul* by Jack Canfield, an inspirational book that contains 101 heartwarming stories. I still remember the recommendation which came from a close friend, not normally the kind of guy to read this kind of book. So I bought it myself, read it in a couple of days, and was impressed. It really is a beautiful and inspiring book. The commercial success it had proved that. What's interesting about the book, though, is not just that 144 publishers turned down the book initially. Even more intriguing is that what drove initial interest was not media attention or celebrity endorsement, but word-of-mouth from people who bought the book and loved it.

In just a few months *Chicken Soup For The Soul* sold so many copies that it appeared on almost all major bestseller lists in the USA and Canada. Today more than 500 million copies have been sold of the first title alone[2].

Chicken Soup For The Soul is a fantastic book, because people love the stories and it really touched the pulse of the time it was published. It was just a perfect match. It filled a niche gap and had a team behind it who did all they could to make it a success.

On the contrary, we are all familiar with follow-up books by famous authors, such as J.K. Rowling's first book for adults, *The Casual Vacancy* or *Twilight* author Stephanie Meyer's thriller *The Chemist*. They had all it normally takes, like a famous author, respected publishing house, media attention for the launch, etc. But after the initial interest, the books failed commercially.

The point I want to make here is that the strength of the manuscript, the raw power of the book, its inner

2 https://www.chickensoup.com/about/facts-and-figures

beauty, is still the ultimate foundation for long term success.

> *"The strength of the manuscript, the raw power of the story, the book's inner beauty, is still the ultimate foundation for a book's long term success."*

When I say "the book is the star" I am not just referring to the manuscript, however, but also the 7 book marketing keys that you will learn in Chapter 2. It's the whole package you see when finding a book online or holding it in your hand physically in a bookstore, friend's house, or library.

Secret #1 is the most important secret, as it is so fundamental to an author's or publisher's mindset. But in order to understand what a fantastic book is, how it is described and can be spotted, we will have to give much more meat to it. Using a term like "fantastic book" without giving it any substance is too vague for actionability. The true question is how an author or publisher can make a book fantastic and what he/she needs to focus on.

The three main questions that need to be answered are:

1) *How do we spot a fantastic book, and what are the metrics?*

2) *What are the areas a publisher needs to work on?*

3) *How can a book be tested and improved in order to become fantastic?*

You will find the answers to these questions in detail throughout this book. For now, though, I want to give a quick overview to lay the groundwork.

1. **How do we spot a fantastic book? What are the metrics?**

There is only one metric that truly counts: customer satisfaction. A fantastic book is loved by its target audience, has ratings that average at least above 80%, has conversion rates of 10%+, and ideally achieves some form of organic growth or even virality with little or no advertising expense.

2. **What are the areas a publisher needs to work on?**

There are 8 critical areas for book success: The book manuscript, and the 7 book marketing keys that you will learn more about in Chapter 2.

3. **How can a book be tested and improved in order to become fantastic?**

The method that I recommend is "lean book publishing." You will learn more about it in Secret #4. This is a process of developing or improving an existing book based on feedback and interactions with the target audience.

A fantastic book will make its own way in the world, once seen by enough targeted people. You will learn about this in Secret #5.

Ultimately, "the book is the star" (Secret #1) is most importantly a mindset. It means a focus on creating a fantastic book, a book that is loved by readers and a book that the author can be proud of. A book that has the power to leave a legacy.

Secret #1 Checkbox

Core Insights:

- ☑ Having a strong book is still the best foundation for long-term book success
- ☑ Strong books enjoy high levels of customer ratings
- ☑ Investments into your book pay off more than investments into marketing and advertising

Exercise: Take the "Book Awesomeness Test"

Answer the following three questions. The more you answer "Yes," the further you are in your journey. The more you answer "No," the more room you have for improvement.

1) Does my book have the metrics of a fantastic book?
2) Do I know more than 10 readers who really loved my book?
3) What is my honest answer to the question: "Is my book amazing?"

Read on to learn how to get more "Yes" and how to make your book fantastic.

2

THE 7 BOOK MARKETING KEYS

"Give me a bad manuscript, and by polishing it with the 7 keys to book marketing success, I will still make it sell."

"Give me a bad manuscript, and by polishing it with the 7 keys to book marketing success, I will still make it sell."

This sounds like a pretty bold statement, but I have seen it numerous times: good marketers can make a bad-to-average manuscript sell well, simply by improving the 7 book marketing keys. And of course, the improvement of the 7 keys is also one of the most important jobs that I do in my daily practice working with authors and publishers.

Changing and improving a manuscript is often difficult or almost impossible, especially for fiction books once they are on the market and have reached critical mass and circulation. That's why marketers often have to turn exclusively to the 7 keys, which you will find out about in this chapter. Hold on tight, here they are:

The 7 Book Marketing Keys	
Key 1	Book Cover
Key 2	Book Title [+subtitle]
Key 3	Book Description
Key 4	Book Layout
Key 5	Author and Publisher
Key 6	Reviews [editorial, consumer]
Key 7	Marketing Strategy

Key 1: Book Cover

We all know the saying, "Don't judge a book by its cover," and we all know that it is impossible. We see the cover first before we ever get the chance to read a book. There is no way around it. And it has not changed with digital publishing, either. A book cover is the face of a book. Even more, it's really the whole body. Analytics have shown that good covers can increase Click-Through Rates by a couple of hundred percent[3], as well as decide whether a book becomes a commercial success or not. Saving your budget with the cover is one of the worst things you can do. You have to get the cover right.

Christiana Miller from *Self-Publishing On A Shoe String* says it well: "A book cover is an invitation — a way of seducing the reader. It beckons, inviting them to enter

3 https://en.99designs.at/blog/tips/impact-book-cover-design-on-sales/

the world of your book and dance with your characters for awhile. It makes a promise about what kind of music they'll be dancing to. Your cover should convey the tone and genre of your story, be eye-catching and, most importantly, look like it's been professionally done."[4]

Creating beautiful and commercially successful covers is a topic with enough meat to write a whole book about it all on its own, so I do not want to dive too deep. Nevertheless I want to share with you the "formula" that I use when creating or assessing client covers, so you can use it for yourself.

The cornerstone of my formula is the concept of "genre matching"[5] which I see as one of the most useful and simple concepts for creating commercially successful covers. The basic idea is to look at bestselling books in the relevant genre and to match book covers accordingly with respect to the overall styles. Just by matching core styles (such as typography, visuals, etc.) you not only match reader's expectations but also automatically match key selling factors in specific genres, such as the importance of looking fresh and up-to-date in the field of "how-to" books, or dreamy and warm with romance novels.

The second and third parts of my formula relate to communicating benefits and matching book title and visuals. Ideally, the book title already contains the core benefit. If not, I recommend using the subtitle on the cover as well. What's often overlooked, but also critical, is to match the title with the visual. If you have a book title that says *Book Sales Explosion* (one of my

---

4 https://www.huffpost.com/entry/selfpublishing-on-a-shoes_2_b_4325962

5 https://blog.flipsnack.com/how-to-design-a-book-cover-based-on-its-genre/

upcoming books) and you do not add a visual that looks explosive, you will not properly communicate your title. It is important that both title and visual click, that they are symbiotic.

Nevertheless, genre-matching, title/visual matching, and benefit communication are not enough. Even with these, you won't necessarily stand out. And book publishing is so competitive that you have to stand out. You need to catch the reader's attention as he browses through the list on Amazon or walks through a book store. Just take a look at the book cover of Donna Tartt's *The Goldfinch: A Novel*[6] and you will understand what I mean.

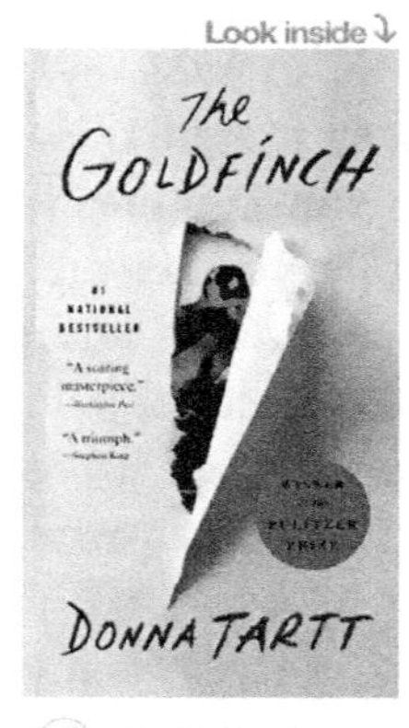

© Screenshot of Amazon — Nov 11, 2019

That's why the cover formula that I apply contains "adding unique twists" as well, elements that are out of the ordinary. This in the book cover formula you see below, which I use with my clients.

6 https://www.amazon.com/dp/B00BAXFECK

Book Cover Formula:
Genre Match + Title/Visual Match + Benefits + Unique Twists = Wow Effect

Let's look at the cover of this book and apply the formula to it.

It matches the genre of "book marketing educational books" (advice and how-to), the visual "magic book" matches the book title *Book Marketing Secrets*, the title includes the core benefit, and the unique twist is the simplicity. It catches my eye, and I am happy with it. For me, the cover gets 4x yes, which brings the desired wow effect.

Could it be better? Yes, it always can. But based on my XP, this is a solid book cover. Apply the book cover formula for your own covers and put the formula to the test. I would be happy to hear your results.

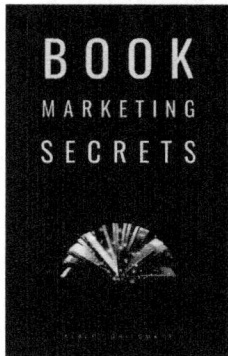

Book Cover Formula Check: Book Marketing Secrets	
BOOK MARKETING SECRETS	Genre matching: yes Title/Visual match: yes Benefits communicated: yes Unique twist: yes ――――――――――― Resulting wow effect: yes

The 7 Book Marketing Keys | Exercise 1 (Cover)
Apply the formula to your own book covers and see how well they perform.

Key 2: Book Title

The second book marketing key is the book title. Over the years, I've created a formula that helps me to check for the main characteristics in book titles, to make sure that my clients' titles work. The formula calculates the score of the strength of four characteristics (0-25 points) to reach a total score between 0 and 100 points (100 points being the top value) The simplified version, which we will use now, gives either a Yes or a No to achieving a characteristic, with 4 Yes answers as the highest score. You can see the formula below.

Magic Book Title Formula	
Characteristic	**Count or Y/N**
Short and Memorable (easy to read, easy to pronounce, easy to listen to)	0-25 (Y/N)
Unique and Attention Grabbing (immediately engages emotions)	0-25 (Y/N)
Story Match (theme, cover, tone, content)	0-25 (Y/N)
Built-In Benefit	0-25 (Y/N)
Total Score	0-100 (X/Yes)

Books that achieve scores between 90-100 points, or alternatively 4 Yes answers, pass my assessment. All titles that are below 90 points, or with 3 Yes answers or lower, are candidates for improvement.

Let's take a closer look at the characteristics by looking at three popular best-selling book titles. These also share one common trait: they have exceptionally well-crafted, high-performing book titles, created by publishing professionals who understand their art superbly. These are superb book titles that we can learn from.

The titles I have chosen are the thriller *Blue Moon: A Jack Reacher Novel*[7] by Lee Child, the book *The Goldfinch: A Novel* (Pulitzer Prize for Fiction)[8] and the book *Educated: A Memoir*[9] by Tara Westover.

Let's do a quick check and see why these titles are performing so well. First of all, they are all short and memorable. This is even with the added subtitle, as presented in my examples and as displayed in online book stores.[10] They are easy to read, easy to pronounce, and easy to listen to. They are also all unique and attention grabbing, and immediately engage the emotions. This is especially true for *Blue Moon*, which on an unconscious level immediately draws us to the book, because of the unique combination of the color and the object, combined with the ease of sound.

But most importantly, all of these titles have built-in benefits, even although none of the titles are

7 https://www.amazon.com/Blue-Moon-Jack-Reacher-Novel-ebook/dp/B07NCNVZ5P

8 https://www.amazon.com/dp/B00BAXFECK

9 https://www.amazon.com/dp/B072BLVM83

10 For digital book sales, subtitles get added to include important SEO-relevant keywords, such as the category, as well as important purchase factors, such as an award or prize, as shown in the example for *The Goldfinch*.

"how to" or a typical non-fiction book.[11] The built-in benefits are easily recognizable in the subtitle (price winner, category, brand name). However, what's more remarkable is that the built-in benefits are also to a good extent communicated through the core titles themselves. In *Educated* the benefit is very clear, as it appeals to an educated target audience. The other two titles are more subtle, but they do their job as well. They draw readers into their stories due to the excellent match of title and story/theme.

Now it's your turn. I invite you to take a look at your book titles and apply the "magic book title formula" to them. How well do your titles perform? What can you do to improve them?[12]

The 7 Book Marketing Keys | Exercise 2 (Title)
– Check your book titles and see how many times they receive a "Yes" – What can you do to improve your book title/ subtitle?

Key 3: Book Description

Bestselling author Sarah Gribbles gets it right when she says: "Your book description isn't a summary of

11 *Educated: A Memoir* is a work of art in non-fiction, but is nevertheless close to fiction. That's why, for illustration purposes, it is not described as a typical non-fiction book, such as cookbooks, advice books, etc.

12 Even if your book is already published and you can no longer edit the title (for print versions), most digital publishing platforms allow you to at least edit the subtitle, which can be used to communicate benefits and improve scores of the four characteristics described.

your book — it's an ad meant to hook your readers and sell your book."[13]

Having a powerful book description is a key element in book marketing. The main point is to get targeted readers to purchase the book. It is as simple as that. The details change depending on whether you create descriptions for fiction or non-fiction, for different genres and topics, as well as formats and places the descriptions appear, such as the back cover, an Amazon sales page, a PR text, or a newsletter. However, the core elements you need to master and communicate are the same. I want to share these critical elements with you and present you a powerful toolbox that not only helps you to craft powerful descriptions, but also to check them for effectiveness.

The following toolbox gives you six tools that I like to work with when creating and assessing book descriptions. The first four tools are process-oriented, which means you can use these tools to create your descriptions from scratch.

The latter two are ingredients you add in order to spice up your description and also test your descriptions for effectiveness. I will briefly explain each tool.

Let's start with the first four tools. I recommend that you rely on only one of these core tools for each description you create, as this keeps complexity low.

The first tool is the "Scribe Book Description Writing Method for Non-Fiction Books"[14], which shows how

13 Source: Sarah Gribble, https://thewritepractice.com/how-to-write-a-book-description/

14 Source: Scribe Writing https://scribewriting.com/write-book-description/

to hook readers, how to create pain and pleasure, legitimacy, and an open loop as a closing. It's a solid method that you can learn more about by visiting the Scribe website (see footnote).

Another great method is to answer the "Who, Why, What & How" questions in your description, as Russell Brunson suggests for creating short but powerful video messages. This method is especially useful for authors who already have credibility in a certain area (Who), as the method suggests starting with the introduction of the author.

A technique that I like a lot is the one I created specifically for non-fiction books: use a great first sentence to "hook" readers, explain what the book is about in the next two sentences or "blurb," followed by "benefits" (presented in bullets), and close with a strong call-to-action (CTA).

Finally, the well-known AIDA model[15] can be applied excellently to book descriptions as well, in order to move readers step-by-step from attention, to interest, to desire, to action.

Book Description Creation Toolbox* *outcomes to be assessed from reader's perspective	
Tool	**Description**
Scribe Book Description Writing Method for Non-Fiction Books	"Hook, Pain, Pleasure, Legitimacy, Open Loop"
Russell Brunson Intro Format	Who, Why, What, How

15 Source: Wikipedia https://en.wikipedia.org/wiki/AIDA_(marketing)

Albert's Non-Fiction Technique	Hook, Blurb, Benefits (bullets) + CTA
AIDA Technique	Attention, Interest, Desire, Action
Cialdini Principles	6 Principles of Persuasion (7th principle added in 2016)
Reader's Perspective Cooking Tools	– Use "you" – Use SEO keywords – Use power verbs – Active and present

One of my favorite ingredients for spicing up any book description come from well-known psychologist Robert Cialdini. His classic book on persuasion and influence[16] describes 6 principles, which you can use like spices in your book description "dish." The 6 principles (a 7th principle, "unity," was added in 2016) are reciprocity, consistency, social proof, liking, authority, and scarcity. I personally use these principles like salt and pepper throughout my own marketing. They are a powerful arsenal for every marketer. Concrete applications include: "Bestselling author, read by XY people, award-winning, limited bonus offer, etc." I recommend that you make sure that your book description covers all these principles in some form, for best results. Closing book descriptions with scarcity works especially well (eg. bonus offer inside the book is only available for first 1K readers, limited book edition, or introductory price), as this kind of scarcity is rarely used for books in general.

---

16 Source: Robert Cialdini. *Influence: The Psychology of Persuasion* (1984) https://www.amazon.com/Influence-Psychology-Persuasion-Robert-Cialdini/dp/006124189X

Finally, the sixth tool is all about writing and checking your book description from the reader's perspective. You have to make sure that your prospective reader understands what is in it for them. Enter the mind of the prospective reader and read the descriptions from their perspective.

The four core elements I suggest you look at are the use of the verb "you" in order to communicate with the reader (eg. You will learn, your best read of the year, etc.), the use of "power verbs"[17] (such as because, exclusive, quick, simple, etc.), "active voice"[18] and "present tense,"[19] and keywords that your readers will actively look for (especially by typing them into search engines). Once you know exactly what terms your readers are looking for, you can use them in your copy. Not only does this help you be found and rank higher, but also reminds your readers why they were looking for your book as they read your description.

The following chart shows why it is so important to rank as number 1 for specific keywords. You will get 27%[20] of all clicks for a keyword on Amazon, and data for other search engines is similar. Ranking high for your reader's search terms is an important aspect to consider when writing your book description.

---

17 Source: Copy Write Matters https://copywritematters.com/copywriter-words-that-sell/

18 Source: Crazy Egg https://www.crazyegg.com/blog/double-power-of-content/

19 Source: Susan Green https://www.susangreenecopywriter.com/articles/write-website-content.html

20 Source: Kindlepreneur: https://kindlepreneur.com/how-to-choose-kindle-keywords/

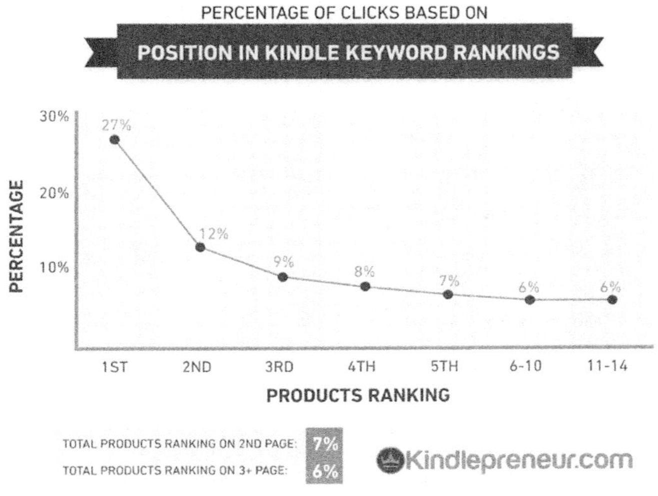

Source: https://kindlepreneur.com/how-to-choose-kindle-keywords/

The 7 Book Marketing Keys | Exercise 3 (Description)
– Pick one of the tools of the "Book Description Creation Toolbox" and start to write a description for an upcoming book project you have in mind. – Check if your book descriptions apply some of "Cialdini's Principles" as well as the "Reader's Perspective Cooking Tools."

4) Book Layout

The next book marketing key is the book layout. This refers to how well the book is formatted, which influences the experience a reader has when reading your book, both as a paperback and as an ebook. Of particular importance for us are typography, images, and the use of quality elements like drop caps, breakout boxes, sidebars, contents, the first pages of the book, and the absence of typos, widows, and orphans.

Experienced publishers know that a good layout makes a huge difference in the perception of a book. However, layout is often not treated as importantly as it should be. In my experience, improving the layout is often a quick win, especially compared to re-writing manuscripts. Investing in a good formatter usually pays off, especially in the area of "advice and how-to." In this genre, authors can achieve a lot by investing in well-designed content, breakout or takeaway boxes, as well as chapter summaries and checklists.

In the following you'll find a table showing important elements to add to and improve your book layout, in order to increase the positive perception of your book:

Important Book Layout Factors	
Non-Fiction	**Fiction**
Typography (fonts, typeface, line height, font-size, drop caps, sinks, whitespace)	Typography (fonts, typeface, line height, font-size, drop caps, sinks, whitespace)
Use of Images/Illustrations	Use of Images/ Illustrations
Nicely Designed Content	Nicely Designed Content
Margins, running heads, page numbers	Margins, running heads, page numbers
Absence of typos, widows, and orphans	Absence of typos, widows, and orphans
Use of breakout boxes, chapter summaries, infographics, sidebars	

Use of references, like footnotes, sources, indexes, links	

One element I want to draw your attention to in particular is the very beginning of the book, namely the first couple of pages. They are especially important online, as retailers allow readers to look at your first pages and get a reading sample for free. We all know Amazon's "Look Inside" feature. Optimizing your beginning pages can have a profound impact on your book sales, not to mention your publishing business as a whole. Why? I will explain that in a second.

So, first of all, it is important to understand that almost every Amazon reader uses the "Look Inside" function before purchasing a book[21]. That means that not only people who eventually purchase your book take a look, but also all prospects (often 10x more than actual buyers).

Smart marketers understood that and started to not only optimize their "Look Inside" in order to get more readers, but also to market other services and to drive people to their websites, as readers can click on links within "Look Inside" to open external webpages as well.

One of my favorite uses of "Look Inside" is the "surprise gift"[22] or "added bonus content." The basic idea is to communicate visually striking bonus content within the

21 As I did not find data on this, I did a quick online survey with 10 respondents, where 8 out of 10 respondents said that they always use "Look Inside" before purchasing a book on Amazon.

22 You can learn more about my surprise gift application by taking a look at this presentation: https://www.slideshare.net/griesmayr/how-to-get-book-reviews-2020-edition

first couple of pages (normally before the actual content), in order to give people added value to the book purchase. This also presents non-readers with an offer on your webpage as well, ideally accessible by signing up with their email. By following this approach, you are able to build email lists much faster and in a very targeted way.

Investing in a good book layout pays off. It's also mentioned as a quality factor from reviewers in 15% of reviews for non-fiction and 5% of reviews for fiction books[23], as my team and I found out in a study of 500 top reviews analyzed on Amazon. I will talk more about that when we look at Secret #6.

The 7 Book Marketing Keys | Exercise 4 (Book Layout)
– Take one of your most important books and make a list of layout elements that can be improved. – Read your book's reviews to see if any of them are referring to layout. If yes, take appropriate action, such as fixing typos or adding drop caps.

5) Author and Publisher

Another book marketing key is the perceived quality of the author and/or publisher. This key seems obvious, as books are linked to their authors and publishers through the whole branding experience. Still, in my practice working with authors and publishers worldwide, I notice that especially the more inexperienced players significantly underestimate this book marketing key.

---

23 Data comes from a 2019 Scribando study that analyzed the contents of more than 500 Amazon reviews of 100 books, both in fiction and non-fiction.

It is obvious that first-time authors often do not have a lot of credibility in the market and are shy to compete with big household names. However this should not lead to actions like practically hiding author names on book covers and book retailers. Not everything is about credibility. It's just as important to show readers who you are as well. A strong story can have such a profound effect on sales, it is vital that authors and publishers think deeply about how to present themselves in a favorable way.

You should definitely create a strong author biography. Explain who you are, why you wrote the book and why it's important, what is in the book, how your readers can purchase it, get the most out of it, connect with you, etc. You do not need to be rock star right out of the gate. A good story behind your book and why you wrote it can make up for a million sales. Include your author biography in your book, as well as online on your webpage and via online retailers. Very often the reason someone purchases a book, or why they don't, is because it really is "all about the author."

While the name of the publisher is less important, it still helps in most cases to be published with a respected publishing house (or at least not directly identified as "self-published"). Readers look for that information as well, in order to assess "credibility" and to reduce risk.

The 7 Book Marketing Keys | Exercise 5 (Author/Publisher)
– Take a look at your author/publisher profiles on your webpage, Amazon, LinkedIn, etc., and make a list of elements you can improve. Think deeply about the reasons why you wrote the book (your story) and credibility factors you have. Improve your story and add credibility to your author biography.

6) Reviews

One of my favorite book marketing quotes is, "Reviews are the lifeblood of books in the digital age." Actually, how to get reviews is normally the #1 task that I discuss with my clients during my consulting sessions. A study by the Spiegel Research Center[24] in 2017 showed that 95% of buyers read online reviews before making a purchase. 95% — a very high number, but I am not surprised by that. Not only based on my personal experience (I always check reviews before purchasing a product), but also based on my experience with client books (books with bad average reviews are extremely difficult to market).

> *"Reviews are the lifeblood of books in the digital age."*

So the task is obvious: having lots of good reviews is one of the most important book marketing keys to focus on, so it is best to start collecting them as early as possible. Simply said, there is no better time to start getting reviews than before having launched your book. This is especially important, as the first reviews set the tone for what's to come.

> *"The first reviews set the tone for what's to come."*

And the best way to get reviews early is to include potential readers, inviting them into your writing

24 Source: Spiegel Research Center (2017): https://spiegel.medill.northwestern.edu/_pdf/Spiegel_Online%20Review_eBook_Jun2017_FINAL.pdf

process as early as possible. Some call it their "launch team," others their "following," but in the end it's about engaging readers before actually launching your book. Not only to get "editorial reviews" from respected players in your field that you can use for your blurb and in your marketing, but also "customer reviews" that you can "activate"[25] when your book is launched.

I'll talk more about different ways to get reviews, including my favorite and most suggested methods, in a later secret. So I'll close this section for now. What's important is that you remember reviews are one of the most relevant book marketing keys, a factor that truly makes or breaks books.

The 7 Book Marketing Keys | Exercise 6 (Reviews)
– Take a look at the reviews your books have received. Rank them according to their average rating and rethink your book prioritization based on customer feedback. – Make sure that for upcoming book projects you make getting both editorial and customer ratings before book launch a priority and take appropriate action.

7) Marketing Strategy

Creating winning book marketing strategies is one of my core areas as a book marketing consultant. Over

25 Most retailers do not allow posting reviews for books that are not released yet (eg. pre-order books). "Activation" refers to a process of securing a review from a reader through an ARC, and asking him to post the review once the book is available.

the last 10 years, I have created more than 100 book marketing strategies for clients from all over the world. In basic terms, a book marketing strategy is about providing a clear step-by-step action plan for how to reach the marketing-related author/publisher goal[26] within a predefined time frame and a given budget.

The crucial question in most strategies is how to reach a substantial amount of targeted readers in the most cost-effective way. Marketing strategy is mostly about using the right channels with the right tactics and messages.

Book marketing strategies can be seen as stand-alone products. They have value regardless of the quality of the underlying book. However, every skilled marketer knows that each strategy is based on the power of the product, and success or failure greatly depend on that quality.

That's why it is no secret that every strategy will greatly benefit from a fantastic book and already-optimized book marketing keys as a foundation. Below, you'll find a simple "book marketing strategy creation cheat sheet" that includes 4 questions to answer to come up with a basic strategy.

By answering these 4 questions, you will already have made significant progress toward creating a winning strategy for your book. However, I recommend authors and publishers without much experience in book marketing to reach out to a book marketing expert for

26 In most cases the goal is to reach certain sales numbers, supported by sub-goals, like getting reviews.

advice in this important strategic area.

Book Marketing Strategy Creation Cheat Sheet
1) What is the goal I want to reach? (eg. sales numbers) 2) Who are my perfect readers? Who likes my book? 3) How many people do I need to reach? (to reach my goal) 4) What are the channels I have to use? (to reach my audience) 5) How good does my product need to be? (to reach my goal)

Having the right strategy means being able to do the right things from the start, which results in dollars invested the right way and increased chances for success.

The 7 Book Marketing Keys | Exercise 7 (Book Marketing Strategy)
– Take a book you are marketing right now, and answer the 5 questions in the "Book Marketing Creation Cheat Sheet."

By mastering the 7 book marketing keys, you will be able to reach targeted readers with a product that they will buy.

Once you have achieved this, it really comes down to your manuscript and the inner power and beauty of your book. Master book marketing Secret #1 (the book is the star) together with #2 (the 7 book marketing keys), and you will have everything you need to create a true bestseller.

Secret #2 Checkbox

Core Insights:

- ☑ Master the 7 book marketing keys, and be able to sell solid books with ease
- ☑ Know the 7 book marketing keys by heart and optimize them relentlessly

Exercises

Get pen and paper and take notes:

1) List the 7 book marketing keys
2) Which of the 7 keys can be improved for your book?
3) Make a list of steps to improve your 7 keys by doing the 7 exercises described in this chapter

3

THE 80/20 RULE OF BOOK MARKETING

I still remember when I first heard about the Pareto Principle, also referred to as the 80/20 rule. It was back in university, when I was a student at the University of Economics and Business Administration in Vienna, taking a basic class in economics. It puzzled me when the professor said that, for many events in economy and life, roughly 80% of the effects come from 20% of the causes.[27]

The professor talked about wealth distribution and business processes, as well as personal finances. It was the first time that I'd heard of the 80/20 rule and was one of the main principles I learned at university that really stuck with me. Over the years to come, I learned what a great rule it was and the many practical applications it had.

So, years later, when I started to consult for authors, I started to wonder whether the rule was true for book marketing as well. Do 80% of royalties, or in a broader

27 Source: Wikipedia: https://en.wikipedia.org/wiki/Pareto_principle

context book sales, come from only 20% of efforts? Do publishing houses have 1 winner out of 5 that covers the marketing expenses of all others?

So I dug deeper and found out that the Pareto Principle was also valid for a lot of relationships in book publishing. When analyzing client projects, I found that it was often only one particular sales channel that brought income, and one good book that really sold.

What struck me the most, though, was that I figured out that the rule applies to other aspects as well which are quite unique for books. And those other aspects are the following:

The 80/20 Rule Of Book Marketing [3 Underlying Facts]

1) 20% effort brings 80% outcome
2) 80%+ is invested into the manuscript, but only 1%-20% is invested in the 7 book marketing keys
3) But 80% importance is in book keys when purchasers make a buying decision

So let's take a closer look at the second and third application of the secret. The second application says:

80%+ of time/effort is invested into manuscript, but only 1%-20% is invested into the 7 book marketing keys

If you are a true author (and not a publisher only hiring ghostwriters) you will most certainly agree with me on this. The huge effort is writing the book itself, filling the story, putting it all together, editing it, etc. The effort put into the 7 book marketing keys, though, is way less. We often take this even as a byproduct of finishing a book. This is especially true if we start out with just the manuscript and add on the 7 keys at the end of the process. Then we are often already out of energy or even funds. We just can't wait to see our baby on the shelves and online.

However, what we learned in Secret #2 is that around 80% of your success depend on the 7 book marketing keys. The 7 book marketing keys which we only give attention and resources to for around 20% of our time.

So we see that something is wrong here. Most of us are investing too much time into something that does not bring much of an outcome. Or, what's even worse, into something that might never be discovered, if your 7 book marketing keys are not convincing. You could have an amazing book, but with average book marketing keys, you will lose a lot of ground or might not even make it past the first reader.

So I suggest you take the following two insights from the facts above:

1) Find the 20% of effort that brings 80% of results and focus on them.

2) And join me for an experiment: Why not do it the other way round and invest 80% of resources into the 7 book keys, and only 20% into the manuscript?

That sounds crazy, right? Impossible. But it isn't. And that's why it is so powerful. In a second I will show you how it works, where it works, and why it works so well.

I invite you to enter the world of "zero or low content book publishing."

It is a world in which the focus is on creating books with minimum effort but maximum outcome. Books that have zero or low content (easy-to-create manuscripts), while on the other hand are driven by their 7 book marketing keys.

Notebooks and creative books, summaries, quote books, etc., all brought down to their essentials. Some of the publishers in this market are there for the quick book. So not all of them pay attention to the 7 keys. But there a couple of great publishers who are masters in their field, and that results in truly amazing book projects.

*Two examples I want to share with you. One is **The Little Notebook For Big Ideas**[28] by Rob Cubbon. Another is **Writers Block**[29] by me.*

These are great projects that apply the 80/20 rule of book marketing and show what is possible by focusing on the 7 book marketing keys at first. Do they match the criteria because their manuscripts are so thin? Yes, that's true. So they are not 100% representative. But I am sharing those to inspire you and to ask you a question:

"What would be possible with your book projects if you invested 80% of your efforts into the 7 book marketing keys instead of your manuscripts? What would happen if you started to focus on those first, before finishing your manuscript?"

28 Source: https://www.amazon.com/LITTLE-NOTEBOOK-Motivational-Journal-Entrepreneurs/dp/1724026372

29 Source: https://www.amazon.com/Writers-Block-What-feels-about-ebook/dp/B00NVKDT68/

"What would be possible with your book projects if you invested 80% of your efforts into the 7 book marketing keys instead of your manuscripts?"

I believe that we have already entered an era of book publishing in which the focus shifts dramatically away from the manuscript to the 7 book marketing keys. We are already seeing the change today: business-oriented market entrants such as Kindle Publishing are competing on Amazon daily, SEO is critical, book editors and translators are supported and threatened at the same time by technology doing their job, the growing demand for audio brings formats[30] that reduce production times significantly, and speech-to-text technology enables faster ways to produce manuscripts.

Digital marketing knowledge has become paramount in an increasingly competitive and global technology driven market. Not all of these developments are rosy.

And what's more, we are on the brink of a new era. An era that not many see yet, but which I believe is close. The era of "artificial intelligence" in book publishing. We are writing late 2019, and AI regarding the creation of books is still in its very early stages. However, given the rate of development and adoption of technological advances in the last decades, it is only reasonable to assume that AI will literally write books faster than we can dream of today.

30 Formats such as audiobooks, CDs, or Alexa Skills. [Time of writing: October 2019]

> *"AI will literally write books faster than we can dream of today."*

As a result, AI will create a book publishing landscape in which the resources invested in the 7 book marketing keys vs. the manuscript will have changed dramatically. AI will literally write book publishing history. Today is the best day to start to invest big time into the 7 book marketing keys (Secret #2) and to apply the 80/20 rule of book marketing to your advantage.

The 80/20 Rule Of Book Marketing [2 To-Dos]

1) Find the 20% effort that brings 80% outcome and focus on it
2) Invest at least 20% (or, better, 50%) of your resources into the 7 book marketing keys

My rule of thumb and core recommendation is that you not only give the 7 book marketing keys the same importance as your manuscript right from the beginning of your book project, but that you also spend at least 20% (but better 50% or more) of your resources on those 7 keys, in order to make your book a success.

Secret #3 Checkbox
Core Insights:
☑ 20% effort brings 80% outcome ☑ 80%+ is invested in manuscript, but only 1%-20% is invested in the 7 book marketing keys ☑ But 80% importance is in book keys, when purchasers make a buying decision
Exercises
Take pen and paper and answer the following questions: – What is your 20% that brings 80% of results? – Did you invest at least 20% of your time in the 7 book marketing keys? – What are low-hanging fruits [tasks with low effort/big outcome ratio] you can grab now to improve your book sales?

4

THE POWER OF LEAN BOOK PUBLISHING

When I started my book publishing company Scribando | Novelify in 2012, there was one concept *en vogue* in the world of internet startups. This concept was "The Lean Startup" by Eric Ries.[31]

The corresponding book was published in 2011 and quickly became a bestseller in the business field and, ultimately, even a New York Times bestseller. Every small company wanted to become lean, more efficient, and reduce the risk of failure by being more customer-centric.

The lean startup movement was huge, and swept across startup hubs globally in no time. Eric Ries was right, and he still is. Applying lean startup principles is profoundly the right way in order to achieve product-market fit quickly, as many successful technology companies born during that time, such as Dropbox, Wealthfront, or Airbnb, showed in later years.

I applied lean principles in my company as well, and was able to innovate quickly. Not everything turned

31 Source and further information: http://theleanstartup.com/

out to be successful. What I learned was that being in touch with your customers from the early stage onwards helps you to find product-market fit way more quickly.

Soon I started to wonder whether lean principles would also be useful for the process of book publishing. I quickly learned that authors such as Guy Kawasaki, Aaron Hurst, Ksenia Anske, and Paulo Coelho, and publishers such as O'Reilly were experimenting with lean startup principles. New publishing platforms like Leanpub and the now-closed Pubslush were providing ways for publishers to write and publish the lean way.

I felt the need of a knowledge resource about lean publishing, and so I registered the domain www.leanbookpublishing.com, created presentations sharing principles and insights, and uploaded them onto the website. I talked to authors, shared knowledge, and even presented Lean Book Publishing at a Pecha Kucha Night. It was an inspiring time. The webpage and concept is still online and, more importantly, more valid than ever today.

"The core idea of lean book publishing is to publish books readers love and to find out what works and what doesn't as quickly and cost-efficiently as possible. That is what Lean Book Publishing is about at its core."

Visit www.leanbookpublishing.com to learn about the principles, tools, and benefits of lean book publishing.

Little has changed regarding the core concepts. What has evolved, though, are the tools that we have access to in 2019, around 7 years later. Almost everyone today can use social media and blogging platforms to test ideas or to find audiences for publishing and launch teams. Authors are way more familiar with technology, as well, and the share of authors who have webpages has grown drastically, too.

Testing book ideas, finding the right audiences for a book, as well as "sequential publishing," are now easier than ever, due to communities like Wattpad, private groups on Facebook, and easy access to book publishing tools, like Amazon's KDP. Still, the concept of lean book publishing did not celebrate a huge success.

So why is that? There are 2 questions emerging:

1) Did applying lean startup principles simple not make publishers and authors successful? or
2) Do not enough authors know about the concept?

Let's take a closer look at the answers. I want to start with looking at the historic development of the book publishing landscape, as well as the current iteration. Historically, writing books has always been a very private process. We all have the image in mind of authors sitting — separated from the world — in dimly lit work rooms, writing their book until, after years of hard work, it is done and can see the light.

Many of the best books ever created, have been created by writers in very isolated situations, deep inside their own brains. And most books, I would assume around 90%[32], are still primarily written this way, with little or no interaction with others before the manuscript is

32 Estimated number that is based on my personal work with more than 100 authors worldwide.

finished. Following the writing process like this seems very much ingrained to us, which makes it difficult to change. Writing a book is still something very personal, a treasure that we as authors guard in our heart, a treasure that is very vulnerable in its making. It seems that this is a major reason why "lean publishing" has not yet found wide adoption.

So even if lots of authors and publishers knew about "lean book publishing," it still seems somewhat counterintuitive to apply it. What's more, we as authors sometimes fear copyright problems, or are overly confident about our writing as well. We all believe we have a great book in the making — if not a bestseller — otherwise we would not devote that much time to writing a book.

> *"Writing a book is still something very private. It's like a vulnerable treasure in the making that we as authors guard in our heart."*

And frankly, bestselling authors like Stephen King, Scott Westerfeld, or John Grisham, as well as big publishing houses, like Random House, Simon & Schuster, and Hachette, will not want to rely on communities to give feedback on chapters, or even co-write whole books, simply because they have learned that they are able to publish bestsellers with their own expertise alone.

And this makes a lot of sense. It has worked in the past and still works like this to a large extent for experienced professionals. For others, though, it very often doesn't, mostly because they lack the professional experience to know what is needed to succeed in this competitive market. For unexperienced professionals, applying "Lean Book Publishing Principles" can not only drastically improve product-market fit, but also save months of work and substantial amounts of money.

Let's go back once more to the initial question, why LBP is still not as widespread as the lean concept is in other industries. Let's take a closer look at success stories, and go on an expedition to the largest writing community today, Wattpad, which has an audience of more than 70 million readers[33]. Wattpad, at its core, is a lean publishing platform. It enables writers to share their stories with readers during the writing process, to get feedback, and to grow fanbases long before books actually get published.

On such a big platform like Wattpad, we have to be able to find successful authors, right?

Yes, we do. We not only find thousands of authors who use Wattpad on a daily or weekly basis to connect with their readers and to generate consistent sales from their books, we also find authors who sold millions of copies[34] and got published by Big 5 publishing houses, such as NYT bestselling author Anna Todd[35] , the well-known author of the *After* series, who even sold the rights to Paramount Pictures for a movie adaptation[36]. Read what Anna says about Wattpad:

---

33 https://en.wikipedia.org/wiki/Wattpad

34 Source: https://publishingperspectives.com/2017/11/anna-todd-foreign-rights-sales-wattpad-rights-edition/

35 http://www.annatodd.com/

36 Source: https://deadline.com/2014/10/after-movie-rights-wattpad-book-anna-todd-paramount-852926/

"I found Wattpad through reading fanfiction and from the second I laid my eyes on the platform, I fell down the rabbit hole. It was a place I couldn't have even dreamed existed with people just like me, an entire world of people who read and write on the internet. I found a community, a home really, with these people who were writing in the hours off of work, school, parenting, life, and I loved every second of it. And I wrote. And wrote. And wrote and then wrote some more. I couldn't stop!"[37]

For me the quote is a beautiful description of how rewarding lean book publishing can be on a personal level. Two other successful authors using Wattpad are Lilian Carmine[38], the author of the *Lost Boys* novels and Brittany Geragotelis[39], author of the young adult series *LIFE'S A WITCH*. Both authors have not only been able to build substantial fan bases on Wattpad, but have also secured publishing deals with well-established publishing houses. So, many authors on Wattpad prove that "lean book publishing" works.

But do we need a dedicated platform for "lean book publishing" at all anymore? The straightforward answer is no. Social networks like Facebook have features like dedicated groups, which could be a way to lean publish and get feedback. Crowdfunding platforms like Kickstarter[40] have shown and still show outstanding potential for applying lean publishing successful. Just

37 Source: http://www.annatodd.com/my-story/

38 Lilian Carmine: https://www.penguin.co.uk/authors/1072451/lilian-carmine.html

39 Brittany Geragotelis: https://www.simonandschuster.com/authors/Brittany-Geragotelis/405274297

40 Kickstarter (www.kickstarter.com) is an often overlooked channel that has a lot of potential for success for publishers and authors.

go to Kickstarter.com and search for projects like "Hello Ruby," "Masters of Anatomy," or "The Leader's Guide by Eric Ries," to see examples of very successful projects that used "lean publishing elements," such as getting feedback and finding followers early. These projects raised hundreds of thousands of dollars from ten thousands of supporters. A priceless support, often even before the first chapter is written.

Also, Amazon has a couple of built-in features for applying lean book publishing principles. In addition, authors and publishers have found ways to use Amazon in a way that allows them to publish quickly and align with the feedback of their target audience.

Let's take a closer look at what is possible with Amazon, as well as other direct publishing platforms like Kobo Writer Life. First of all, Amazon's KDP platform provides an interface that allows authors to test variants of the 7 book marketing keys as well as the manuscript. This allows for adaptation on an ongoing basis and, with ebooks, almost instantly. Simply upload a different book cover, show a different book description, or present a new manuscript. With Amazon, you can do that by clicking a couple of buttons. Amazon's approval normally follows within a couple of hours as well, resulting in a great platform for testing elements quickly.

But what about the core idea of finding out if readers like your book quickly, by publishing raw ideas and first chapters? Amazon does not provide a way to do that. At least, that's what we assume at first sight.

But what you will learn now might surprise you. Because both fiction and non-fiction authors have found ways, often without knowing about the concepts behind it, to publish the lean way. And this with big success!

I invite you to take a look at the author profile of well-known British writer Mark Dawson[41]. He is the creator of the John Milton series.

For non-fiction low content and 10 instead of 50 rules and pdf downloads, do not write a 500 page book. Break it into 5-10 parts instead, whether it is fiction or non-fiction.

This has many benefits. Not only is it faster to put on the market and provide the option for quicker feedback, but also offers advantages like better visibility in Amazon search (because there are more keywords) and higher total sales (when adding up individual prices). And what's more, LBP through Amazon also reduces failure rates. Realizing that you've failed with part 1 of a series is much easier than with a whole series/book published at once. And finally, LBP is also in line with a trend. People have less time to read big books. They want instant gratification.

So, to sum up, LBP is more relevant than ever before, and has found its way into book publishing. It is, however, not noticed for the most part, and when it is, it's not described as LBP.

For you as an author and publisher, this does not really matter anyway. What matters for you is that you are aware of the advantages that applying lean publishing principles to your books have. By relying on Secret

41 https://www.amazon.com/Mark-Dawson/e/B0034Q9BO8

#4, you will not only reduce costly failure and find the right target audiences for your book faster, but more importantly get closer to publishing books that your readers will truly love.

There is a popular quote that says "starting is the hardest."[42] However, I would argue that with books "finishing strong" is the harder part. And lean book publishing provides a fantastic way to not only start quickly, but also to stay motivated through the often lengthy writing time. Most importantly, it helps you to finish strong, based on a good product with an already established fan base.

> *"Being able to finish strong is a powerful and rewarding skill for publishers and authors to master."*[43]

42 Quote by Simon Sinnek. "The hardest part is starting. Once you get that out of the way, you'll find the rest of the way much easier."

43 You will learn more about that skill throughout this book, mostly in Secrets 9 and 10.

Secret #4 Checkbox

Core Insights:

- ☑ LBP is all about creating books that readers truly love
- ☑ LBP reduces failure rates and is a win-win for both authors and readers
- ☑ LBP is everywhere (in launch teams, book series, ebook first launches, podcasts, etc.)

Exercises

1) How could you apply lean book publishing principles to your books?
2) Do you have a story in the making that you could publish the lean way? And if yes, what are possible actions?

5

THE IMPORTANCE OF 10,000 READERS [A BOOK LAUNCH]

What I have learned from my experience working individually with hundreds of authors from all over the world is that around 50% of authors who come to me are not aware of two critical points when launching their books:

1) It needs a substantial amount of targeted readers (ideally aiming for 10,000) that need to connect with your book, in order to give it a true chance for success
2) And secondly, it needs an investment into paid advertising and/or promotional campaigns in order to target these readers

Let's look at both points more closely.

The first point is constructed around a simplified calculation that is based on experience in the market. It says that if you manage to get around 10,000 targeted readers notified of your book launch (eg. via newsletter, high-quality online advertisement, radio, etc.) and convert 10%, to get 1,000 people on your book sales page (or in the physical world in touch with your book), you can expect around 10% to actually purchase your book, leaving you with 100 targeted readers, which are the minimum amount of readers needed to have given your book a true chance for success. If you continue the calculation with the simplified 10% conversion rate, you end up with only 10% of readers being an advocate[44], which means they give you feedback, spread the word, or write a review.

The Importance Of 10,000 Readers [Simple Calculation]		
Impressions	10K	10%
Sales Page	1K	10%
Readers	100	10%
Advocates	10	

Suddenly looking at a number of only 10 advocates or 100 readers, compared to the initial 10,000 people targeted, changes the perspective quickly. When also taking into account that 50% of books only get half read[45] and that having just a handful of brand advocates is seldom enough to trigger virality, we get closer to an understanding that in book marketing, as well as in

44 "A brand advocate is someone who elevates your brand through word of mouth marketing. Brand advocates leave positive reviews about your product. They also refer new customers and create content on your behalf. Brand advocates even contribute useful insights to your user personas." Source: Sprout Social, 2019: https://sproutsocial.com/glossary/brand-advocate/

45 Source: https://www.theifod.com/how-many-people-finish-books/

digital product marketing as a whole, we need to target and think bigger numbers in order to reach critical mass.

Interestingly, we can learn the most in this respect from the book launches of successful online entrepreneurs and business owners. Just think of Peter Voogd (founder of the Game Changer's Academy[46]), Sabri Suby (founder of King Kong[47]) or Russell Brunson (founder of Click Funnels[48]), who have successful online businesses and were able to apply their digital marketing knowledge of creating profitable paid advertising models to their book launches.

To give you a couple of numbers from their campaigns, Russell Brunson sold 66,000 books in 12 weeks in 2017[49], Peter Voogd earned $200,000 in royalties in 2 years from 2 books between 2016 and 2018[50], and Sabri Suby's book *Sell like Crazy*, launched in summer 2019, makes $10,000 on Amazon alone every month, just three months after launch[51].

I am not sharing these numbers to line up with the digital marketers out there screaming big numbers in order to create hype. No, I am sharing them to show you that sales numbers like this are possible for digital marketers, who are not coming from the book publishing industry and are not published by big publishing houses.

---

46 Game Changer's Academy: https://gamechangersmovement.com/

47 Australian digital marketing agency: https://kingkong.com.au/

48 US-American software company: https://www.clickfunnels.com/

49 Source: https://marketingsecrets.com/66k-books-sold/

50 Information from Meanwhile Private Podcast

51 Private research using paid software

What these entrepreneurs do is to combine paid advertising (focusing on big numbers that go way beyond my recommended 10K+) with high-converting book sales funnels. And they apply a process that works over and over again.

By looking at entrepreneurs like this, we are able to more quickly change our thinking and to move away from the traditional and sometimes a little romantic book marketing model, in which we initially market our books to 10, 50 or 100 targeted persons and wait for the bestseller to happen.

For experienced digital marketers, these numbers are just ridiculously small. And for the sake of our books and the time, sweat, love, and effort we invested into them, we are wise to learn from them in this respect and apply "bigger numbers" thinking as well.

As a side note, I want to add that bigger publishing houses can also learn a lot from this thinking. Distribution is just different in the digital world. In bookstores publishers have the visibility for these basic numbers automatically, without giving it too much thought. But in the digital world, it is easy to overlook that the base distribution is often just not where it has to be in order to reach critical mass.

The second point I want to address is that it needs an investment in paid advertising and/or a launch campaign. This means allocating a budget for your book that allows you to pay for marketing campaigns reaching 10,000 targeted readers or more. And sometimes also for experts who are able to set up and monitor campaigns for you.

The truth is that you need to be prepared to invest the base amount needed [I suggest that this amount is at least $1,000 USD[52]] into paid advertising and/or promotional campaigns, in order to give your book a true chance to succeed.

So when looking at the campaigns of publishing houses and digital marketers, we know what is necessary. But what does the reality look like? What do I see in the market when working with authors and publishers?

What I observe is that there is still a widespread assumption in the market that a good book will make its own way. Or that, once the book is uploaded to Amazon, it will get found in search and discovered.

This could not be further from the truth.

The fact is, if you upload a book on Amazon today, you can upload some random text, swear and do crazy things, and without marketing this book it is unlikely that someone will ever purchase it and discover what you did. At least that's true for new KDP accounts and first time authors. You want to give it a try? Do so. But of course, proceed at your own risk and be careful if you are an established author, publisher, or writing non-fiction based on clear user search intent. You might get caught.

The point I want to make clear is that without investing in having an audience to start with, you will not be able to get enough eyeballs on your book to give it a chance for

52 At the time of writing (Nov 2019) $1,000 USD is a good ballpark figure for the budget needed to reach 10K+ targeted readers through a book launch, by using email newsletter services or paid advertising campaigns. The expense includes advertising rates, as well as having a freelancer to help you with the basic setup if needed.

success. You need to give your book a substantial push in the beginning. And I am not talking about a little nudge, like you give your kid the first time she goes sledding or rides a bike. No, I mean a substantial push out into the cold, out of your comfort zone, into new territory, so that you see if it stands and starts to thrive on its own.

Here is what I have developed as a rule of thumb over the last couple of years, consistent with the calculation shared at the beginning of this chapter: if you manage to reach 10,000 targeted prospects[53] through advertising and, out of them, around 1,000 highly-targeted readers visit your book sales page (eg. Amazon or personal book landing page), you get a lot of valuable data and feedback about conversion rates for your book marketing campaign.

And if you apply the calculation for your book launch and are able to convert 10% into readers who actually buy your book, you will not only get the base amount of readers needed for proof-of-concept, but also start to be on a good track for creating profitable campaigns in the future. You will have given your book the chance it deserves for success. That's the secret of 10,000 readers.

"The calculation behind giving your book the chance for success is the secret of marketing to 10,000 readers."

53 Key is the conversion rate, in order to get 1,000 highly targeted readers visiting your book sales page. The 10K work if they convert at 10%. To give you an example: In case you run display ad campaigns on Google, you will not manage a 10% conversion rate, you will need way more impressions. So in the end, the 10K work in case you are running high-quality ads with the right advertising method chosen.

But how much does it cost to reach 10K readers and to do a proper book launch?

From my experience, you do not need more than $1,000 USD[54] to do a basic book launch, including a paid advertising or email marketing campaign that reaches 10K+ targeted readers. Listing recommended campaigns at this point would go beyond the scope of this chapter, as well as doing calculations on CPCs for digital advertising campaigns, debating the suggested $1,000 ballpark figure, or going into details about my simplified 10% conversion rate, which will not hold up for many campaigns.

So I want to keep that short at this point. These are very simplified numbers, and will vary widely from book to book and depending on the actual advertising or marketing campaign selected.

What's really important for me is to give you a simple and memorable recipe, based on my experience working on hundreds of book projects over the last couple of years. And that is what I am doing with the 10K reader secret.

Can the numbers be different? Yes, they can.

Do you need to invest $1,000 or more all at once, in order to push your book launch? No, you don't.

You can think lean and divide your advertising amount in 2-4 investment phases as well. This gives you the chance to learn from your campaigns and, ideally, also create revenue along the way to fund your expenses. You also don't need to invest everything into paid

54 At the time of writing in November 2019.

advertising services like AMS, Facebook, or Bookbub ads. There are also cheaper options to advertise and different ways to get eyeballs at lower cost. The opportunities are diverse and would go beyond the scope of this book, but just to name major areas, think about online PR, blogging, newsletter campaigns, collaborations with other authors, social media, etc.

As a first step, especially if your budget is limited and you need more feedback, you can also aim for at least 1,000 readers (ad impressions do not count, though). At a 10% conversion rate, you would get 100 readers, which is often the absolute minimum in order to create any form of virality and word-of-mouth or to have an effect on discoverability in Amazon search.

Are there exceptions to the rule?

Yes, most certainly. There will be exceptions, such as very targeted non-fiction books or truly amazing fiction books; however, you should not expect to be the exception. It's better to prepare for reality.

So ask yourself:

- Did I give my book a real chance to succeed?
- Did I invest enough money to get 10K readers (or as a minimum 1K readers) to my book sales page?

If you didn't and you believe in your book, come up with ways to get this exposure. Give your book the chance it deserves in the competitive landscape of book publishing.

Secret #5 Checkbox

Core Insights:

☑ Aim to reach at least 10K targeted readers (mere display ad impressions do not count, high-quality ads, mentions and interactions do), in order to give your book a chance for success

Exercises

- Did you market your book to at least 10K targeted readers? If not, take appropriate action.
- Did at least 100 targeted readers read your book? If not, take appropriate action.

6

THE ONE FACTOR MAKING OR BREAKING BOOKS

There is one decisive factor that makes or breaks books: reviews. In the offline world, publishers are still able to keep the influence of reviews limited. But in the online world, reviews are almost everything. And this is supported by hard facts.

As already shared with you in Chapter 2, a study conducted by the Spiegel Research Center[55] in 2017 showed that 95% of buyers read online reviews before making a purchase. 95%. An incredibly high number, but I am not surprised.

Truth is, and I have seen it with clients numerous times, without a substantial amount of positive reviews, books will almost certainly die. Or, at the very least, not become very successful.

The basic rules regarding online reviews are:

55 Source: Spiegel Research Center (2017): https://spiegel.medill.northwestern.edu/_pdf/Spiegel_Online%20Review_eBook_Jun2017_FINAL.pdf

Basic Rules Regarding Book Reviews

No reviews = No sales

The more reviews -> The more sales

The more positive reviews -> The higher the conversion rates, and the other way around

I am still surprised how often authors approach me with books that have 0 reviews and wonder why they have no sales. The first thing I always tell them is that the reason no one buys their book is because it has no reviews. Getting this external validation from an expert is often an eye-opener. That's the point when they realize that they absolutely need to fix this one problem first, before doing anything else.

And yes, if the book is good, your first step is to get 10 reviews for it, so that you can rise from the ashes.

For well-established authors and big publishers, getting the first 10-25 reviews is comparably easy. Just put together a proper book launch and inform the author's previous readers about the new book.

For first-time authors, self-published authors, and small publishers, however, the task of getting the first 5-25 reviews is difficult. And it does not get easier with Amazon's strict terms and community guidelines, prohibiting asking family, friends, and business associates, and not allowing to you to offer anything in return for the review.

For market players who want to do everything correctly, developments regarding online reviews have become a true burden. And I do not exclude myself here. Getting the first 25 reviews and doing everything properly and correctly is one of the most critical results that I have to achieve for my clients.

Over the years I developed a fantastic strategy though. Authors and publishers can use this strategy to get reviews ethically and at very high conversion rates. I call the strategy the "surprise gift strategy." It uses the "Look Inside" pages of a book to communicate the offer for a surprise gift that readers can access on the author's or publisher's webpage. After signing up with their email address, they get bonus content and also a request for feedback and a review.

When done properly, this strategy not only increases the conversion rates of getting reviews substantially, it also creates email lists of readers at incredible speed. I also use this strategy with my books. You can go through the process to see how, and learn how I do it to build my list and to get reviews.

Once you have this strategy in place and create a decent list of readers, it gets easier and easier to promote book launches and to get those first critical reviews.

First-time authors just starting to apply the "surprise gift strategy," or authors publishing for a new target audience, will still need to make an initial push for reviews. For those clients, I mostly recommend that they work with selected ARC-services and/or to research power reviewers who are not only highly interested in the respective niche, but also frequently provide reviews. By approaching power reviewers correctly, authors and publishers are not only able to get more reviews, but also to establish powerful business relationships in their fields. You can learn more about my latest advice for getting reviews by visiting my personal website www.albertgriesmayr.com.

Another critical aspect regarding reviews is that, interestingly, the quantity of reviews is generally more important than the quality. Books that have garnered 100+ reviews on Amazon, for instance, communicate "proof of concept" and give readers security and social proof that the book is established in the market.

However, the threshold between a perception of overall positive ratings to a perception of overall negative ratings is thin and has to be monitored closely. On Amazon, the threshold is at a rating of 4.25. It is visually visible by the amount and the extent of stars filled. Below, I'll show you two book examples with a rating of 4.2 and a rating of 4.3. You can easily see that there is a big difference in the perception of these ratings, although the actual difference in quality is very small.

Star Rating above 4.25 (to 4.7)	Star Rating below 4.25 (to 3.8)	Star Rating below 3.75 (to 3.3)
★★★★☆ (128)	★★★★☆ (62)	★★★☆☆ (65)

As a rule of thumb, you should always aim for a rating of over 4.25 in order to sell well. If you are below this rating, your sales will suffer. Being in the range between 4.2. and 3.8 is still acceptable for some books (depending on the competition, the genre, etc.) as well. However, below 3.75, click-through rates, sales, and perception get ugly quickly.

But more importantly, you should not only look at the economic message overall ratings provide, but carefully read all reviews and take criticism in order to improve your book. This leads me to the hidden core message of Secret #6. When I say "reviews make or break books," I do not only refer to the economical side of it. I also refer to the important "feedback mechanism" that reviews provide, in order to literally "make a book."

It's absolutely eye-opening to read through the reviews of a book that has 50 or 100+ reviews, because they reviewers say so much about the book. They talk about the quality of the writing, the book layout, their feelings, knowledge learned, and even typos with page numbers.

Doesn't it make you shake your head when you see an established book on the market with reviews dated from a couple of years ago, complaining about typos and layout mistakes which are still present 5 years later? It tells us that some publishers or authors do not read reviews. But more often, it says they do not care enough about little pieces of advice that can be used to improve a book's layout, resulting in an updated edition.

Once publishers and authors really start to take all reviews seriously, to see their books as works in progress, and to take appropriate action, they significantly increase their quality of books, sales, and satisfaction rates. Too often we just move on to a more promising project or a new interest, before taking the time to improve what we already have.

To further illustrate the importance of reviews, as well as their critical feedback mechanism, I want to invite you to visit the Amazon page[56] of young adult author Amanda Hocking, who was one of the early self-publishing Kindle stars.[57] When you browse her books, you will notice that some of them have over 900 reviews, while others have 0 or just a handful of reviews. How is it possible that a successful author with millions of copies sold has such a huge spread between the books?

One obvious answer is that Amanda has different formats in her list (such as a hardcover version or a CD), as well as some "orphan files" with weird titles or very high prices. But what you also see by taking a closer look is that some books reach "critical mass" and others don't. The ones who don't simply die. And not surprisingly, out of the ones with less than 10 reviews, ratings are low as well. When analyzing such statistics mathematically, you see that there are clear correlations and data points supporting the three review rules stated at the beginning of this chapter.

Basic rules for book reviews

1) No reviews = No sales
2) The more reviews -> The more sales
3) The more positive reviews -> The higher the conversion rates, and the other way around

So what's paramount is to give reviews the importance in book marketing that they really have. They truly make or break books.

56 https://www.amazon.com/kindle-dbs/entity/author/B003H4L762

57 https://www.theguardian.com/books/2012/jan/12/amanda-hocking-self-publishing

To finish this chapter, I want to share with you the results of private research I did with my team. We analyzed the qualitative content of "top reviews" of 100 books on Amazon (51 fiction books, 49 non-fiction advice books)[58] in order to test assumptions and to get a deeper understanding of characteristics readers care and communicate about.

What we found out, by analyzing almost 600 reviews for these books, was that — supporting our core assumption — there is a big difference in what is important in fiction and what's important in advice books. Also, factors that often do not get taken so seriously, such as layout (formatting, typos) or language (easy to read, clear language), get referenced often.

As you can see by looking at the results, in non-fiction books "value" is a primary factor, mentioned in 74% of all reviews. What was interesting to observe for me was that in 14% of all NF reviews, layout was an important factor, although many books were not outstanding in this field. In most cases where the layout was really good (including checklists, nice typography, illustrations, etc.) this was also mentioned in the reviews. This shows that layout is indeed important and has the power to be a convincing factor if done properly.

In fiction books, the factors "storytelling" and "language" are critical and mentioned in even more than 90% of analyzed reviews. The paramount take-away is to focus on these characteristics in order to improve ratings and reader satisfaction.

58 Private Research conducted on Amazon.com in October 2019

Number of books analyzed — 100 (NF- 49 , F- 51)
Number of reviews analyzed — 581 (NF- 299 , F -282)

NF (299 reviews)
Storytelling mentioned in only 6.5% of the reviews
Providing Value mentioned in 74% of the reviews
Layout mentioned in 14% of the reviews
Language mentioned in 17% of the reviews

F (282 reviews)
Storytelling mentioned in 72% of the reviews
Providing Value mentioned in 10% of the reviews
Layout mentioned in 5% of the reviews
Language mentioned in 33 % of the reviews

I want to finish Secret #6 by sharing my favorite quote about reviews, which is:

"Reviews are the lifeblood of books in the digital age."

"Reviews are the lifeblood of books in the digital age."[59] They not only have critical economic importance but also provide much needed feedback to learn and to improve books.

So my advice is to not only focus on having lots of positive reviews, but also to analyze the content carefully, in order to grow your sales and to make you a better writer, author, and publisher.

59 Personal quote, October 2019

Secret #6 Checkbox

Core Insights:

- ☑ Reviews are the lifeblood of books in the digital age
- ☑ 95% of online shoppers read online reviews before purchasing products online [according to 2017 study]
- ☑ Providing value is the most critical satisfaction factor mentioned for non-fiction reviews, whereas storytelling is in fiction
- ☑ Remember the basic rules for book reviews [No reviews = No sales, The more reviews -> The more sales
- ☑ The more positive reviews -> The higher the conversion rates, and the other way around

Exercises

- What is your strategy for getting reviews right now?
- Do you already use a tactic similar to the "surprise gift strategy"?
- What can you learn from the qualitative message of the reviews you already have?

7

THE EARLY BIRD CATCHES THE WORM

In 2007, I went for an exchange semester to the US, to Oregon State University. It's still one of the best memories I have from my time as a student. The campus was huge, modern, and overall student life on campus was fantastic. I also met a lot of international students and established connections for life.

After having been asked a couple of times to connect with them on Facebook, which I had never heard of, I decided it was time to check out what Facebook actually was.

I went online and registered for the site to connect with students I met. I was hooked quickly and I realized that this social network was onto something. I also realized that creating a Facebook page was easy, and that pages could grow really quickly from just a few members to thousands or even tens of thousands of fans.

Eventually, I started to work in a social media agency which was fully focused on Facebook. We had a great time designing and implementing social media campaigns for corporate clients. Growth rates were fantastic.

At that time, I was not sure about the main take-away from this episode. But years later, when I was already in business with Scribando | Novelify, it became very clear to me that the core insight was how powerful it was to latch on to a trend early. The rewards for early entrants catching a big wave in business are so much higher than the rewards for the players catching the second wave. Very often, it is also not possible to really profit from trends if you are too late. You need to be early.

We have seen the importance of being early[60] and catching a trend numerous times in business, such as with Google, which was not the first search engine of course, but still within the first wave of major players fulfilling the growing need of a great search experience; with Zynga[61], one of the early social game developers on Facebook, the creator behind viral games such as Farmville, reaching 10 million daily active users (DAU) within just six weeks; or with "Toniebox"[62], a more recent example of a German company, whose "listening boxes for kids" have grown into a household name in German-speaking countries within just two years.

And the importance of being early is not any different with books. Especially when we focus on book marketing. The big publishing houses had to learn their lesson painfully regarding e-commerce, when they had to sit still and observe Amazon taking over the online retail space for books, as well as consuming a huge portion of self-publishing with its Kindle Direct Publishing service.

---

60 The emphasis is on being early and not first. Google, Facebook, and Amazon have certainly not been the first companies in their fields, but their growth was still fueled by catching the immense wave of a trend being created.

61 Source: Wikipedia: https://en.wikipedia.org/wiki/Zynga

62 https://tonies.de/

And authors realized quickly around 10 years ago that self-publishing was more than a short-lived trend, but instead a bigger shift that would alter the playing field forever. Today Amazon's KDP service is the absolute market leader in self-publishing, with sources referencing its book market share in self-published books as up to 85%[63]. Amazon definitely caught the wave early and grew tremendously. Early self-publishing stars like Amanda Hocking[64] in the U.S.A. or B.C. Schiller in Germany have profited immensely from being early.

However, I would not draw a complete picture by only talking about areas related to book marketing, such as distribution and availability. Trends are relevant for the core field book publishing a lot as well, such as with formats (eg. ebooks, audiobooks), publishing processes (eg. lean book publishing), as well as book genres (eg. growth and decline of genres).

A fantastic example was provided by J.K. Rowling with Harry Potter. When she published the first novel, *Harry Potter and the Philosopher's Stone*, in 1997, nobody wanted to touch fantasy stories, as Michelle Smith, senior lecturer in literature at Deakin University[65], told ABC. Fantasy stories were seen as old-fashioned. But Rowling created something new. She added wizards, witches, and magic, bringing new life to the formula. Belle Alderman, the director of the National Centre for Australian Children's Literature at the University of

---

63 Source: Kindlepreneur: https://kindlepreneur.com/best-self-publishing-companies/

64 Source. Learn more https://www.theguardian.com/books/2012/jan/12/amanda-hocking-self-publishing

65 Source: https://www.abc.net.au/news/2017-06-26/harry-potter-effect-how-seven-books-changed-childrens-publishing/8630254

Canberra, even said "the series was the first to blur the line between children's and adult's books."[66]

Rowling's success could be more related to catching a trend early than we had assumed so far. We can also learn that there are frequent opportunities in classical aspects of book publishing, such as new or changing book genres, hot and trending book topics (eg. the latest cooking trend, a new celebrity, a hotly debated phenomenon, etc.) and trending formats (such as short stories, audiobooks, podcasts and conversational stories), to catch and to benefit from.

However, talking about the benefits of being early is one thing. What's even more important, from my experience working personally with more than 100 authors and publishers from around the world, is to talk about the costs of being late and of trying to be successful in a market where you have little experience.

A good observation can be made by looking at job postings related to "book launches," "ghostwriting," and "book marketing support" on freelancer webpages, such as Upwork. Many postings unveil author and publisher intentions to follow outdated tactics, combined with inexperience about book marketing. You can read about requirements and expectations, such as "launching book to 100K copies sold," "social media management for aspiring influencer," "getting Amazon bestseller badge quickly," or "ghostwriting Keto Diet book" (which is probably book number 10,000 on that topic already on the market).

Being active on portals like Upwork as a professional[67] can get a little crazy sometimes, but of course I am not

66 Source: https://www.abc.net.au/news/2017-06-26/harry-potter-effect-how-seven-books-changed-childrens-publishing/8630254

67 Here is my Upwork profile: https://www.upwork.com/freelancers/~01a883a70099dc1746

here to throw blame. Upwork is a place for connecting with professionals who can help, so that is all fine. What I want to make you aware of, though, is that unfortunately lots of these postings find an agency or a freelancer who will fulfill the client's need without much questioning or a specific background in book marketing, resulting in actions and campaigns that are simply far from being effective in the current landscape.

And honestly, my heart is bleeding every time I see great book projects petering out because of outdated marketing tactics.

Here you have the author who invested a year writing his book, months into polishing, editing, and formatting it with professional help, often investing thousands of dollars, who is finally able to publish it on the market, only to realize that the current approach is not good enough. For me, personally, it is painful. It's one of the factors that keep me most motivated about what I do on a daily basis, as I want to keep as many authors as possible from this painful cycle.

It definitely is one of the aspects I am most passionate about regarding my job, namely, to help my clients with the latest strategies for success, and to save them from going on overcrowded paths that, most of the time, lead to nowhere.

The good thing is that I see a development in the market. Both publishers and authors see more and more that it is beneficial to catch marketing trends early. Clear indicators are the commercial success of self-publisher support companies, like Self Publishing School[68], Kindlepreneur, or KDSPY, as well as outcomes,

68 Source: Self Publishing School: https://self-publishingschool.com/

such as sales figures of self-publishers, and the strong performance of established publishers in the audiobook sector over the last couple of years.

I've even developed my own contribution to helping support authors and publishers in caching book marketing waves early, with my company Scribando (www.scribando.com). In case you haven't, I highly recommend that you sign up for the service and give it a try. My goal is that this service becomes the best investment for a publisher in terms of staying up-to-date on the best book marketing opportunities in the market.

So what should you be doing as an author right now[69], in order to catch the worm? What are the main marketing trends?

My answer at the time of writing (late 2019) is straightforward: right now you should be on the forefront of "audio first," "automated book sales funnels," and "AI related to content production." Audio is already happening, as you can see by the growth rates of audiobooks and the success of Audible in recent years. But there is still big potential for audiobooks related to ebooks (just do a search for a keyword on Amazon vs. Audible, to compare the numbers of audiobooks and ebooks on the market).

The most important aspect, though, is to think "audio first." This means you should at first think about questions like, "How would that sound?" "Is that a topic for audio?" etc... Ideally, start with producing an audiobook first.

The next area is Amazon's Alexa. Amazon says it sold over 100 million Alexa-powered gadgets before the

69 Time of writing: December, 2019

beginning of 2019[70], and the catalogue of skills has grown from just 130 upon its release in 2016 to over 100,000 skills as of September 2019.[71] Once you have an audiobook, creating an Alexa skill in order to promote your book or creating added value for your audiobook is the next step. Today, almost no one is doing that, but my data and insight suggests that this will change quickly and provide a big opportunity in the upcoming years.

The next major area to be in early is AI related to content production. There are already numerous applications and companies offering services in the following three areas, all substantial for authors.

- Content production: Speech to Text (related to speed) makes producing a book much faster
- Content production (content automation): Content automation supported by AI. You start a text, AI continues to write a story
- Book editing (with AI): You provide the raw manuscript, software makes a book out of it

It will take some time for commercial readiness in these applications. But once that readiness for marketing has been reached, the wave will grow quickly, and you should not miss it.

I want to finish this chapter with my perspective on the popular quote: "The early bird catches the worm but the second mouse gets the cheese"[72] by advising: "Be both."

---

70 Source: CNBC https://www.cnbc.com/2019/09/28/amazon-alexa-growth-has-investors-questioning-the-business-model.html

71 Source: Statista: https://www.statista.com/statistics/912856/amazon-alexa-skills-growth/

72 Source unknown: https://quoteinvestigator.com/2013/01/25/second-mouse/

> *"Be both the early bird that catches the worm and the second mouse that gets the cheese."*

The most successful authors and publishers I work with have a great attitude toward staying on top of the latest market developments and opportunities. But they are also wise enough to wait for proven concepts and tools to develop around an opportunity. You do not have to have the expenses of the first mover. That's why, at Scribando, we have also decided to test opportunities whenever possible ourselves, before communicating the insights with our members.

The next secret will teach you how not only how to be the early bird, but more importantly how to be the second mouse which gets the cheese. So read on and discover a proven concept for reverse-engineering successful book publishing models and businesses.

Secret #7 Checkbox
Core Insights:
☑ Publishers and authors who catch trends early can exploit advantages and quick growth
☑ It is not about being first, it is about being early and being the second mouse that gets the cheese
Exercises
– Are you using services or processes in order to stay up to date on the latest book marketing developments and opportunities? If not, establish a process.
– What are great opportunities you are aware of that you could tap right now?

8

FOLLOW THE MONEY [AND REVERSE ENGINEERING BOOKS]

What do the fields of mechanical engineering, military or commercial espionage, e-commerce, and software engineering have in common with book publishing?

You have no clue? Gotcha! I totally understand. Hopefully I've got your attention, because I'm about to tell you. Secret #8 is worth gold to everyone who applies this secret to their book publishing businesses.

What these fields have in common is that they all benefit from the application of reverse engineering. Reverse engineering is the process of developing detailed design information from an existing part or product and an understanding of how it works.[73]

Reverse engineering is about finding something that works, analyzing and understanding it and, in

73 Source: NPD Solutions: https://www.npd-solutions.com/remethodology.html

a consequent step (technically distinct from reverse engineering)[74], using the knowledge gained for improving and modeling your own processes. And this is exactly what many successful authors and publishers have done for years, in order to be commercially successful and to beat their competition. I recommend you to do the same. And you should do that by starting to "follow the money" as a first step.

So how do you start with "following the money"? The quickest way to do that is by opening bestseller lists and analyzing sales rankings of books at major retailers, such as Amazon. Go through the first 10 books of major lists, and analyze their book marketing keys. Figure out what they do to be successful. Check out their webpages and observe how they present themselves and their books. Once you take a deep look at the most successful players and start learning from them, you realize more quickly the gap that stands between you and them.

Once you see the gap, you can start to close it by modelling and adapting what successful market players do. Success often speaks for itself. It is hard to hide.

"Success often speaks for itself.
It is hard to hide."

So modelling successful authors and publishers is one important aspect of Secret #8. True mastery cannot be achieved, though, if you are not clear on what you want to achieve in the first place. Goal clarity will help you

74 Source: Wikipedia: https://en.wikipedia.org/wiki/Reverse_engineering

to look for exact role models, as well as envisioning the kind of books and marketing tactics that you need to create in order to reach those publishing goals.

I have recently created a Slideshare presentation on that topic, "How to reach your author goals by reverse engineering your dream book."[75] I recommend you take a look at it.

Source: Reverse Engineering your dream book, © Albert Griesmayr, 2019 https://www.slideshare.net/griesmayr/how-to-reach-your-author-goals-by-reverse-engineering-your-dream-book

In the following, I invite you to do an exercise with me, based on the presentation. It's an exercise that you can apply either to a book project you have planned or a book project you are marketing right now.

75 You can find the presentation by following this link: https://www.slideshare.net/griesmayr/how-to-reach-your-author-goals-by-reverse-engineering-your-dream-book

Follow The Money Exercise
1) Get clarity on your publisher goals (Full-time author? Amount of copies sold, visibility, or sales?)
2) Modeling and defining the needed outcome (Go through the 7 book marketing keys)
3) Create the action step to reach goals (Make a plan to get the results)

The exercise is all about finding the best way to reach your author goals, with the help of modeled players who have already achieved your goals. Defining your goals is quite straightforward (1); what's more difficult is to model and define the needed outcome and the key elements as closely as possible (2). To make things more concrete, I am sharing with you a personal story and my concrete example for the "Follow the money" exercise.

The person that I am modeling is Russell Brunson, founder of Clickfunnels, who has sold at least 250,000 copies of his books *Expert Secrets* and *DotCom Secrets* (April, 2018)[76] through Amazon, his publisher, and his own book funnels. I am a big fan of Russell, as he is a true marketing genius and keeps inspiring the digital marketing industry not only with his wisdom, but also with his concrete applications of sales funnels, which he and others have applied very successfully to books as well. So my choice is quite obvious and a well-suited example, as he has already reached the exact goals I want to reach with methods that align with me as well.

So here is my exercise based on an analysis of Russell's books and business.

76 Source: Marketing Secrets Blog, Russell Brunson, 2018: https://marketingsecrets.com/sell-book-amazon-sales-funnel/

Follow The Money Exercise [Modeling Russell Brunson, Founder ClickFunnels]
1) My goals: – more visibility and sales – book sales automation important – testing webpage based book sales funnels – promoting Scribando.com – adding credibility – having more time for consulting by sharing already formulated insights with clients 2) Needed outcome: [primarily based on Russell as an example] – Need to have strong manuscript and 7 book marketing keys – Particular focus on the funnel on my page and Scribando.com – Funnel needs to have upsell products, so that I can invest in paid advertising – Podcast or video series on the 10 secrets 3) Action steps: – Going the extra mile for creating a great book – Building funnel on my webpage and integrating upsells – Once the book is out, create YouTube- and Facebook video series on the 10 secrets – Get help for paid advertising campaign on FB and YT

I invite you to visit some of Russell's websites, such as "Expert Secrets,"[77] "Clickfunnels,"[78] or his marketing

77 https://expertsecrets.com/freebook

78 https://www.clickfunnels.com/

blog "Marketing Secrets,"[79] so that you get a better understanding for my analysis. Examining and studying a process that brings you the results that you want to achieve online is priceless. The internet has made reverse-engineering so much easier. It opens up true shortcuts that will free your time for what truly matters most to you.

Here are some important notes for your personal "follow-the-money" process. These will help you to avoid common pitfalls. Make sure that you:

- Do not get blinded by something that looks good or brings results indiscriminately; pick a role-model that has achieved what you want to achieve (be specific)
- Analyze potential success elements with care (sometimes there are tiny things that make a huge difference)
- Simplify whatever you can. It's difficult to start with the most advanced system. Break it down and start with something very simple, based on your role model
- Understand the underlying principles, formulas, and mechanics behind processes in order to learn correctly

Now, it's your turn to do the exercise. Find at least one publishing role model who has achieved what you are striving for and who you want to learn from. Analyze what they are doing and create your own action steps to get the results you are looking for.

Applying Secret #8 will put your publishing business and author career on steroids, as you will be able to reach your goals much faster by following proven recipes and formulas.

79 https://marketingsecrets.com/

Secret #8 Checkbox
Core Insights:
☑ Follow the money and look for authors and publishers who have reached what you want to accomplish ☑ Reverse-engineer their books and systems and get an understanding of why they are successful
Exercises
– Do the "follow the money" exercise and reverse engineer one of your role models

9

POST SALES MAGIC

I want to start this chapter with a question. What do you think: How much more expensive is it to acquire a new customer versus retaining an existing one?

- 2-3 times
- 5-10 times or
- 5-25 times

According to numerous studies, acquiring a new customer is anywhere from 5 to 25 times more expensive than retaining an existing one[80]. So if you guessed c) you chose the correct answer.

> *"Acquiring a new customer is anywhere from five to 25 times more expensive than retaining an existing one.[81]"*

And still, we as marketers behave in quite an unorthodox way. Most of us (including myself) have the natural tendency to focus on acquiring new customers

80 Source: Harvard Business Review, 2014 https://hbr.org/2014/10/the-value-of-keeping-the-right-customers

81 Source: Source: Harvard Business Review, 2014 https://hbr.org/2014/10/the-value-of-keeping-the-right-customers

and making new sales, instead of nurturing existing ones and focusing deeply on the customer journey of existing clients. Based on studies, our behavior is simply a mistake, a trick that our mind is playing on us. This chapter is aimed at convincing you that it pays off disproportionately. We need to break this wrong mindset and to focus on "post sales phases" instead. I invite you to follow me on a journey, an adventure to "Post Sales Magic Land" [PSML].

"Post Sales Magic Land" is a place that is filled with happy clients. They have crossed the border by paying their entry fee and realized after entering that they not only got what was promised, but even more than that. Their expectations have not only been fulfilled, they have been excelled. And now as clients are feeling happy, they are starting to make the new land their own. They start exploring for further opportunities. They prepare themselves for a long stay. They start shopping around and spreading the word about their great experience by calling their friends. And as long as they are not disappointed, they will stay happy customers of Post Sales Magic Land.

Wouldn't it be great to be the mayor of PSML? I bet it would. PSML is full of "post sales magic." Let's explore further.

Post Sales Magic is about making a fundamental shift: a shift in thinking. The shift away from the focus on "making the sale" to "starting with the sale." It is all about acknowledging that making a book sale is just a start or a stopover in the relationship with the reader, always embedded in a bigger process. It's about realizing that our job as authors and publishers has not been completed when we have sold a book; it has just started, instead.

In this chapter, you'll not only learn why focusing on the post-sale phase is so beneficial. Even more importantly, you'll learn how to create reader experiences that celebrate "post sales magic" in a way that not only makes your readers happy, but which is also financially profitable. So stay with me.

Let's explore the question of why investing in an amazing post-sales phase is so beneficial. We already talked about the high costs of acquiring new customers vs. selling more to existing ones, but there is way more than that.

In fact, by focusing on the post-sales phase, you are able to create happy customers who, in turn, will help you to sell more books and grow your business. Think about yourself! What do you do when you find a product that not only fulfilled your expectations, but even over-delivered? You will likely use the product, share it with others, maybe give feedback or provide a review, and want to buy more of the same brand. You will not complain to customer service, cause negative experiences with company reps, or make the product designers unhappy.

A happy customer (in our case a happy reader) will bring you the results you are striving for. Focusing on the customer experience and designing an amazing "post sales experience" is one of the best things that you can do as a publisher or author.

I now invite you to take a look at the following checklist, which shows you 15 proven tactics to create "post sales magic" for your readers. Most of these tactics below are used by my clients and other publishers with success.

Post Sales Magic Tactics [15 Proven PSM Tactics To Improve Reader Satisfaction And Increase Book Sales]
– Create the best book you can (apply secrets 1,2,3,..) – Work with a fantastic surprise gift – Add bonus value on your webpage – Put a "feedback request box" into your book – Offer useful upsell products – Create email automation that adds value – Invest in creating a launch team – Work with book publishing professionals (eg. editors, formatters, translators, marketers..) – Apply lean book publishing principles (such as testing your book before launching big) – Write a book series – Promote other books from you at the end of your book – Have upsell products in place – Read your book reviews and fix what can be fixed (publish revised editions) – Trigger built-in virality (eg. include partner exercises, surprising book elements, etc.) – Add unadvertised bonuses that readers did not expect (eg. thank you gift, book summaries, audiobook free, etc.)

Once you have achieved a high level of customer satisfaction, it gets far easier to earn more by offering related or upsell products. Take a look at the following list of possible related and upsell products that you can use to earn more from the readers and clients that you already have.

List of possible related and upsell products
– other book formats (eg. audiobook, paperback, etc.) – other books in a series – online courses – paid webinars – online or real-world workshops – affiliate products – related books and products – online programs – member areas

Post sales magic creates true win-win situations. Readers win because they get product experiences they truly love. And publishers win because they receive positive feedback, reviews, and more sales down the line.

In order to make things easy, I boiled Secret #9 down to a simple formula: the post sales magic formula. Apply the formula and be rewarded.

Post Sales Magic Formula
Create a fantastic reader experience that not only fulfills but excels reader expectations and provides plenty of opportunities to stay in touch and to purchase more from you.

One of the most important questions that you should ask yourself is: "What should my readers do after they have purchased and read my book?" Take a break for a second, get a pen and paper, and do the following exercise:

Exercise: Post-Sales Reader Behavior: "*What are*" vs. "*What should* my readers be doing after having read my book?"
Get pen and paper and answer the following questions about your readers post-sales experience. Then write down a concrete action step that you can implement for getting desired results. – Do your readers think that they have read a fantastic/valuable book? – Do they tell a friend about it? – Do they post on social media? – Do they visit your webpage and leave their contact information? – Do they purchase a different book from you?

Once you have done the exercise, you will have concrete action steps for getting closer to creating "post sales magic." Act on them and increase reader satisfaction bit by bit.

I want to finish Chapter 9 with a quote by management professor Michael LeBoeuf[82]:

> *"A satisfied customer is the best business strategy of all."*
>
> —Michael LeBoeuf

A satisfied customer *is* the best business strategy of all. It should come as no surprise when I tell you that

82 Source: Wikipedia: https://en.wikipedia.org/wiki/Michael_LeBoeuf

without satisfied, loyal customers, you will never have a successful business.[83]

I couldn't agree more with Michael LeBoeuf, and this is certainly true for books as well. Do not fall for the mistake a lot of authors make of focusing on the sale and missing the big opportunity of "post sales magic." Act like a skilled book marketer instead. Understand that your job and the real opportunity for book wealth has just started with a book sale.

Change your focus towards reader satisfaction and stop seeing the book sale as the end point. Always see it as a starting point or interstation before receiving feedback, getting a reader on your email-list, making another book sale, selling an upsell product or spreading word of mouth. Change your mindset and increase your odds of success substantially.

83 Source: By Michael LeBoeuf: https://therestaurantboss.com/leboeuf-satisfied-customer/ (exact source of original publication unknown)

Secret #9 Checkbox

Core Insights:

- ☑ Post Sales Magic is about focusing on reader satisfaction and realizing that the book sale is just the start
- ☑ Use the "Post Sales Magic Formula" [Create a fantastic reader experience that not only fulfills but excels reader expectations and provides plenty of opportunities to stay in touch and to purchase more from you.]

Exercises

- Analyze how you can apply the post sales magic formula to your books.
- Do the post-sales-reader behavior exercise and list action steps to increase your PSM

10

THE HOLY GRAIL: BOOK SALES AUTOMATION

Book Marketing Secret #10 is the holy grail of book marketing. It is the ultimate ideal outcome of all author and publisher efforts and the result of mastery of all previous book marketing secrets. It also shows a core element of the beauty of book publishing. It is the chance for creating a stream of passive income.

A stream of passive income created from an "automated book sales system" that lives and breathes on its own, a stream that makes your book publishing venture profitable. That means I am not talking about selling 50 copies, for instance, that bring $4 USD royalties/book a month, resulting in a revenue of $200 USD.

No. What I am talking about is the type of passive income that stays in your pocket at the end of the month. Profit. Revenue/royalties from book sales, minus advertising and other costs, resulting in pure profit from your book ventures. That's the kind of income that has made selected publishers and top authors truly wealthy over the last decades. Due to increased competition, achieving market success has certainly become more difficult over the last 10 years. But passive income from books is still a very achievable goal and a reality for many authors, publishers, and publishing businesses in the market.

I just recently talked again to owners of a Kindle publishing business, who were able to scale up their business from 0 to more than 300 books (which they fully control), bringing in a revenue of more than $25,000 USD per month, all built in less than 2 years. Pretty amazing. Is their business profitable? Yes, it is.

These founders are ambitious and they have far bigger goals. That's why they invest heavily in new titles, education, and advertising. So they might not generate a big profit at the end of a month yet; but if they stopped investing and publishing today, they would already have built a very solid passive income business, all made from books.

To fully understand different ways of how book sales automation can work, you need to understand your "book sales system" first.

Below, find my visualization of the "automated book sales system" for this book, *Book Marketing Secrets*. It is based on the 3-step model "Attraction — Conversion — Retention."[84] Attraction involves steps to attract customers. Conversion refers to the process of making them a customer, requiring that they are in touch with your sales page. And retention is all about keeping and growing revenue from existing customers. The model is simple, beautiful, and effective. You can also draw it out quickly (once you have the data) and make your "automated

84 Source: Albert Griesmayr, 2019

book sales system" understandable quite easily. As I created the model before I launched, the cited numbers, such as the cost for acquiring a reader and the expected conversion rates, are my estimates and plan to launch with. I am planning on updating the numbers in a revised future edition. Let's take a look at my model below:

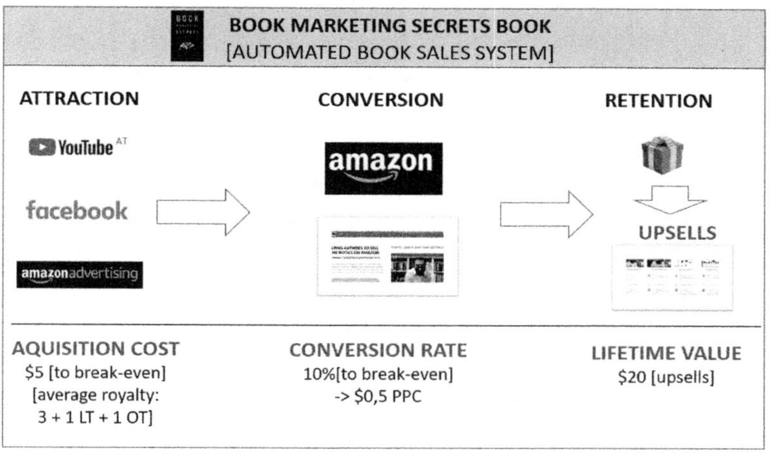

"Automated book sales system" — Book: Book Marketing Secrets" © Albert Griesmayr, 2019

Traffic should primarily come from:

- YouTube video series + paid YT advertising
- Facebook video series + paid FB advertising
- Amazon ads + Amazon organic search

Conversion [rates & sales pages]:

- There is one sales page on Amazon and one sales page on my website
- I am willing to spend up to $5 for each new reader who purchases the book (to break even)

Retention [upsell products]:

- Readers should sign up on my webpage (50% of my readers), because of my thank you gift

- As long as they are on my list, I can make them aware of my other (upsell) products, such as my online program, the Scribando service, and other books

So in a nutshell, that's my plan and visualization of my book marketing system. I will launch the book to 10K readers [Book Marketing Secret #5], and have the goal of getting 200 new readers at break even [$1,000 revenue] at $1,000 expense. To make this calculation work, I calculate with $5 in revenue ($3 revenue + $1 lifetime value + $1 organic sales increase), as below that point paid advertising gets increasingly difficult, even for a very targeted product.

On the other hand, when looking at the lifetime value of my audience, I estimate a new reader to be worth much more than $5, so I am totally fine with my calculation of spending $5 for each new reader, without any loss and with acquiring new readers basically for free. When you combine that with the fact that you can scale up such a system, it quickly gets very powerful for authors and publishers who are able to make such a system work.

You can also see that this book is not a passive income machine for me. My main goal is to share my knowledge at an affordable price (because that's my passion) and most importantly to acquire new customers basically for free. These will hopefully, ultimately, spend more later, as my business is 100% focused on making them more successful with their books. I truly hope that you will be one of those customers that I can convince to stay longer and do more business with me along the line.

So, summed up, *Book Marketing Secrets* is primarily a marketing tool for me. But let's go back to you and your "automated book sales system." I invite you to get pen and paper and to draw your own current (or intended) version of your book sales system.

Draw Your Own Book Sales System | Exercise
Take pen and paper and draw your own book sales system with the help of "Attraction, Conversion, Retention" and the visual example of the "BMS book sales system" displayed in this book.

Start with the channels your readers are coming from, and put concrete numbers if you have them (if not, your homework is to get those numbers).

Afterwards, look at your point of sale(s). What can be done there to improve your conversion rates? And as a final step, look at your retention. What are you doing to keep in touch with your readers (eg. email signup), to keep them engaged (eg. built-in virality elements), to drive them to your other products (eg. other books)? Make a list of things to improve in this area.

The ideal scenario is that you are able to optimize your system to a level where it keeps itself running. A system in which you put $1 USD in, and $2 USD emerges at the end of the day. Ideally, a system that is scalable with paid advertising. Once you have achieved this level, you have achieved true mastery. With mastery, you can bring it to a level where you can live on your books and writing, the dream of every writer, but which so few of us achieve in the end.

I hope that my calculation also reminded you once more why it is so important to have upsell products. If you have only one book on the market and you generate a royalty of around three or four dollars, then it gets almost impossible to achieve positive return on advertising spent with the book alone. That's why most successful authors and publishers have lines of products such as book series, and related products on top of that. Your tolerable cost of acquisition of a new customer changes dramatically with just one more product down the line. Imagine you are selling an online course for the price of $37 on top of your non-fiction book. Suddenly you are able to spend up to $10 for a new client. Without the upsell product, you can spend only $3.

And don't forget that you do not always need to create your own products. You can also act as an affiliate and earn commissions for products that are already on the market. Summed up, your calculations change dramatically with upsell products and also decide if you are able to compete in the market with paid advertising at all. I highly recommend that you dive deep into your own book sales system. Invest time and resources to make that work and to achieve the point of mastery, which frees you to spend more time on writing and creating and all the things you truly love.

Never forget Book Marketing Secret #10. Strive for it, make it one of your ultimate goals, in order to achieve true book marketing mastery.

Secret #10 Checkbox

Core Insights:

- ☑ Books are fantastic products for getting passive income
- ☑ Every author/publishers should have an understanding of their automated "book sales funnel" which covers Attraction, Conversion, and Retention

Exercises

Take pen and paper.

- Draw your "book sales funnel." Include numbers whenever possible.
- If you advertise, do you have a positive ROAS?
- What steps can you take to improve your level of book sales automation?

CHEATSHEET

BOOK MARKETING SECRETS CHEATSHEET

DISCOVER ALL SECRETS AT A GLANCE | PERFECT FOR PINBOARDS

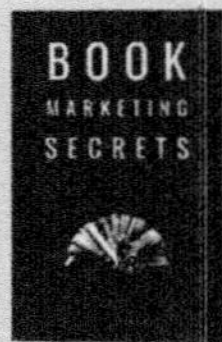

SECRET 01 THE BOOK IS THE STAR

-> CREATE THE BEST BOOK YOU CAN

SECRET 02 THE 7 BOOK MARKETING KEYS

-> COVER, TITLE, DESCRIPTION, LAYOUT AUTHOR/PUBLISHER, REVIEWS, MARKETING STRATEGY

SECRET 03 THE 80/20 RULE OF BOOK MARKETING

-> 20% EFFORT / 80% OUTCOME | 80% IMPORTANCE BOOK KEYS

SECRET 04

LEAN BOOK PUBLISHING

-> PUBLISH LEAN - GET FEEDBACK

SECRET 06 REVIEWS

-> GET AS MUCH AS YOU CAN

SECRET 08 MONEY

-> FOLLOW & REVERSE ENGINEER

SECRET 05

10K READER LAUNCH

-> 10K -> 1K -> 1H-

SECRET 07 EARLY BIRD

-> CATCH TRENDS EARLY

SECRET 09 POST SALES

-> MAKE READERS HAPPY

SECRET 10 AUTOMATE YOUR BOOK MARKETING

-> UNDERSTAND READER FLOWS AND AUTOMATE YOUR PROCESSES

www.albertgriesmayr.com

FINAL WORDS

Dear author,

First of all, I want to thank you for taking the time to read this book. It means a lot to me, as the core of my business career is to help authors like you to create successful book projects and publishing careers.

If there is one thing that I would love you to take away from this book, it's an improved mindset toward the critical success factors described in the secrets, such as having a relentless focus on producing great book, performing data-driven marketing, and applying a lean publishing approach.

If you have the 10 secrets in mind consistently then I am very confident that having bought and read this book will bring a positive ROI for your books and career as well.

I truly hope that this book was of high value to you. I hope that you have learned skills which will help you to better market your book. If you have not yet taken a look at Scribando (www.scribando.com), I highly recommend that you do so, as my service will help you to not only stay up-to-date on what is happening in the market, but also be informed about the latest success strategies on how to sell books.

In the end, to win big as an author, you need to master both timeless book marketing knowledge and the latest success strategies. With this book and Scribando, you have the perfect knowledge setup for selling lots of books.

I also want to invite you to check out the surprise gift that I have prepared for you. It will also help you to grow your author career. In addition, when you sign up at my webpage, you can stay in touch with me and won't miss new releases and book marketing insights.

CLAIM YOUR SURPRISE GIFT

Thank you for purchasing this book.
To show my appreciation, I've prepared a special gift for you that will help you to sell more books.
Access it by visiting:
www.albertgriesmayr.com/thank-you

As a writer you also know how important it is to get reviews. I always say, "Reviews are the lifeblood of books in the digital age." They can truly make or break books. So I hope that, as a fellow author, you review this book and post your review on Amazon or any other book retailer you purchased the book from. It would mean a lot to me. You can be sure that I read each review. I am happy with each positive one and try to learn from each critique as well.

ASK ME YOUR QUESTIONS
GIVE FEEDBACK AND REVIEW THE BOOK

The most important thing for me in business is to provide value and to leave you, as my reader, satisfied. That's why I invite you to ask me questions and to send me feedback about the book to hello@scribando.com. I will try to get back to you within 24-48 hours. I would love this to be the start of a great relationship between us!

And, of course, I would also love to see an official review posted to Amazon or other book retailers. I read each and every review personally.

I want to close this book by sharing a last quote. It is from the creator of the 100 Day Challenge, Gary Ryan Blair[85], who says, "Finishing strong is the only respectable way to finish."

> *"Finishing strong is the only respectable way to finish."*
>
> — Gary Ryan Blair

And I could not agree more with him when it comes to creating successful book projects. Finish strong and

85 Source: Gary Ryan Blair: Creator of the 100 Day Challenge https://www.100daychallenge.com/gary-ryan-blair/

make what's already good great. That's an easier way to success than starting all over again.

I wish you all the best in the world, and that you have the success with your books that you dream of.

Best wishes,

Albert Griesmayr
Founder & CEO of Scribando | Novelify
December 1, 2019, Vienna, Austria

THE END
&
THE BEGINNING OF YOUR NEXT CHAPTER

BOOK 2

BEST SELLER

How to Land a Long-Term Bestseller on Amazon and Earn Passive Income Every Month

1

INTRODUCTION

> *"Simplicity is the ultimate sophistication."*
>
> Leonardo da Vinci

I would like to start with a story. Listen closely.

As you know, one of my core services is offering book marketing strategies to publishers and authors. This is one of my most successful services, and I have created thousands of strategies. Last year alone, I was designing a couple of strategies per month for a wide array of clients.

These strategies commonly get a bit complicated. I usually give my clients comprehensive ten-step plans which demonstrate what they can do with their books. However, there were two particular experiences that made me stop and think.

The first was a client I had in 2019. My client was a fantastic person who was writing a book on recruiting and how to find a job that you love. I created a strategy for him. Afterward, he came to me and told me that it was an amazing strategy, but it was too complicated for him. He wanted to have a straightforward blueprint to follow and wanted me to show him how this strategy would work in very simple terms.

I worked with him, and we managed to cut away step five, and then steps eight through ten. After going over it, we managed to cut it down to a very simple strategy, something that was much easier for him to follow and allowed him to focus on what was really important. However, regardless of how simple the strategy is, follow-through is the most critical ingredient.

I had a similar experience with another client, also in 2019. This client was an amazing author who was a chef in hotels around the world. I created a very powerful strategy for him, and he was excited to execute it.

He worked on this strategy for a few months. Then he came to me and said that he had been doing everything in his plan but it was incredibly time-consuming and that he wasn't a tech-savvy person. He was finding the overall strategy challenging to follow through on. So, we sat down and again simplified things. In the end, what I realized was that I should try to create something more simple and easier to follow.

There is so much information out there, and so much of it is good and worthwhile. But, in the end, we all have limited time to follow through.

What you're getting with this book is the result of simplifying all my past strategies. You're getting a clear blueprint on how to have a long-term bestseller on Amazon. Here, I've simplified things to give you a three-step process that is basic enough that you can even memorize it.

However, don't assume that simple means easy. The execution and details will always be more difficult. If things were easy, everyone would do it.

What you learn in this book isn't easy, but the blueprint that I provide you with is easy to understand. By focusing on understanding this core blueprint and adding concrete action steps to it, then your goal becomes manageable and achievable.

I want to give you more than just the best book on how to create a perennial bestseller that provides you with passive income every month. I want to give you a blueprint that's so simple and clear that you can execute it and achieve success. Let's summarize this three-step blueprint.

Step one: Create an irresistible book offer. This offer consists of an amazing book and bonuses that will form an incredible package in the eye of the client. You must be able to communicate this offer in your marketing. We'll discuss how to do this in greater depth.

Step two: Launch (or relaunch) with a bang. Make sure that you have the audience and will reach enough people to give your book a fighting chance.

Step three: Automation. In this step, we'll discuss automating your book sales system so that this runs on autopilot and brings in consistent book sales and income very month.

So, to keep the story short: What you hold in your hands is the result of simplification. It's the result of cutting away everything that's not perfect from a strawberry bush before spring, leaving only what's truly necessary.

To achieve long-term success, these three steps are necessary:
1) Having a fantastic book offer
2) Launching with a bang
3) Creating a system that brings consistent income

You don't need anything more or less than that.

However, the challenge, of course, is in the HOW, and you will learn that in this book.

Before we jump right into it, we need to answer three vital questions:1) Why do we focus so much on Amazon?2) What is a perennial bestseller?3) Why a long-term focus is so important?

Let's talk about the importance of Amazon first (Q1). Let's take a look at why I recommend focusing on Amazon and why it makes sense. First of all, we need to see the size of Amazon and the reach that a high ranking will give you.

Regarding size, it is not easy to get detailed numbers, but most analysts agree that Amazon's share of the e-commerce market in the US had reached 50% in the US[86] in 2018; more importantly for us, Amazon's market share for books in the US (including print books sold in bookstores and other retailers) reached 42% in 2018. The e-book market share in the US was already high for many years, and is now around 85% or even 90% as of 2018/2019, depending on the source[87],[88].

---

86 Source: https://techcrunch.com/2018/07/13/amazons-share-of-the-us-e-commerce-market-is-now-49-or-5-of-all-retail-spend/

87 Source: https://www.bloomberg.com/graphics/2019-amazon-reach-across-markets/

88 Source: https://kindlepreneur.com/best-self-publishing-companies/

2018: Amazon is by far the largest U.S. book retailer

Books
807M
unit sales

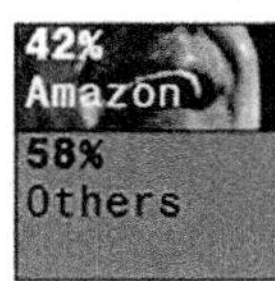

E-Books
560M
unit sales

Source: © Bloomberg 2019
https://www.bloomberg.com/graphics/2019-amazon-reach-across-markets/

What's also interesting is that the rewards for being high in rankings are significantly higher than on smaller marketplaces; on the other hand, the difficulty of rising in the rankings is comparable low, due to proven blueprints and a surrounding ecosystem for promoting books on Amazon, something that you won't find on this scale in competing book retailers.

Finally, Amazon has also become a very accessible marketplace through services like Amazon KDP. Everyone can publish on Amazon quickly, with access to the more than 100 million users per month shopping on Amazon in the USA alone[89].

The rule of thumb is simple:

> *"If you make it with your book on Amazon, you have made it with your book."*
>
> – Albert Griesmayr, 2020

The three reasons above show why Amazon is a good choice. It is not only the primary book publishing

89 Source: https://www.oberlo.com/blog/amazon-statistics

platform for applying the "Perennial Bestseller Blueprint," but also the sole publishing platform you will need.

The second aspect (Q2) is the term "perennial bestseller." I want to explain this term in more detail so that it is clear what it means and what goal is our target.

Dictionary.com describes "perennial"[90] as "lasting for an indefinitely long time, enduring, lasting or continuing throughout the entire year, perpetual, recurrent or everlasting."

The term "bestseller" is described as a book that is among those having the largest sales during a given period[91]. If we combine both terms we end up with this basic definition:

Perennial bestseller: "A book that is among those having the largest sales over an extended time period." To make our definition even more specific I am adding two details to comprise our final definition:

Perennial bestseller: A book that is among those having the largest sales in a specific category over extended time periods, such as many months or years

What I added was targeting a specific category and the clarity on timing. Why is this important? Primarily because of setting the right expectations. When I talk about landing a perennial bestseller on Amazon, I am always referring to a bestselling book in a specific category, such as "love & marriage," "writing & editing," or even sub-categories, such as "new age self-help" or

90 Source: https://www.dictionary.com/browse/perennial

91 Source: https://www.dictionary.com/browse/bestseller

"marketing for small businesses." Only the absolute top books (normally from the major publishing houses with big advertising budgets and physical bookstore distribution) land bestsellers on aggregated lists, such as "Top 100 in Paperbacks." We are not competing with the big guys. Instead, we are competing with the books within our genre and categories. And Amazon not only displays hundreds of book categories to their customers, Amazon also promotes category bestsellers beautifully, by having separate bestseller lists for each book category. This allows us to get visibility on Amazon directly for the audience who is interested in reading our genres.

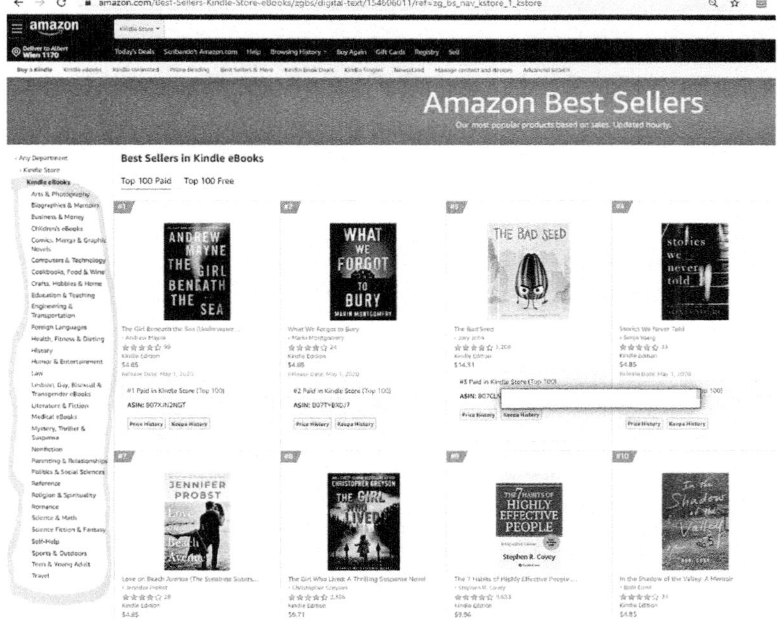

Illustrating book categories shown on the left. Each category can be expanded to open new subsets of categories. Amazon Kindle Bestsellers, April 2020. Source: Amazon. Screenshot © Albert Griesmayr 2021

The second important aspect is "time." Although I would to help you create an everlasting bestseller that exists indefinitely, I have to be clear on this: I am not currently able to circumvent the laws of business and life. As we all know, no success in business is indefinite, especially in today's digital world, in which even the most successful companies, like Google, Amazon or Facebook, are only around for some 20 years. Even the CEOs of these big businesses say that at some point they will become extinct[92]. And the same is true for books as well. Sure, there are outliers and classics, such as *The Little Prince* by Antoine de Saint Exupery, *Chicken Soup for the Soul* by Jack Canfield, or the *Harry Potter* series by J.K. Rowling. These may be bestsellers for decades[93]. However, normal book life cycles are much shorter, usually achieving most of their sales in their debut year. The lifecycle that we are targeting is the one between 1-3 years. That's the timespan referred to when we talk about a "perennial bestseller."

The timespan we are certainly *not* referring to is the "one-day-bestseller." Although achieving bestseller status even for a day can be valuable – and you'll learn the techniques to do so – it's much less valuable than a long-term bestseller, especially when viewed from the perspective of economics and what true success really means for authors and publishers.

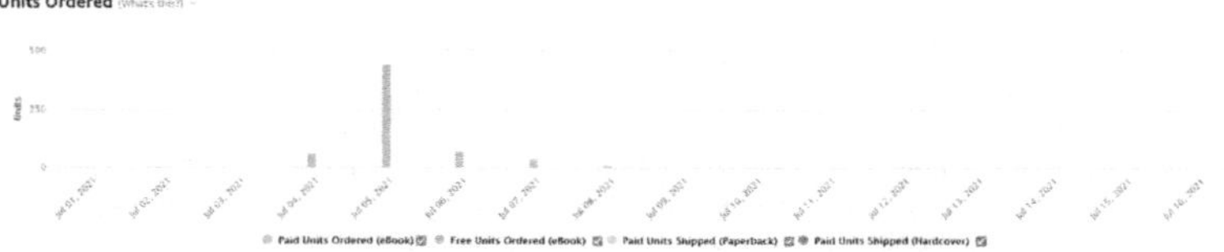

Screenshot of KDP sales dashboard showing a sales spike – unwanted outcome for long-term success.
Source: KDP Screenshot © Albert Griesmayr 2021

92 Source: https://www.cnbc.com/2018/11/15/bezos-tells-employees-one-day-amazon-will-fail-and-to-stay-hungry.html

93 Source: https://www.indiatoday.in/information/story/here-are-the-10-best-selling-books-of-all-time-1546429-2019-06-11

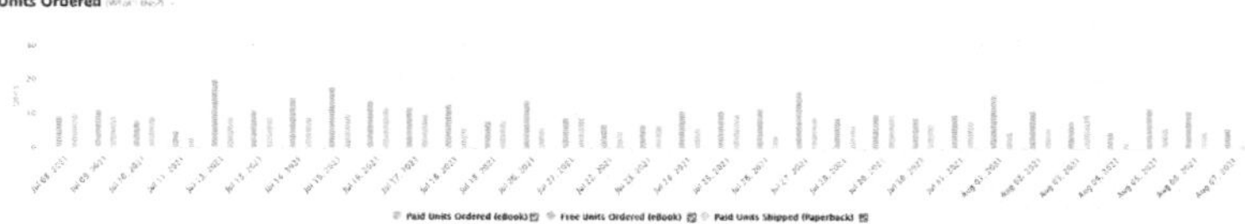

Screenshot of KDP sales dashboard showing consistent sales – the desired outcome for long-term success.
Source: KDP Screenshot © Albert Griesmayr 2021

Our target is long-term book success. It's the joy of creating a great book that is received well and bought in plentiful supply. It's also the joy of seeing persistent passive income, month after month. That's what I want you to achieve, and that's what I'll teach you in this book.

Fantastic! Now we understand the power of Amazon, what "perennial bestseller" actually means, the important difference between a short-term and a long-term bestseller, and what kind of timespan we are targeting. We're all set!

You are now ready to start learning the "Perennial Bestseller Blueprint." Before I launch you into that, though, let's get some clarity on your goals. This will help you not only to focus on the aspects of the blueprint that are most relevant to you, but help you to start thinking in the right direction as you read.

2

YOUR GOALS

> *"Setting goals is the first step in turning the invisible into the visible."*
> Tony Robbins

This chapter is all about YOU. What YOU want. What you want to achieve with your book.

Having clarity on your goals will help you to define your strategy and tactics. Strategies and tactics vary depending on your goals. They're different for someone who wants to land a perennial bestseller without a financial motive, and someone who wants to build a book publishing business making thousands of dollars each month.

It's very important to do this session properly, as it will sharpen your focus and help you to choose the right tactics and action steps later. The point of this exercise is to create clarity on your true motivations and goals before you create your book marketing strategy.

So let's define your goals. Make yourself a coffee, take 20 minutes, grab a pen and paper and answer the following questions.

[Please rate the answers from 1 (low, not important) to 5 (high, very important), or circle your desired answer]

1) How important are the following outcomes of your book project for you?
1a) increasing authority (1 2 3 4 5)
1b) getting good reviews and positive feedback (1 2 3 4 5)
1c) earning money with the book (1 2 3 4 5)
1d) being proud of your book project (1 2 3 4 5)
1e) landing a bestseller (1 2 3 4 5)

2) How much money do you want to generate from your book project? *(Please do not consider this question as wishful thinking. Approach it like a realistic expectation that you truly want or need to reach!)*
2a) I don't need to make money with the book
2b) I would be happy with $100 extra profit a month
2c) I would be happy with $200-$500 extra profit a month
2d) I am targeting $500 and more profit a month

____

(Please write down your target number)

3) How many copies do you want to sell in a year to consider your book project a success?
3a) I would be happy with selling 100 copies
3b) I would be happy with selling 250-1000 copies
3c) I want to sell at least 1000 copies a year
3d) I am targeting to sell 10000+ copies a year

____

(Please write down your target number)

4) How important are the following aspects for you? *(Please compare 4a and 4b before answering)*
4a) Making money with the book (1 2 3 4 5)
4b) Getting many readers and visibility (low prices and free giveaways are welcome) (1 2 3 4 5)

5) What's your primary motivation behind doing this book project? (e.g. is there a cause, do you have a related business, is money or visibility important, etc.)

(Please write down your answer)

6) Do you strive to become a full-time author or publisher, creating more books down the line? (Is this a one-time project or do you have further plans, is it a financial side-project or full-time business, etc.)

(Please write down your answer)

7) When landing a bestseller on Amazon, what's more important to you? (Please choose only one answer)
7a) Getting the bestseller tag (Bestseller just for a couple of days is fine, I most importantly want to use the title for my marketing)
7b) Being ranked as a bestselling book consistently (I want consistent rankings on bestseller lists in the Top 100 in suitable categories)

Excellent! Now you have more clarity on your goals and are ready to advance to learning more about how to land a perennial bestseller.

Based on your goals, I suggest that you target different project-related goals in terms of sales and visibility and analyze the different action steps that will help you reach each one.

The core target of this book is to help you to create a perennial bestseller, which requires effort. However, after going through those questions, you may well have learned that you're primarily motivated by getting the bestseller title or using your book as an authority tool. There's nothing wrong with either of those goals! The important thing is recognizing your goals, having clarity on what you want, so you can create the best book marketing strategy specifically to achieve those ends.

In this book, I've included insights that will help with any goal, whether to create an authority tool, a short-term bestseller, or a perennial bestseller that brings passive income every month.

For a perennial bestseller, you will need the full program (the Perennial Bestseller Blueprint). For a short-term bestseller, you won't need to invest in book sales automation. For creating an authority book, your actual sales won't be very important, so we will primarily focus on creating a killer book project that gets strong ratings and looks good.

Now that you have more clarity on your goals, it's time to learn about the Perennial Bestseller Blueprint. You're about to find out how to create a bestselling book that will bring in passive income every month. You'll also learn how likely you are to land a bestseller with your book idea, how many sales you'll need to do so, and your goals are realistic based on the tools you have now.

It's time to lift the curtain. Say hello to the Perennial Bestseller Blueprint.

3

THE PERENNIAL BESTSELLER BLUEPRINT

"One picture is worth a thousand words."
Fred R. Barnard

It's kind of unusual to use a quote like the one above in a book. Books usually consists of words, and words are still one of the most effective ways to teach and to communicate concepts.

Still images are extremely effective, however, especially if someone is able to connect deep meaning and understanding to a visual. Getting this understanding requires experience and knowledge.

The 50,000 words of this book will give you what you need to understand the following illustration. For now, it gives you an overview. Later you will learn to understand all details.

The Perennial Bestseller Blueprint consists of three steps.

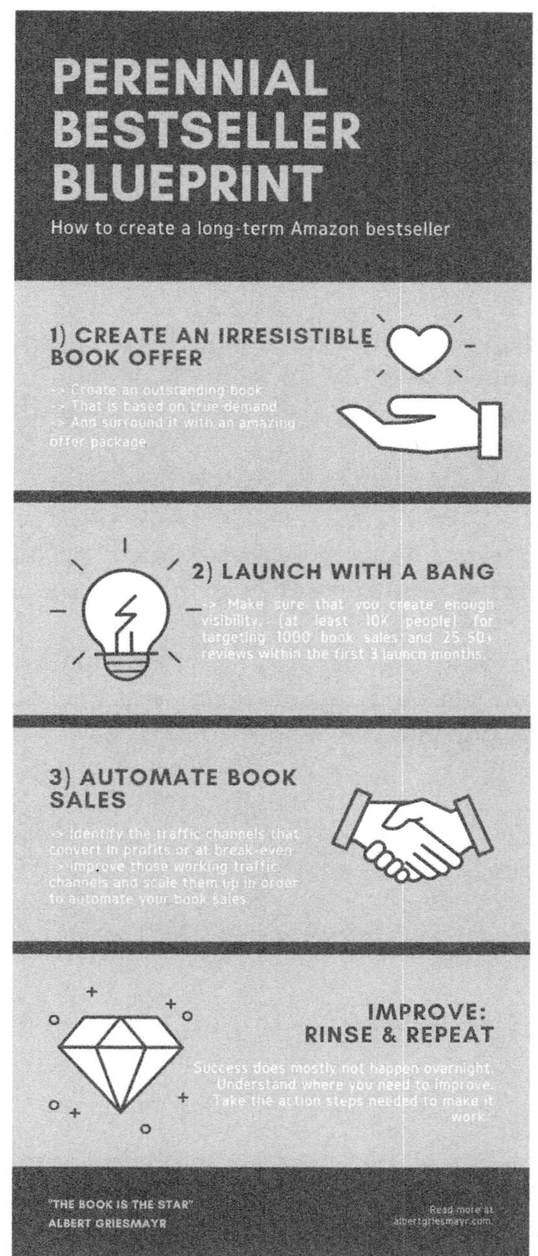

PERENNIAL
BESTSELLER
BLUEPRINT
How to create a long-term Amazon bestseller
1) CREATE AN IRRESISTIBLE BOOK OFFER
-> Create an outstanding book
-> That is based on true demand
-> And surround it with an amazing offer package
2) LAUNCH WITH A BANG
-> Make sure that you create enough visibility, (at least 10K people) for targeting 1000 book sales and 25-50+ reviews within the first 3 launch months.
3) AUTOMATE BOOK SALES
-> Identify the traffic channels that convert in profits or at break-even
-> improve those working traffic channels and scale them up in order to automate your book sales
IMPROVE:
RINSE & REPEAT
Success does mostly not happen overnight. Understand where you need to improve. Take the action steps needed to make it work.
"THE BOOK IS THE STAR"
ALBERT GRIESMAYR
Read more at
albertgriesmayr.com

Perennial Bestseller Blueprint © Albert Griesmayr 2021

Step one: Create an irresistible book offer. A book offer consists most importantly of the book itself, but also the marketing package around it, such as the USP, the bonuses, upsells, etc. It's also important to have "sub-offers" for your two most important target groups (readers and enablers).

Step two: Launch with a bang. Most importantly, you must reach at least 10K people and make sure that you receive at least 25+ ratings (5-10 reviews, 15-20 ratings), plus at least 250 book sales within the first 1-3 months after launching your book (ideally all reached in the first month)

Step three: Create a system for book sales automation that ensures profitably converting leads on an ongoing basis, allowing you to reach your passive income goals.

The book you are holding in your hands, reading digitally, or listening to will teach you all you need to know. Let's get into it!

4

CREATING AN IRRESISTIBLE BOOK OFFER [STEP 1]

"There is nothing more beneficial for book success than having a strong book that is presented in the right way and with the right tactics, to become a truly irresistible offer that a target audience can't turn down."

Albert Griesmayr, 2021

What I've learned working personally with more than a hundred authors over the last ten years is that having an irresistible book offer is the most important step for book success. By focusing on the creation of a kick-ass book, you are laying the foundation for book success later.

And the importance of a strong book is going to increase further over the coming years. Why is that?

While more and more books are being published and Amazon's visibility-providing digital shelf spaces are getting more and more crowded, there is only one way for Amazon to decide who to feature – and who not to feature. This is based on sales and conversion data. Books that perform well get up-ranked by Amazon, while lower performing books get down-ranked.

And this is not only true in regards to organic search, but Amazon ad performance as well. Already today, I see many campaigns getting low impressions or becoming dried out simply because Amazon detected that it's not worthwhile to give those books shelf space, as the return is not good. In the end, it is in Amazon's self-interest to feature books that sell and produce profits. Amazon will continue to get better and better at handling the marketplace in their best interest.

In addition, competition will further increase in an ever-expanding global digital market, therefore leading to higher advertising and promotion costs to make, and keep, your book visible.

One of the best ways to bypass this problem is to create word-of-mouth caused by a fantastic product with built-in virality.

One of the main points of this book is to teach you how to create a book that fits this criteria.

Once you have a strong book on the market, you have the foundation for success. Excelling in this stage usually leads to further book success later. On the other hand, going to the market with an average or even lacking book offer is an almost surefire way to fail in today's competitive publishing landscape – unless you market exceptionally well.

Please note that here I am talking about a "book offer," not a book. Our goal in this chapter is to create an irresistible book offer, one that your target audience can't turn down.

Before we start with crafting an irresistible offer, though, we need to do one thing: we need to understand our reader. We need to understand his wishes, expectations, and wants – the outcome that the readers longs for in reading this book. The following exercises will help to create this understanding.

Exercise [Answer the following questions]
1) What do my readers want?
2) What is the reader's desired outcome from my book?

Make sure to have the answers above in mind, when crafting your irresistible offer below.

First, you need to understand the three core elements of irresistible book offers:

1) A great book (manuscript + title, cover, etc.) [book is the start + 7 book marketing keys)
2) Based on true demand (clear search volume, low competition)
3) Supported by a great offer package (bonuses, etc.)

The combination of those three leads us to the irresistible book offer formula:

IRRESISTIBLE BOOK OFFER FORMULA
1) Create a fantastic book (manuscript + title, cover, etc.) [book is the start + 7 book marketing keys)
2) Based on true demand (clear search volume, low competition)
3) Supported by a fantastic offer package (bonuses, etc.)

In order to create an irresistible offer, you have to have all three.

Let's look at those three elements in more detail and learn how to make each element irresistible.

Creating a Fantastic Book

First, let's look at the element "a fantastic book." What is a fantastic book? It's much more difficult to describe and to create than to spot.

To illustrate this, take a look at the books below.

Source: Amazon. Screenshot © Albert Griesmayr 2021

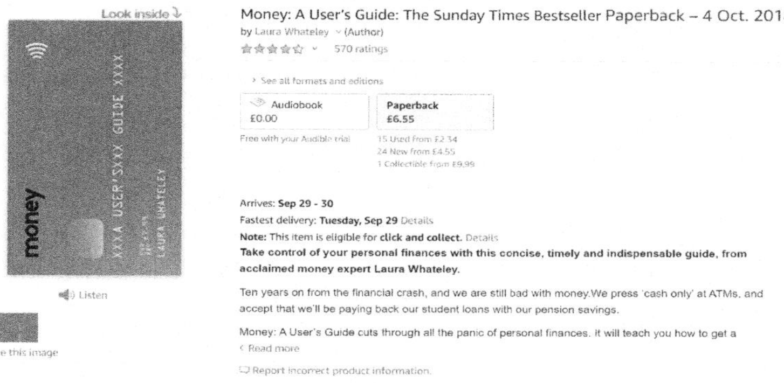

Look inside
money
XXXA USER'S XXX GUIDE XXXX
LAURA WHATELEY
Money: A User's Guide: The Sunday Times Bestseller Paperback – 4 Oct. 2018
by Laura Whateley (Author)
570 ratings
See all formats and editions
Audiobook
£0.00
Free with your Audible trial
Paperback
£6.55
15 Used from £2.34
24 New from £4.55
1 Collectible from £9.99
Arrives: Sep 29 - 30
Fastest delivery: Tuesday, Sep 29 Details
Note: This item is eligible for click and collect. Details
Take control of your personal finances with this concise, timely and indispensable guide, from acclaimed money expert Laura Whateley.
Ten years on from the financial crash, and we are still bad with money.We press 'cash only' at ATMs, and accept that we'll be paying back our student loans with our pension savings.
Money: A User's Guide cuts through all the panic of personal finances. It will teach you how to get a
Read more
Listen
See this image
Report incorrect product information.

Source: Amazon. Screenshot © Albert Griesmayr 2021

Look inside
HOW TO TELL STORIES TO CHILDREN
How to Tell Stories to Children: And Everyone Else Too Paperback – Illustrated, August 10, 2019
by Joseph Sarosy (Author), Silke Rose West (Author)
126 ratings
See all formats and editions
Kindle
$7.76
Read with Our Free App
Paperback
$8.99
4 Used from $7.95
6 New from $8.99
"This book will help to promote storytelling as a key education tool." - Dr. Jane Goodall, DBE, Founder of the Jane Goodall Institute & UN Messenger of Peace
This whimsical little book combines the science of storytelling with a step-by-step method for parents, grandparents, educators, and anyone interested in a lasting relationship with children.
Storytelling helps children build empathy and remember life lessons. It hones their concentration, boosts their vocabulary, and expands their imaginations. Most importantly, storytelling fosters the connection between parent and child. It also happens to be a lot of fun.
Read more
See all 2 images

Source: Amazon. Screenshot © Albert Griesmayr 2021

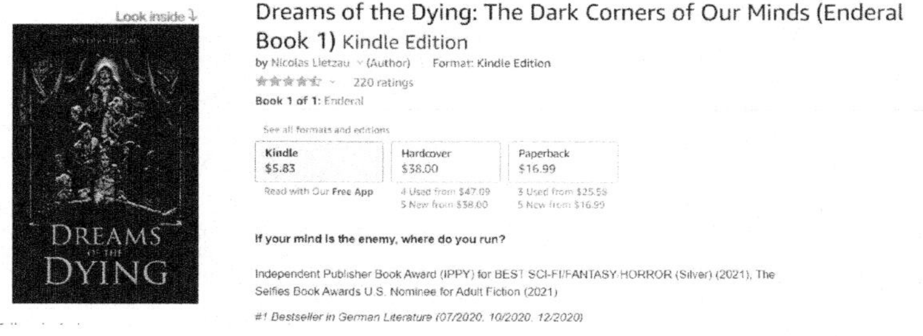

Look inside
DREAMS OF THE DYING
Dreams of the Dying: The Dark Corners of Our Minds (Enderal Book 1) Kindle Edition
by Nicolas Lietzau (Author) Format: Kindle Edition
220 ratings
Book 1 of 1: Enderal
See all formats and editions
Kindle
$5.83
Read with Our Free App
Hardcover
$38.00
4 Used from $47.09
5 New from $38.00
Paperback
$16.99
3 Used from $25.55
5 New from $16.99
If your mind is the enemy, where do you run?
Independent Publisher Book Award (IPPY) for BEST SCI-FI/FANTASY/HORROR (Silver) (2021), The Selfies Book Awards U.S. Nominee for Adult Fiction (2021)
#1 Bestseller in German Literature (07/2020, 10/2020, 12/2020)

Source: Amazon. Screenshot © Albert Griesmayr 2021

To me, all of those books are masterpieces. They have a special magic that can be difficult to describe.

When you look at the specific elements that go into creating strong books, you can understand the reasons for the magic – and the success. Luckily, I've worked personally with hundreds of authors and publishers. I've seen first-hand what a difference a strong book makes. You change the cover, and suddenly campaigns become profitable. You spice up the description, the title, or even improve the manuscript, and suddenly it's a whole different ballgame.

The fact is that a fantastic book is the most important element for book success.

Learn below what to look for and what to master to create a great book.

Brilliant books have seven key elements, which I call the "Book Success Keys." In this book, I will not discuss the seven elements in detail, as I could easily fill a book with them alone. However, I will share the most essential insights and show you the core steps for making your seven book success keys work.

As further reading I recommend that you read my book *Book Marketing Secrets*, which covers those elements in more detail in the first two chapters.

1. A Great Manuscript

Firstly and most importantly, content is king. The book is the star! Your book must be well written, accurate, and compelling to read. The text must flow and draw the reader into the story.

Take any work in the literary canon and they all succeed at this. A book such as Tolstoy's *War and Peace* is immaculately written and provides great entertainment value as well as insightful knowledge into 19th century Russia and the human condition. Although you do not have to be on Tolstoy's level, you must ask yourself honestly whether your text is well put together and whether your readers will get benefit out of your work.

For works of nonfiction, it is particularly important that your readers find compelling value in your book. Nonfiction is made valuable by expanding the reader's knowledge.

If you have experience in your chosen niche (for example, you're an expert on your topic, an experienced genre fiction author, etc.), it's easier to assess your ability to create a great manuscript. As a new author, or when working with ghostwriters (which I generally do not recommend as a good long-term strategy in book publishing nowadays), this is more difficult.

The surefire way to test your manuscript is always external feedback. The more unbiased, the better. I recommend that you get feedback as much and as often as possible during the creation process (from readers, experts, etc.) and make sure that your target audience is in love with the raw power of your book. In the end, your readers are the ones who matter; they will decide about your book's success in the market.

2. A Great Book Cover

They say that you shouldn't judge a book by its cover; however, that's really just a saying. Your book cover is the first thing people see. It has to create a good impression.

Do not cut corners and do the cover yourself if you are not an artist. Don't opt for the cheap version. Hire a professional to do a proper cover for your book.

Screenshot of book covers from Amazon.com comparing visual arrangement. Source: Amazon Screenshot © Albert Griesmayr 2021

Have a look at the two covers above.

They are two book covers, one done by the author himself on some free software, the other done by a professional. Which of the two books are you more likely to buy? Which book will look better on your bookshelf? They are exactly the same book; however, I'll safely bet that nobody will choose the one on the left.

In *Book Marketing Secrets* I introduce the book cover formula that helps you to check if your cover has what it takes before final approval.

The core essence is that a good cover must be visually appealing, be clear in regards to the title and the core visual, appropriate for content, and with a touch of uniqueness to it. Make sure that you and viewers say "Wow" when seeing the cover in a bookstore or online. Your book must stand out.

The lesson is clear: do not skimp on a mediocre cover, as it could be your downfall. As with the manuscript, I recommend getting external feedback – not only from readers, but book cover experts as well. Tell them to be critical. Remember, in the creation stage you have much less to lose than post-publishing.

3. Book Title / Subtitle

After the cover, the next thing your potential readers will notice is the title.

Your title must be attention-grabbing, short, unique, and relevant to the content of the book. Don't underestimate the importance of your subtitle, either; both must work together as one compelling element.

Over the last decade, SEO was an important factor for book titles, and especially for subtitles. However, nowadays it's becoming ever less important to include core keywords in the title. This is especially true for Amazon. But SEO may still be more relevant for smaller retailers, which have smaller shelfspace and less sophisticated algorithms, which can lead to a heightened focus on keywords.

I recommend that you do not favor keywords over accuracy or uniqueness when deciding on your book title. Just remember that for some titles, especially in nonfiction, strong keywords may still have a profound effect on visibility in the smaller retailers.

Below are a few book title examples. They work well and fit the criteria I've outlined.

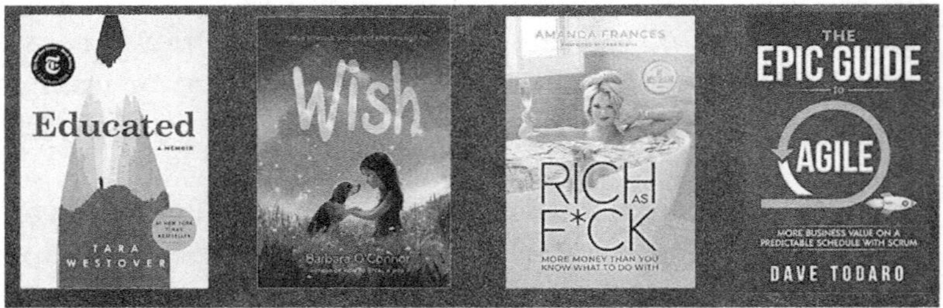

Screenshots of book covers from Amazon.com, illustrating visual arrangement. Source: Amazon Screenshot © Albert Griesmayr 2021

Please note that the title-cover match also plays a significant role. The visual needs to support the title. The titles displayed as examples make your head turn when you read them and make you want to read more. They use emotionally loaded words which provoke an emotion in book shoppers and intrigue them into investing in the book.

4. Book Description

The book description is a major driver for book sales as well.

A good description has four elements: the hook, the blurb/benefits, built-in credibility, and an open loop or call to action.

The hook line gets the attention of the reader right at the beginning. A hook should be emotionally loaded and brief, such as "*Sick of hangovers?*" or *"If Agile is so amazing, why is it hard to produce reliable results?"* Hooks are often questions which prompt the reader into wanting to find the answer, leading them to read the rest of the description.

The next element is the blurb. For fiction, you will want to briefly describe the main story; for non-fiction, focus primarily on the benefits your reader gets from the book. Benefits are the bread and butter of non-fiction book descriptions. List the advantages your readers will take home after reading your book. How will you enrich their lives? Terrify them? Shock them? Make them cry with emotion? Your blurb must outline what your reader will get out of the experience you are providing.

Credibility is obvious but it is surprising how often people omit it from their description. People are much more likely to buy a book if it has been recommended by someone else, so show the reader that it has been. A quick sentence like, "Jason Phillips from *The Guardian* says this is an absolute shocker and will have you turning the pages like crazy!" will boost your description and give you material proof. Include at least one review to give your description credibility. If you have strong credibility as an author, make sure to include that as well. One of the best credibility boosters is having received awards and accolades – and bestseller status of course. I will cover tactics for achieving both later in the book.

A call to action is a statement at the end of the description. Studies have shown that readers respond to "doing" words. Tell your potential reader what you want them to do next. Tell them to open the first page and read on for the rest of the story. Make them feel as if they have to buy your book, or otherwise they'll feel incomplete.

A secret weapon at the end is known as the open loop or open question. This technique involves asking a question at the end of the description that can only be answered by buying and reading the book. "Will June find true love?" "How much does it take? Find out by clicking Add to Cart."

Once you have crafted your description, it's vital to format it for online retailers. You can use the HTML formatting tool presented by the Kindlepreneur or format directly on KDP. Luckily, Amazon has finally added this tool; however, it's still in Beta, so you have to check if it's available.

5. Book Layout

The book layout refers to the finer points of your book: the accuracy of typing, the lack of typos, the references, fonts used, summaries, the table of contents, and the pictures in your book.

Look at any professional book you have read. They are usually referenced correctly, have accurate summaries, have no typos, and utilize a good balance between text and pictures as is appropriate for the type of book. You should be just as precise with your book as the professionals are with theirs. Do not omit these vital aspects of your book as you put on the finishing touches.

Layout is sometimes taken lightly by authors and publishers. However, its importance as a book success key is profound, as the layout sends a powerful message that is processed subconsciously by the reader. Choose the wrong font, font size, or TOC layout, and you can quickly reduce the perceived value of the book. On the other hand, a good layout can win points for your professionalism and authority.

An important point is also to format differently for e-book, paperback, and hardcover. My recommendation is to work with a professional, as book layout is not easy and can cause true headaches if you try to do it yourself or on the cheap.

From my experience, you can get good results at affordable prices by choosing an existing title that fits the genre/subject, and advising the formatter to use the title as a reference and model. This is an effective, cost-saving approach to decisions on font, sizing, TOC design, and more.

6. Author/Publisher

The next book success key is the author and/or publisher. It's no surprise that books by well-known authors published by major publishing houses sell significantly more easily than self-published titles by unknown authors.

It's also important to add that the author is significantly more important than the publisher. However, some readers to look for the publisher when making purchase decisions, and put a higher value on books that are published by respected printers. I recommend filling out the publisher field on your Amazon listing with your company or "[Author Name] Publishing."

Most important is that you have a strong author/ publisher profile. Make sure to use Author Central, and to submit your bio and a photo that is professionally done. Your name is displayed next to your book, and many readers will click on your name to learn more about the author.

Invest time in writing your profile, and make sure to assess the quality of your biography from the perspective of your readers. Is it engaging and interesting? Does it communicate that you are an expert and experienced in your field? Did you include available credibility?

Some of the authors I work with have low credibility at the beginning of their career, so it's important to know that you can add credibility by framing aspects of your bio in the correct terminology. Regardless of your profession and experience, or lack thereof, descriptions like "business owner," "consulted with X clients," "worked on projects worth X," "created designs for Fortune 500 clients," and "expert" immediately add credibility. You don't necessarily need to have won awards and accolades, but it's important to realize what you do have to work with.

Choosing a professional-looking picture of yourself is critical as well. In the non-fiction arena, you might choose a picture in which you are speaking, presenting, or being interviewed. Stay away from selfies, blurry pictures, or CV-like pictures.

Screenshot of Amazon Author Profiles of Patrick McKeown, Theresa M. Lina, and Sarah J. Maas Source: Screenshot © Albert Griesmayr 2021

The authors in the above example have a list of their successful works, well-shot profile pictures, and detailed descriptions of themselves.

Make sure your profile looks as good as the examples above.

7. Reviews & Ratings (Customer and Editorial)

Reviews and ratings are integral to your proof as an author. They're social proof that someone has read and valued your material. Back in 2019, I said, "Reviews are the lifeblood of books in the digital age," and not much has changed since then. Reviews are one of the main purchase factors, often the most important one. To put it another way, they are the most important reason *not* to purchase a book.

A decade ago, I read a marvelous book created by former advertising executives of Danone and other brands. This book described identifying and eliminating factors to *not* purchase specific products as substantially more important than creating compelling reasons *to* buy. The book was called *Break Brakers*[94] but unfortunately it's not available anymore. It was a profound read and I see its supreme relevance in regards to negative reviews. They can truly break your book and substantially limit your chances of success.

It's important to understand the difference between ratings (a star rating without a written review) and reviews (actual written reviews consisting of a text/image review and a star rating). Until 2019, Amazon was only allowing reviews; however, they have since changed their system and are allowing customers to leave a rating (1-5 stars) without leaving a written review. It seems that this information has not yet become widely known in the publishing community yet, so it

94 Brake Breakers now active as an agency: https://www.brakebreakers.com/

remains a valuable insight for pro publishers. Amazon now makes it much easier to get ratings from your launch team, supporters, and readers. I recommend informing your audiences of this, as it's much more likely that someone would leave a star rating if they're not compelled to type a review.

There are three main places where you should have reviews/ratings displayed:

a) Include a brief but compelling review in your book description as described in step 4
b) Include editorial reviews on your author profile as described in step 6[95]
c) Make sure you get at least 10 reviews/ratings initially (ideally 25+), and 50+ customer ratings (consisting of both ratings and reviews) over time

Later in this book, we will discuss the best tactics for getting customer reviews and ratings, so stay with me.

If you combine the seven steps above, you have the key ingredients to make a successful bestseller. Go through this list several times and make sure they are all up to speed.

Based on True Demand

But having a fantastic book is not enough. There needs to be a strong demand for it as well. And as competition has increased so rapidly over the last decade, it is no longer enough to say: "Well, I am an expert in this field, so I will write a fantastic book in that field. The demand will supply itself."

95 You provide editorial reviews through Author Central.

The problem is that competition has become so fierce that it must be taken into account as well. If there are already a hundred books on your topic in the market, it's imperative that you get your book across and stand out. In some cases, it may be that you are commercially doomed to fail from the very beginning if you pick the wrong target market. At the very least, it can make your life much more difficult.

So how do you make sure that there is demand for the book that you want to write?

There are basically two ways of doing that:

A) The pro approach. Load up with paid software (namely Kdspy and/or Publisher Rocket) that will give you all the intel you need, such as how much traffic certain keywords get, how many books you need to sell to rank on a bestseller list, how many sales specific books are making, how competitive niches, keywords, or categories really are, and much, much more.

B) The common sense approach This is recommended if you have a lower budget, a single book, or simply if you're focusing on other areas. Use two free software tools (DS Quick View and KDP Sales Rank Calculator by Kindlepreneur) to get the most important data and to make sure that there is demand. Combine this with your understanding of the book you are writing.

Before we start to take a closer look at A) and B), one word of warning: Software is fantastic to get accurate data; however, those tools can sometimes lead to wrong assumptions, especially from new authors unfamiliar with digital marketing.

To give you an example from my personal experience, I had a client in the historical romance niche, who calculated her expected sales based on the top sellers in her niche. Using sales trackers, she noticed that the best books sell thousands of copies a month. As her book would naturally be much better, she reasoned, her sales would be similar. Of course, a calculation like this can lead to disastrous outcomes when it comes to reality. My recommendation is to make sure that you not only understand the data you are getting, but also to keep realistic expectations.

Most importantly for this book, since we are targeting long-term bestseller status in a category and top rankings for your core keyword, write down the numbers you get using the tools so that you know how many copies you need to sell and how difficult it will be.

When assessing the demand, we want to make sure that we have a clear understanding of our one to three main keywords and main book category. When you upload your book to Amazon at a later step, we will come back to the category and keyword selection in more detail. However, you need to be aware of the main SEO elements in order to assess your book demand.

Target	
My Target Sales (per month)	
Main keyword 1	
Main keyword 2 (optional)	
Main keyword 3 (optional)	
Main category	

Target	
How many books need to be sold for both my main keywords and main category in order to be Top 10?	
Result: Target Sales per month/day to get SEO visibility	

Please fill out the table above to note your main SEO elements and to get an understanding of the sales necessary for visibility.

A) The Pro Approach (using software like KDSpy[96] and/or Publisher Rocket[97])

When using software, we want to find out two things:

- Is there enough demand for my keywords and categories?
- How many copies are the competitors selling?

The demand for specific keywords, or more specifically search queries, can be assessed by using Publisher Rocket. Simply navigate to "keyword search" and get an orientation on traffic and competitiveness for your target keywords.

Once you know that the keywords you are targeting have healthy search traffic, it's time to confirm this by looking at sales data from the books coming up in the Top 10 for your keywords and/or categories.

96 KDSpy is a paid software for tracking book data. Source: https://www.kdspy.com/

97 PublisherRocket is a paid software for tracking book data. Source: https://publisherrocket.com

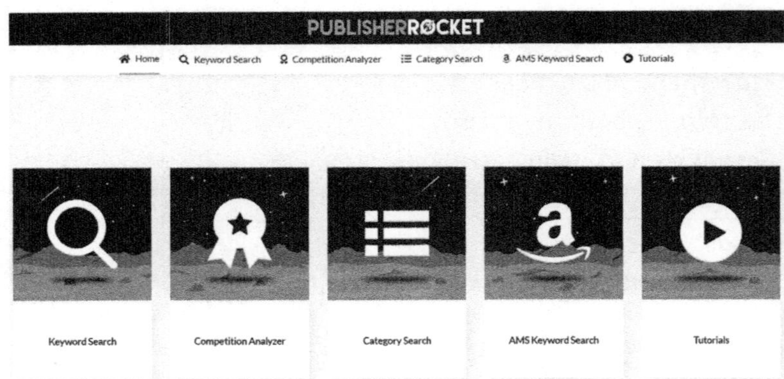

Screenshot of Publisher Rocket Software
Source: Screenshot © Albert Griesmayr 2021

You can get this data from Publisher Rocket or from KDSPY.

It's important that you take into account that your top-selling competition are likely out of reach. So don't fall for the trap of thinking that you will outperform them quickly. It's better to keep your expectations realistic in assessing the true demand for your title.

By using Publisher Rocket or the free Sales Rank Calculator from Kindlepreneur you can also quite easily calculate how many copies you need to sell in order to land a bestseller.[98]

With Publisher Rocket you also see right away in the category search how competitive specific keywords are. This is highly useful when selecting categories for your bestseller campaign later. I will describe the exact process for finding and submitting winning categories in detail when I talk about Step 2 of the blueprint, *Launching with a Bang*.

98 Source: https://www.creativindie.com/how-many-books-do-you-need-to-sell-to-become-a-bestseller/

Kindle Spy https://www.kdspy.com/
Source: KDSpy. Screenshot © Albert Griesmayr 2021

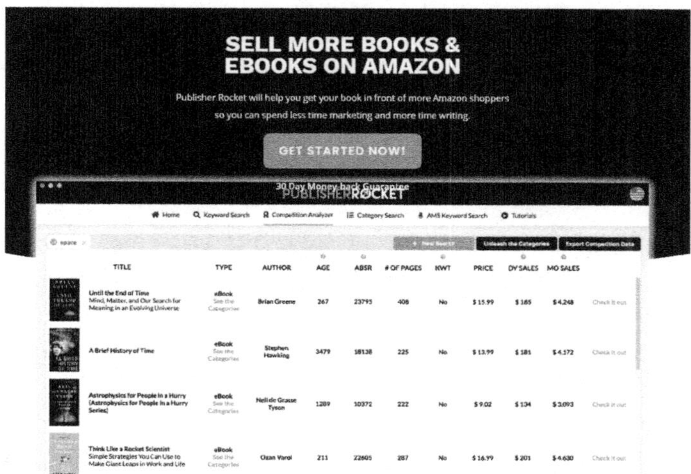

Publisher Rocket https://publisherrocket.com/
Source: Publisher Rocket. Screenshot © Albert Griesmayr 2021

A great tool to look at is also https://genretrends.com/. It gives you an overview of the competitiveness of your genre.

Your main target at this stage is making sure that your book is based on true demand with associated search queries, and your book is competitive enough to compete with the existing books already performing in the market.

B) The Common Sense Approach

It's also possible to skip paid software for the demand assessment, and instead rely on common sense and free tools. When using this approach, two free software tools (Google Chrome Extension: DS Quick View[99] and KDP Sales Rank Calculator by Kindlepreneur[100]) will supply you with the most important data to make sure that there is demand. You can combine that data with your understanding of the genre you work in and the book you create.

Additionally, I recommend using the Amazon search bar (auto complete) to make sure that your search term comes up. As an example, let's check the auto-complete results for the keyword "consilience," which is one of the main keyword targets of one of my previous clients, Tom Beakbane.

When entering the term "consilience" we get the results shown as in the screenshot below. Next to our main target keyword "consilience," we add "consilience book" as keyword 2. The reasoning behind this method is that Amazon only puts data into autocomplete if are enough search queries for a term.

---

99 DS Quick View: https://chrome.google.com/webstore/detail/ds-amazon-quick-view

100 Sales Rank Calculator: https://kindlepreneur.com/amazon-kdp-sales-rank-calculator/

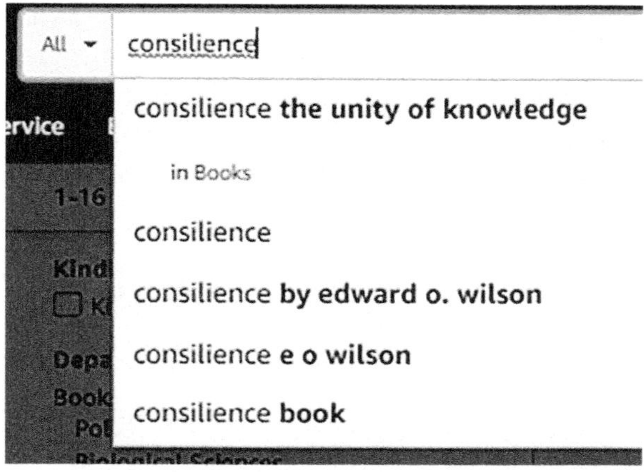

Source: Amazon. Screenshot © Albert Griesmayr 2021

Lastly, you need to check again into your competition in regards to those search terms and target categories. Are you able to compete in terms of content? Does your book bring something new to the table?

Make sure that you are convinced of your title when assessing the demand for your book. True demand is necessary to land a long-term bestseller on Amazon.

Supported by a Great Offer Package

It's important to distinguish the difference between your book as an integral part of the offer and the additional elements, such as bonuses, that become part of your offer package.

What might those elements be?

- Pricing: Reduced book prices (especially for launches or special promotions) are important attributes for strong offer packages. I recommend that you price your e-book between $0.99-$2.99 and your paperback between $7.45-$9.95 during launch month. You can increase your book prices once you have reached your launch goals. If your book is not performing well, however, I don't recommend raising prices immediately after that first month.

- Bonuses: Bonuses in any form, such as bonus e-books, videos, audiobooks, etc., can increase the attractiveness of your offer.

- Surprise Gifts (or Thank You Gifts): Including a surprise gift is a very effective element for an attractive offer package. Often, the link to the gift is included in the book (which increases the likelihood for sales) with links to your website where they can locate the gift. It is critical not to unveil the nature of the gift, in order to spark curiosity. You can see example surprise gift placements in my own books. Visit the link in the foot note to see how I implemented this tool[101].

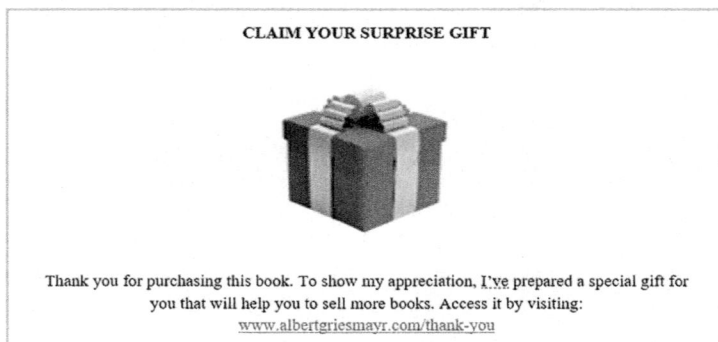

CLAIM YOUR SURPRISE GIFT

Thank you for purchasing this book. To show my appreciation, I've prepared a special gift for you that will help you to sell more books. Access it by visiting:
www.albertgriesmayr.com/thank-you

Screenshot of the surprise gift section included in my books on book marketing. © Albert Griesmayr 2021.

101 Source: Albert Griesmayr, Thank You Gift: https://www.albertgriesmayr.com/thank-you/

- Exclusivity: (Scarcity in time or people) Exclusivity is another important attribute. Make your book scarce in time (such as a limited edition or a reduced price for the first month only) or exclusive to a specific group of people (such as only for your launch team or the first 1000 readers). This has a positive effect on conversion rates and is a worthwhile part of your overall offer package.
- Credibility: Finally, it's important to make your book as credible as possible. This is critical because your book has very little credibility at the launch due to lack of reviews. Make sure that you add editorial reviews through Author Central, spice up your author bio, and present yourself and your book in a way that makes people trust your marketing message and believe that your work is worth reading.

I recommend that you take a look at Robert Cialdini's groundbreaking work *The Psychology of Persuasion*[102]. In this book, Cialdini outlines six principles of persuasion (later, he added a seventh) that work well to persuade people. I've written a blog article on this topic, in regards to book descriptions, and I recommend that you take a look: https://www.albertgriesmayr.com/self-publishing-blog/robert-cialdini-principles-book-descriptions-marketing/

Below, you will find concrete applications for each of Cialdini's principles regarding crafting an irresistible book offer package.

---

102 Source: Robert Cialdini, The Psychology of Persuasion, 1984 https://www.amazon.com/Influence-Psychology-Persuasion-Robert-Cialdini/dp/006124189X

Applications of Robert Cialdini's 7 Principles of Persuasion In Regards To Book Marketing	
Principle	**Application**
Reciprocity	Give your readers something valuable (for free) first to trigger "reciprocity" in return
Consistency	1) Get your readers to commit by signing up or reading part one of your series. 2) Remind your readers of the specific goals your book can help them with ("You want to reach X, so read the book").
Social Proof	Use testimonials, success stories and **reviews** to highlight what other readers liked about your book.
Liking	Present yourself, as the author, in the best possible light. Use pictures/videos of yourself on a stage or presenting on Author Central. Share audience numbers, like the number of your YouTube subscribers. Show reviews of your work by popular, respected figures.
Authority	Include details that establish your credentials, experience, and recognition in your author bio, online profiles, and book description.
Scarcity	Give your readers a sense of urgency and priority. Limit your offer (timespan or quantity) to incentivize engagement.
Unity	Connect with your readers on a deeper level by creating a shared identity around your book and subject—e.g., based on location, traits, personal interests, or challenges.

A question that I often get is what kind of bonus or surprise gift to add to the offer package. I've included a list here that has been used personally by myself and my clients to great success. Take a minute to brainstorm and pick out the bonuses that would work best for your own book.

- A video in which the author talks about his motivation for writing the book or the story behind the book
- A video in which the author presents fresh insight or a unique background story to the book
- Companion courses (primarily suited for non-fiction books)
- Checklists, cheat-sheets, and infographics (primarily for non-fiction)
- Accompanying free audiobook or e-book
- E-book with alternative endings or unpublished content
- Products of other authors/publishers/influencers (especially useful for cross-promotion)

This list makes it clear that there are many options for potential bonuses that can help you to spice up your book offer package.

My recommendation is to add one strong bonus or surprise gift to the core offer, which will help you to sell your book more easily. Important note: Always make sure that your irresistible offer is clearly connected to your book and does *not* make your book weaker.

What do I mean by that?

Overselling is unattractive. If you bombard prospects with the bonus materials in the very first line, you may take away from the compelling nature of your raw book offer. Balance both aspects in order to avoid front-loading the package with bonuses that diffuse the value of your book proposition in the first place. Remember, the core focus should be on the benefits of your book itself.

So far, we've only spoken about creating one irresistible book offer for your readers. However, there's another variation of this book offer – you could even refer to it as a second book offer – that you should have for your influencers (the Magic 100), and in some cases even a third offer for your book launch team. For now, we'll refer to this additional group as "enablers."

Enablers are members of your book launch team, cross promo partners, and/or influencers. In short, this is a unique subset of your readers that will help you to reach your book project goals by spreading the word and bringing additional traffic and credibility.

As you outline your irresistible book offer, you'll want to include a special benefityou're your enablers as well. Ideally, this extra bonus is something exclusive, such as receiving a free paperback version, free access to your online program or course, or visibility.

Visibility works especially well for enablers who also operate online and have platforms and audiences themselves. One of my favorite offers is to feature their work and profile as a "Top Article" on my website or blog.

Imagine you are an expert in the field of pool construction and are about to publish a book with the target audience of pool construction companies, centered on how to build and market pools to homeowners and construction companies. In this case, I'd recommend you publish an article on your website, with a title like "Top 50 Pool Construction Companies in the USA" or "Top 20 Expert Insights For Building and Maintaining Your Dream Pool" or "Top 50 Inspiring Pool Designs." The next step is to find the best experts in the market and invite them to contribute to your article. Even better, show them the content that you would like to see from them, allowing them simply to approve the feature. You'll offer for them to be featured on your website and receive an incoming link. This is quite a strong offer, and in my experience conversion rates are very good with outreach like this.

In the next chapter, I will introduce the Magic 100 concept to you, and you will see that the "Top Article Feature" is a very attractive outreach tactic to this group.

Before we put all the elements together for your irresistible book offer, I would like to introduce to you one more concept which, when correctly applied, can have a profound impact on the word-of-mouth potential in regards to your book and reader retention rates.

An attractive package is a great feature that can boost conversion rates, but the after-sale experience of the reader is even more important in regards to book success. I recommend that you focus on the quality and attractiveness of your book. The next concept that we will discuss pertains directly to this, and can spark word-of-mouth and virality. I call this concept "Built-In Product Virality."

Virality is the dream of all digital marketers; however, it is unbelievably difficult to achieve and sustain. As Andrew Chen, general partner at the venture capital firm

Andreessen Horrowitz points out, "Virality is a business design problem, not a marketing or engineering effort." Therefore, virality has to embedded into your product.

With your book, I wouldn't necessarily encourage you to target virality, as this is difficult to achieve. Rather, I'd aim for a level of word-of-mouth and sharing that will be facilitated by your book. I've developed a few tactics for this, and here they are.

My four favorite tactics for facilitating built-in product virality:

1. Collaborative books:

Remember "friendship books" from your childhood? A book that you could fill out and pass around. One friendship book could easily make its way into ten different households, thereby achieving a high level of virality. Most books, however, are intended for one reader at a time. Nevertheless, there are smart ways to encourage collaboration, both in fiction and nonfiction. In fiction, you can add riddles or quizzes into the content of your book which are sufficiently difficult that they will require the reader to look for help to solve them. In nonfiction, include group experiments, activities, or partner exercise to foster WoM.

2. Two-Sided rewards:

This is a rarely used element in book marketing. We all know this concept from software products that provide referral programs. They are largely rare in books because of a combination of technical difficulties and historic reasons. In my experience, however, two-sided rewards can be highly effective in book projects.

Include a coupon in your book that can be shared with up to three friends in order to receive a free e-book.

3. **Artifacts shared:**

Sharing is powerful and popular in today's social-media-fueled world. When you use powerful language, quotes, stories, and infographics in your books, you can encourage and facilitate WoM and virality through sharing. Make sure that the content is shareable – for instance, include an info box in the beginning of the book to let the reader know that sharing of your content is encouraged, and add a link to your website with the embedded code for specific elements. The better and more valuable your content, the more likely it is to be shared.

4. **Unique book elements:**

An outstanding cover, layout, and content arrangement can go a long way, if your book makes it beyond the first 1000 sales. Jonathan Safran Foer's book cover for *Everything Is Illuminated*[103] is a fantastic sample of an iconic cover that went viral. *The Business Model Canvas*, featured in Alexander Osterwalder's book *Business Model Generation*[104] went viral in the startup community because of its unusual book format, beautiful layout, great typography, and powerful content. A great example for a unique book is also *Whose Boat is this Boat?*[105] by the staff of *The Late Show with Stephen Colbert*. By mocking former

103 Source: https://www.amazon.com/Everything-Illuminated-Jonathan-Safran-Foer/dp/0544484002/

104 Source: https://www.amazon.com/Business-Model-Generation-Visionaries-Challengers/dp/0470876417

105 Source: https://www.amazon.com/Whose-Boat-This-Aftermath-Hurricane/dp/1982121084

president Donald Trump's responses to victims of Hurricane Florence in a creative way, there was a lot of built-in-virality already included in the book (cover, description, content) that helped tremendously with book distribution.

My recommendation is to check your book for built-in product virality features. If it falls short of what it could be doing, be ready to work on these elements. Competition with books is fierce, and facilitating WoM and virality can make the difference between simply a published book and a perennial bestseller.

An excellent article by Gabor Cselle on Medium features more applications and tactics for embedding virality into products, so you might want to take a look for further reading: https://medium.com/gabor/9-ways-to-build-virality-into-your-product-5975e1fe74e3

Exercise and Checklist

We can now put together all 3 elements that we need for an irresistible book offer.

1) A great book (manuscript + title, cover, etc.) [book is the start + 7 book marketing keys)

2) Based on true demand (clear search volume, low competition)

3) Supported by a great offer package (bonuses, etc.)

In a next step, I invite you to do the "irresistible book offer exercise" and create your irresistible book offer.

Exercise Box [Irresistible Book Offer]

After you have learned about how to create an irresistible book offer, it is time to put that knowledge to work. Fill out this worksheet.

1) These are the core elements of my irresistible book offer for my readers:

____

____

____

(List your most important elements, such as reduced launch price, bonuses, SEO keywords and categories, and core benefit of your book)

2) In addition, I am adding the following benefits to my offer for enablers:

____

____

____

(List the add-ons for your enablers, such as members of your book launch team, influencers, and cross promotion partners)

3) I need to prepare the following items before my irresistible book offer is ready and I start the pre-launch phase:

____

____

____

(List action items you need to deliver to finish your offers and to prepare your book launch campaign)

And finally, make sure that you can answer the following four questions with a clear YES before launching your book. If you answer No, I recommend you go a step back and work on improving a specific element (e.g. editing by an experienced editor) or to perform a specific activity (e.g. getting feedback), so that you get four YES answers and are confident that you are ready to launch your book.

Pre-launch Checklist
To finish chapter four and to make sure that your irresistible book offer is truly irresistible, answer the following four questions with a YES. 1) Is my book honestly amazing? (solves a problem, well written, free of errors, etc.) 2) Did I test my book (offer) with a group of people successfully? Did I get feedback on my book and offer? (at least 5-10 people) 3) Is there a true market for my book? (search traffic, beatable competition, etc.) 4) Do I have an enticing offer for my book launch/ relaunch? (added bonus, added scarcity, reduced price, built-in-virality, etc....)

Excellent! You have successfully completed step one of the Perennial Bestseller Blueprint. It's time to cover the book launch phase now! Stick with me, it's about to get exciting.

5

LAUNCH WITH A BANG [STEP 2]

> *"Everything you've ever wanted is on the other side of fear."*
>
> George Addair, 1823-1899

Book launches can be quite frightening. You've spent a long time caring for this infant, and now the baby's going to be released out into the world. It's young, it's vulnerable, and it's clear that there will be a sharp reality check.

All the dreams, all the fluff, all the hope gets threatened by a real book launch, and it's good to be prepared. Prepared not only in terms of launch preparations, but also psychologically.

It's important to push through, through that first negative feedback, through that negative gut feeling, through the disinterested influencer you pitch to. Launching is always a big effort. But without a launch, you won't succeed!

Once you have your irresistible book offer ready, it is time to launch with a bang. Launching with a bang means to launch strongly, with a book launch that gives you enough sales and reviews for Amazon to notice your book. It will provide you with enough visibility to test your book for keywords and to calculate clickthrough rates and conversions for your book. Launching with a bang also means to get enough readership to assess the true potential of your book. You'll find out if it sparks word of mouth, and see what readers truly think about your book.

In simple terms: To launch successfully, you need to do a proper book launch.

Note: What if my book is already published?

If your book is already published, you have two options. **Option A** is to do a relaunch based on the existing book. Ideally, you can add a new book format to the existing sales page, which Amazon will treat as a book launch for the new format. The effects of this are not as strong as a completely new launch. But they are still more effective than simply updating the metadata and running promotions. This is a simple relaunch.

Option B is to launch an existing book under a new title (a standalone book or as a bundle or extended version). If you choose Option B, Amazon treats the book as a new launch. I recommend this option if your existing title has only a few reviews and generates only sporadic sales. With the current algorithm, it is difficult to get an existing book with low rankings to rank high quickly. A fresh launch is much easier, as the Amazon algorithm will evaluate this new product during the launch period and calculate conversion rates for rankings.

Setting Goals

Before we jump into the three different launch phases and tactics for each phase, let's define the main goals of each proper book launch. First, let's define what is needed after the book is three months into the launch. (Ideally, you will reach these numbers towards the end of the first launch month, but up to three months is still fine.) What is the outcome of each book launch when you follow the Perennial Bestseller Blueprint?

- **250+ copies sold (around 50+ pre-orders, and 200+ sales within the first three launch months)**
- **25+ ratings online (10+ in first 14 days, 20+ in the first three months)**
- **Consistent sales (on average at least 2+ copies/ day), without running major promotions**

Why those numbers?

250+ sales because we want to make the launch worth it, as well as making sure that enough people read the book to assess its potential. The theory behind it is simple: If you get 250 readers, you gave your book a true chance to succeed. People read it and Amazon was able to calculate conversion rates for your major keywords. If your book rocks and you outperform your competition, Amazon will reward you for it, setting the stage for further success.

Note that a main goal of your launch is to make sure that you give your book enough visibility. If you've created an irresistible book offer, your book will take wing after you cross 250 sales. Even better would be the 1000+ sales within the first three months. However, I know from experience that it takes quite a push to cross that threshold. Not all authors can or want to invest enough resources to get that many sales so quickly after launch. That's why I suggest 250+ sales as your launch goal. The bottom target should be 100+ sales. This is the minimum needed to get feedback from readers and give Amazon a chance to assess conversion rates.

My clear recommendation is to invest in promotions and advertising (more about that later) so that you cross 100, 250, 500, or ideally 1000 sales. Under that threshold, you may end up with a failed launch, even if your book theoretically has everything needed to perform in the marketplace.

Let us look at the timeline of a proper book launch in more detail.

A good book launch has three important phases:

Preparation Phase: preparing your pre-launch, finishing your offers

Pre-Launch Phase: Usually a three month period before your book actually launches

Launch Phase: Usually a three month period from the moment your book goes live on Amazon (and other retailers).

As a reminder, here are your target numbers. Ideally, we're reaching these outcomes at the end of the launch month, but we definitely want to reach them by the end of the third month.

- At least 250 book sales (or, depending on the keywords or niche you are targeting, even more) [including pre-orders]

- At least 25 book ratings (ideally positive, with average rating above 4.5, consisting of at least 5-10 written reviews, the rest simple star ratings)
- Top 20 keywords rankings for our 2-3 top keywords

The reason why we need to reach those numbers is to show the Amazon algorithm that it's worthwhile to test your title for CTRs and conversions. If you did your job properly and created a book offer that your target audience can't resist, Amazon will see that demonstrated. Your CTRs and conversions will be better than your competition, and will ultimately bring Amazon more income. That's when Amazon will decide to rank your book highly (Top 20 keyword rankings) and give it visibility within the Amazon search system. That's when a book launch is a success, and it's as simple as that.

Phase 1: Preparation Phase

During preparation phase, you are getting ready to start the pre-launch phase. You will create your irresistible offers, schedule promotions, research contact lists, update your website, prepare mailings, etc.

It's important not to mix the preparation phase with the pre-launch phase. You should not use the pre-launch phase to create irresistible offers and update your webpage, for instance; instead, when you start the pre-launch phase you should be ready to go to market.

Phase 2: Pre-Launch Phase

The pre-launch phase is the time period before your book actually launches. Amazon allows putting up a book for pre-order up to one year before the actual book release[106]. However, you don't need to put your book up for pre-order. You can launch without that option. My recommendation is to put your e-book up for pre-order and to make pre-orders one of your goals during the pre-launch phase.

In order to get momentum and to make the most of the pre-launch phase, I recommend a time period of three to twelve months prior to launching your book that gives you plenty of time to get pre-orders, to grow your launch team, to build buzz, and to craft an irresistible book offer.

In reality, though, I know that most of us do not have the patience to wait up to a year for a book launch. Once we have the book ready, we want to bring it to the market. However, I strongly urge you to be patient. The pre-order phase provides a big opportunity for the long-term success of your book, if executed correctly.

The minimum time period you should have for the pre-launch phase is one month, as anything less puts your book launch at risk.

Here is what you need to take care of in the pre-launch phase:

1) Creating a book launch team of at least 100 people within your target audience who commit to pre-ordering prior to launch or purchasing your book during launch week, giving feedback, and ideally writing a review as well.
2) Making sure that your book files, bonuses, and meta data are ready for Amazon at least 14 days prior

106 Amazon terms on preorders: https://kdp.amazon.com/en_US/help/topic/G201499380

to your book launch. (All details, see "book launch checklist" under bonuses)

3) Making sure that your "irresistible book offer" has product-market fit through testing your book and Amazon sales page with your launch team prior to launch.
4) Research and connect with your Magic 100. The Magic 100 is a careful selection of powerful influencers and trafficked websites in your market that you want to connect with to generate traffic and jumpstart your book.

Once you have checked 1-4, you are ready to launch your book. Learn more about creating a launch team, testing book offers, and getting your book ready for launch by checking out the *Book Launch Team Creation Guide* by Self Publishing School[107] and by reading my advice on creating a launch team and working with the concept of The Magic 100.

Do not skip the next two blocks, as they are valuable success secrets for each major book launch! Get ready to learn more about creating your Book Launch Team and the Magic 100.

Creating Your Magic 100

It's time to take a closer look at the Magic 100.

I first heard about this approach from Russell Brunson, who uses the term Dream 100. For Russell Brunson, the Dream 100 is basically a collection of 100 influencers

107 Book Launch Team Creation Guide by Self Publishing School. Source: https://www.youtube.com/watch?v=bNy7hK1S4tc

that you'd like to work with. The idea is to carefully research influential bloggers, business owners, or anyone with a strong following or shared mindset and to build a relationship with each of them so that you have access to them before you need it.

What I like most about this concept is that it jumpstarts your audience and makes powerful shortcuts to the top. I am talking from experience. In today's digital landscape, it takes a lot of time to go from zero to the top. It's much smarter to use aggregators or influencers to build an audience and to get attention that much more quickly. My concept of the MAGIC 100 is quite similar to Russell Brunson's Dream 100; however, I have one major tweak. What I suggest is not only looking for people with an audience of influence, but also for channels and websites with existing traffic that you might be featured on. Here are my suggested tactics:

a) Research 50 influencers in your niche that you'd like to work with, who have a strong following, and who would be a true gamer changer if they give you support.
b) Research 50 channels and/or unique articles/videos/websites within your niche that have strong existing traffic (e.g. rank one to three for your main keywords via a Google search, have the most subscribers on YouTube, appear at the top of a YouTube search, etc.)

Then, reach out to the 50 influencers and try to get featured on your 50 target sites. Easy, right?

Gotcha! Yeah, the implementation is tricky. But that's why I want to show you ways to reach out.

Outreach Example 1 (Straightforward, Benefit-Oriented, Strong Response Rates)

Subject: Request to feature you/your content in upcoming book

Dear <Insert Target Name Here>

I am a big fan of your work and would love to feature some of your insights in my upcoming book <Insert Book Title Here>.

Is it OK with you that I refer to <Insert Insight/Concept/Book/ Content> in my book with a reference/link to your work?

I am looking forward to your reply.

<Insert Your Name + Signature Here>

Outreach Example 2 (Good for establishing connection, works if influencer has time)

Subject: Let's connect

Dear <Insert Target Name Here>

I have been following your material for a long time and have always been interested in your content.

Recently, I have been writing a book called <insert name here> which covers a lot of the content which you go through in your videos/blogs.

I would love to share some of my ideas with you and I feel like we could both benefit from sharing a few tips together.

Please let me know if you are interested.

<Insert Your Name + Signature Here>

Outreach Example 3 (super low-key, works to build a relationship very slowly

Subject: Congratulations on your work

Dear <Insert Target Name Here>

I am a big fan of your work and just wanted to send you a big thumbs-up on your latest <insert concrete feature/project/book/article/etc. here>.

I truly loved it.

Wishing you a great day!

<Insert Your Name + Signature Here>

I personally have had success with all three outreach templates myself in the past. Examples one and three have worked the best for me. It's very powerful to put the interest of your target in focus, either by featuring them or showing your appreciation. We're not doing this to bombard them in follow-up emails or just to be emptily flattering. We're doing it because we want to show genuine interest.

Genuine interest is very important when reaching out to the Magic 100. Use this concept if you are in for the long run and truly interested in building up a longer relationship (ideally, it won't focus just on your book, but on the bigger picture surrounding your core interest or career).

You need to understand that you will reach out to important people in your industry, and you don't want to burn your relationships or credibility by selling too hard.

Do not push too hard. Do not beg for mentions on their blogs and videos, request reviews, or ask for feedback on your book. They get hundreds or thousands of emails from desperate people begging them for free things.

Most influencers are very busy as well. Time is a valuable asset. Don't be that person. Offer them something of value first before demanding something in return.

To decide who should be in your top 100, make a list:

Firstly, contact influencers who you know in your niche and whom you admire. Likely those people will have an audience, connections, or insights that can help you later down the line.

Secondly, see who comes up first in the search engines for your niche. If your area of expertise is car hydraulics, Google it and see who comes first in YouTube, Quora, and even Twitter and Instagram. See what their content is like and you can then decide whether you want to send them a message or not.

As stated above, a needy message just begging for a feature is going to get you anywhere. I would suggest writing a message offering value, such as a feature or a thank you first. A good example is to offer to feature them in your book or to share your success on their channel. Have you had a positive experience which would be good in a blog or a video? Your influencer would probably love to know. Offering a story like this is far more effective than demanding something in return straight away.

As a next step, after contact is established, you can share your project and ask for short feedback.

Some influencers are very keen to show their expertise. If they weren't, they wouldn't be blogging or making videos about their subject matter. After they have given you some feedback, then you can start to grow a relationship slowly. See it in terms of dating – you do not propose on the first date. Likewise, you do not ask your influencers for a detailed review in your first email. Take your time.

Asking for support should be one of the last things on your agenda. Interestingly, if you put that off, often you will be offered support well before you ask for it.

To sum up, give first before taking. Think of content that would be useful to your influencers, build up a relationship with them slowly, and then you will see the benefits further down the line.

Having relationships with someone high up in your industry gives you a huge boost. If you are having trouble with something, you can always reach out to them for a professional opinion. It is not just about getting a small feature on a video, it is about networking with people that can help you far into the future.

A final word of caution: Building your Magic 100 will take time. At first you initiate contact, exchange messages, let things stay calm for some months, follow up, etc. That's why I recommend you incorporate this concept slowly. It's okay to do the first outreach only weeks before the launch (if you do not have the time resources for a longer pre-launch phase); however, do not push your own agenda, such as getting a feature or a review, if you had little time to build the relationship first.

A good tactic is to show what you have in a subtle way that invites the influencer to support you if he/she likes what you do, sees a connecting factor, and has resources available. How can you do that?

Use your email signature, for instance. Here are examples:

< Insert Your Name Here>
Launching soon: < Insert Your Book Title Here >

< Insert Your Name Here>
Author of: < Insert Your Book Title Here >

< Insert Your Name Here>
Learn about being part of my amazing book launch team. (Link to launch team)

The last example brings us to the next topic, which is the famous "Book Launch Team." In addition to building your Magic 100, I highly recommend building a book launch team. Stay tuned.

Your Book Launch Team

What is a book launch team (AKA street team)? It's a group of people who commit to supporting your book launch. Often, book launch teams consist of people from the close and extended network of the author. Contact with the launch team is personal, instead of using mass communication (unless the author has a bigger existing platform).

Important rule for book launch: We will not launch our book without having secured the support of at least 10 people who have given feedback to the book and have committed to spreading the word and, most importantly, to reviewing the book (either as an editorial review or a customer review on Amazon). We need to have at least a small book launch team in place!

It's critical to have this support base in place, as doing a cold book launch is a very risky endeavor that you want to avoid at all costs.

What is the most important job of the members of your launch team?

To provide reviews! Ideally, verified purchase customer reviews on Amazon.

How many people you need to contact in order to get 10 commitments for reviewing your book?

The straightforward answer is: it depends. If you are reaching out to your close circle, it might be enough to secure 25 contacts. On the other hand, if you have a larger email list, you might need to send an email campaign to thousands of subscribers in order to reach your 10 commitments.

Quality beats quantity, so do not assume that having a big audience will make it easy to get launch support for your book. Luckily, you have already created an irresistible offer during step 1 of the Blueprint. This will help you tremendously with recruiting members for your launch team.

In the following pages, I will give you some amazing outreach templates for announcing your launch during pre-launch phase with the goal of recruiting people into your launch team. You can use those templates both for reaching out to your inner circle (via Facebook, personal email, phone calls, LinkedIn messages) and for email campaigns to your subscriber lists.

Should you reach out to your Magic 100 to ask them to be on your launch team as well?

My recommendation is that you should avoid an initial outreach with a potential influencer/enabler via one of these templates. Instead, stick with my outreach templates as provided in the section targeting the Magic 100. Once you've established real contact with the member of your Magic 100, you can consider asking them to join your launch team as well.

The core purpose of being in touch with your Magic 100 is the bigger picture (getting long-term support, visibility, etc.), so make sure to approach them carefully. Weigh the pros and cons of asking them for joining your launch team.

Find some amazing and proven templates for recruiting people to your launch team below:

Email Template for Announcing/Recruiting

Below you find my recommended email outreach for announcing your book launch team. The message is rather long (you can shorten and adapt it for social media messages). Almost as important as the initial outreach is the follow up.

STREET TEAM ANNOUNCEMENT – FIRST EMAIL

Subject: [First Name], You're Invited To My Book Launch Team! 😊

Body:

Hi <first name>, I am happy to let you know that I am only weeks away from launching my new book with the title <insert book title here>. The book is about <describe your book and why it is awesome>.

I can't wait for this book launch to finally happen!

In order to make the launch a success, I want to pick about 100 special people to form my book launch team to help me get the word out.

Are you interested in joining?

Here is what you get as a launch team member:<Insert bullet points describing your bonuses and benefits>

Here is what you have to do:<Insert bullet points describing the to-dos, such as:-> Pre-ordering the e-book on Amazon for only $0.99-> Leaving a review on Amazon during launch week>

That's it! Of course, I'd love spreading the word via social media or helping in any other way as well, but that's totally optional.

---Isn't that awesome?

I have 100 spots and would love to have you on my team.Can I count you in?

Thank you,

<Your Name>

STREE TEAM - FOLLOW UP

Subject: Re: [First Name], You're Invited To My Book Launch Team! 😊Body:

Hi <first name>,Did you have time to read my email? It would be great to have you on the team.Looking forward to your reply.

<Your Name>

Please take a look at a couple of longer examples for street team invitations by checking out a resource provided by Kevin Kruse[108]. A useful resource for book launch teams is also provided by Self-Publishing School[109].

www.youtube.com › watch

Launch Team: How to Launch a Book Effectively ... - YouTube

When it comes to launching a bestselling book on Amazon, the biggest leverage an author can invest in is ...

May 7, 2019 · Uploaded by Self Publishing School

Source: Google. Screenshot © Albert Griesmayr 2021

Make sure to include the creation of a book launch team in your overall book marketing plan. It's okay to have a small team and even to avoid using the term "launch team" when reaching out to your network. But make sure to get the commitments for reviews and support. Don't skip this important step.

108 Email templates for announcing launch teams. Source: http://authorjourneyto100k.com/sample-invitation-join-book-launch-team/

109 Launch Team Guide. Source: https://www.youtube.com/watch?v= bNy7hK1S4tc

Pre-Order Campaign

Another important element of the pre-launch phase is a possible pre-order campaign that you can run for your e-book via Amazon[110]. By putting your e-book up for pre-order you can monetize your pre-launch phase, evaluate the demand of your book and effectiveness of your irresistible offers, show your commitment to the launch, increase your credibility, and create a tangible asset and target for members of your book launch team.

The narrative in regards to launch teams works as follows: "Pre-order the book and get a fantastic surprise gift within every book!" By doing so, you strongly raise the chances that people will actually pre-order your book, as well as read the book when it comes out! It's a double win.

Clearly, pre-orders on Amazon are highly useful.

In 2020, Amazon even extended its pre-order phase up to one year and BookBub started to offer submissions for featured new release promotion (which have less competition than the featured discounted book deals).

The bottom line is that I recommend using Amazon pre-orders for e-books, especially if you are running a proper pre-launch phase.

The only times I wouldn't recommend this feature is if you have a very short pre=launch phase, are not sure about your book launch date, or are not planning to promote your pre-order. It's worth noting that as of May 2021, Amazon allows book launch delays once, by only

110 Pre-orders on Amazon are only possible for e-books right now (not for paperback or hardcover versions). [Last updated: May 2021]

thirty days, and restricts you from further pre-orders if you miss your launch window. Make sure to read the latest terms as I included in the footnote[111].

Pre-order campaigns are also very useful if you have a supporting webpage and marketing campaign in place.

Below, you'll find two examples of pre-order campaigns that I ran for amazing clients during 2021 that communicated pre-orders via an author website.

Simple landing page with email sign up:

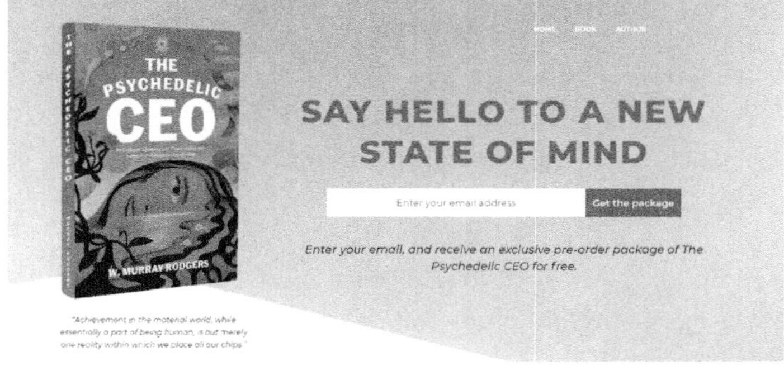

Source: Client Campaign: *The Psychedelic CEO*, 2021.
Screenshot © Albert Griesmayr 2021

Discover a new way to see the world
Special launch offer:

- Low price USD$3.10 (CDN$3.90) for ebook. $9.89 for paperback
- Personalized, signed bookplate
- Join discussion group with the author

Source: Client Campaign: How to Understand Everything, 2021.
Screenshot © Albert Griesmayr 2021

111 Source: https://kdp.amazon.com/en_US/help/topic/G201499380

What we did for both campaigns was connect the action of pre-ordering the book with getting bonuses. Both books had a strong launch based on a clear offer communicated to existing author networks.

In a nutshell, here is my recommended approach for communicating pre-orders:

Pre-Order Communication [Via Website]
Pre-order my book and get a surprise gift/bonuses (worth $XXX): Communicate the following effectively: • Why your book is amazing, has credibility, and is useful to the reader • While the e-book is on pre-order it is super cheap (reduced pre-order price) • Readers get a surprise gift/bonus once the book is out that can only be found within the book. In addition, you can add a bonus available right now after signing up for the pre-order (which helps to convince readers to act right now). ——— Please refer to examples for surprise gifts in the section on bouses discussed in step1 of the Blueprint in this book.

I'd like to introduce you to the Launch Onion. This is a useful concept for understanding the importance of the pre-launch phase with leveraging pre-orders and building support with a launch team and the Magic 100. What we want to do with a proper book launch is target the closer areas first, such as friends and family, then move on to acquaintances and influencers, before reaching out to the general public in a last step.

THE LAUNCH ONION

Screenshot https://pixabay.com/illustrations/onion-vegetable-market-onions-2284992/ (free for commercial use)
© Pixabay, 2021

Inside the onion: You and your book

Next layer: Friends and family, contacts for launch team

Acquaintances, the Magic 100 and email subscribers for launch team, Pre-Launch Phase and launch activities

General public (via promotions, PR, and advertising) after launch week and at least 10 reviews have been secured.

Note: The pre-launch phase is primarily for tapping your network and to establish relationships with the Magic 100.

Cold promotions should not be started before you have 10+ reviews in place and a good support base from your launch team is established.

Important Pre-Launch Activities

Before it is actually time to launch your book and to start the launch phase, there are some important activities that need to be performed. We call them "pre-launch activities." By performing those activities, you are making sure that your launch will run smoothly and that you reduce obstacles during launch week.

You can find a checklist of activities below, with a detailed discussion of the core activities.

STEP 2: LAUNCH WITH A BANG A: LAUNCH PREPARATION (1-12 MONTHS PRIOR TO LAUNCH)	
Making sure that book materials (covers, manuscripts, etc.) are ready at least 14 days prior to launch [Hiring professionals early if necessary]	
Making sure that all marketing materials (website, funnel, author bio, book descriptions, email outreach to subscriber and influencer, etc.) are ready at least 14 days prior to pre-launch phase (or launch in case you have no pre-launch phase) [Hiring professionals early if necessary]	
Website and Funnel	
Author Bio	
Book blurb	
Book Description	
Email Outreach (Sequence) to Subscribers	
Email Outreach (Sequence) to Magic 100/Influencers	
Email Outreach (Sequence) to Book Launch Team	
Email Outreach to Reviewers (People you request a review from)	
Optional: Surprise Gift (Within book, on website, plus email sequence)	
Optional: Preparing social media messages for your book launch phase	
Magic 100 List created (100 Targets)	
Book Launch Team Email List Created (10+ Targets)	
List of Reviewers (people you ask for a review) from your network created	
Optional: If you do PR, outreach message and media kit for journalists created	
Optional: 1 month prior to launch, signing up for Reedsy Discovery and submitting your book for launch (launch date has to be 1 month in the future)	

Optional: If you put your e-book up for pre-order on Amazon, signing up for KDP, filling out payment and tax details and creating an e-book entry for your pre-order (Note: You don't need a manuscript, only an e-book cover, publishing data, and a core book description for the pre-order)	
Optional: If you already have at least one book published, signing up for Pubby.co, submitting a prior book and starting to collect points (Ideally, launch your book when you have 20,000+ points on Pubby)	
Optional: Organize cross promos via Magic 100/influencers	
1 Month prior to launch: Signing up for KDP (and checking out required fields for publishing, making sure you have all info to fill out)	
1 Month prior to launch: Signing up for Amazon Author Central (and starting your author bio and claiming your prior books if available)	
1 Month prior to launch: Checking within KDP that your book files will be approved by Amazon (Previewer for Kindle, Paperback which is available when you upload your book)	
1 week prior to launch: Making sure that you have a professional hired for Amazon ads, so that you have keyword lists and categories to target the moment your book launches	

Those core activities are:

1) Signing Up for Amazon KDP and Author Central (and publishing your book)
2) Making sure that your book materials are publish-ready for Amazon
3) Organizing review and rating generation (via your network, the Magic 100, and your book launch team)
4) Booking launch promotions for visibility, sales, and the bestseller campaign

5) Preparing social media, PR, and network outreach messages

Let us look at those activities in more detail now.

1. Signing Up for Amazon KDP and Author Central

One of the most effective ways of publishing your books is through Amazon's Kindle Direct Publishing (KDP). Although this program supports publishing through more than just KDP (you could use Ingramspark, PublishDrive or Draft2Digital as well), important action steps described, such as publishing your book, entering seven keywords and using KDP Select, are only possible if you publish through KDP. Amazon KDP offers a wide reach (geographies) and a comparably fair royalty structure. And yes, there are other publishing channels, such as Ingramspark, Publishdrive or others. You might decide to publish your book through those because of reasons specific to you. In this book, however, we'll keep it simple and assume that you are publishing through KDP. In my experience, this is the optimal choice for an initial book launch.

Amazon has global distribution to forty different territories, the ability to use book promotions and countdown deals for your readers, and has its own "Author Central" page, where you can set up a hub for yourself, enabling you to market your products and keep track of your sales.

Over the next couple of pages, we'll take a look at how to publish your book on KDP and how to sign up for Author Central. If you already have experience with KDP and Author Central, you can skip those pages.

How To Publish Your Book On KDP

What You Need Before Publishing Your Book On KDP

Using Kindle Direct Publishing is very easy, but you will need the following:

- A completed manuscript formatted for both e-book and print
- The correct metadata (it is recommended to keep this in a separate document)
- An HTML description (Explanation below)
- A KDP account set up in advance
- An e-book and print book cover

How To Publish Your Book On KDP

When you have your print book, e-book, and all the relevant information in order, sign into your KDP account at https://kdp.amazon.com and start the publishing process.

Source: KDP. Screenshot © Albert Griesmayr 2021

After you have signed in, at the top of the page click Kindle eBook and then you will be prompted with three sections (details, content, pricing), all of which will need to be filled out.

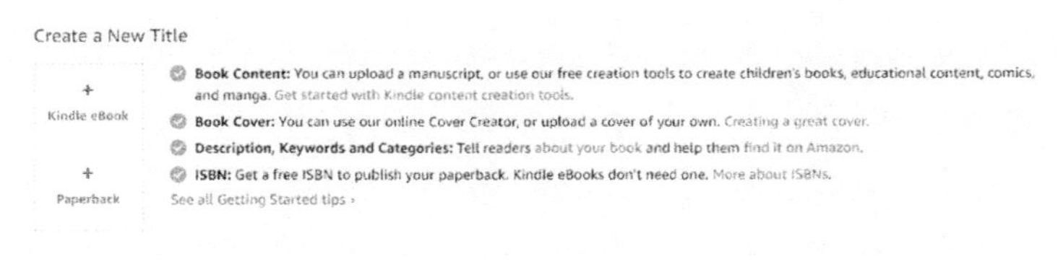

Source: KDP. Screenshot © Albert Griesmayr 2021

Details

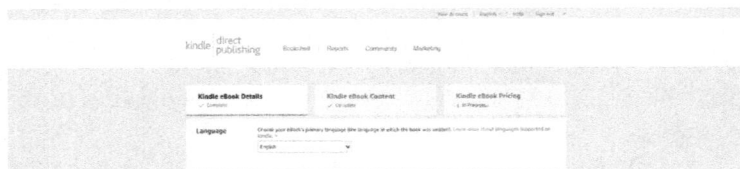

Source: KDP. Screenshot © Albert Griesmayr 2021

- Language of book
- Author name and title of book
- Series name and number if applicable
- Any contributors
- Description: (The description appears on your book's Amazon detail page and it is important because it is what potential readers will see when they are deciding whether to read your book or not. Descriptions must be HTML formatted. Fortunately, there is a resource on Kindlepreneur which takes care of this for free: https://kindlepreneur.com/amazon-book-description-generator/. For more information on the description, you can watch the following video: https://www.youtube.com/watch?v=PES3QoTioYA&feature=youtu.be&ab_channel=Kindlepreneur)
- Publishing rights
- Copyright
- Seven keywords (Up to 50 characters for each keyword)
- Categories (Selecting a category helps Amazon with filing your book in the correct browsing paths; this video explains categories in more detail: https://www.youtube.com/watch?v=Oe1shRiUMZc&ab_channel=RachelHarrison-Sund)
- Age and grade range
- Select pre-order if you need time to promote your book launch; if not, select publish now.

Content

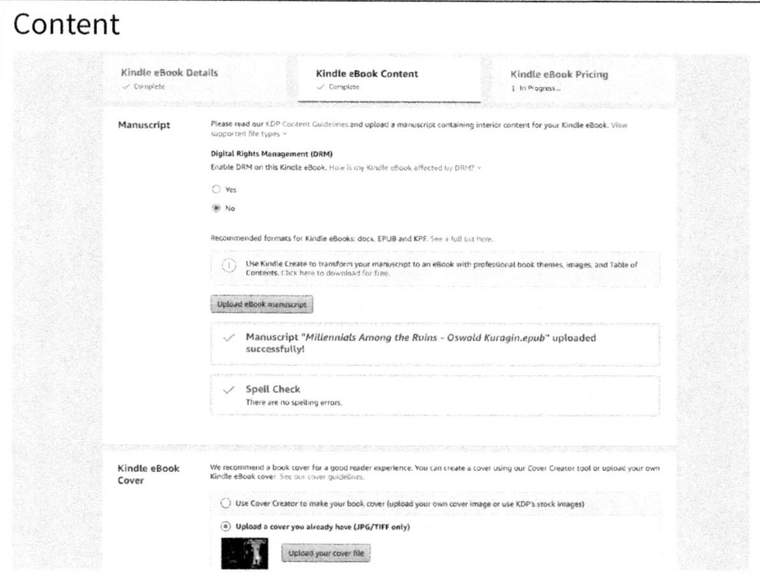

Source: KDP. Screenshot © Albert Griesmayr 2021

Digital Rights Management (DRM) protects your book against piracy. Once you select this option, you cannot remove it. I usually do not select this option, but please decide for yourself

- Upload your manuscript
- Upload your Kindle cover file
- Launch previewer to see how it looks on Kindle; make sure you see how it looks on landscape and portrait as well as different devices
- Spellcheck
- ISBN

Pricing

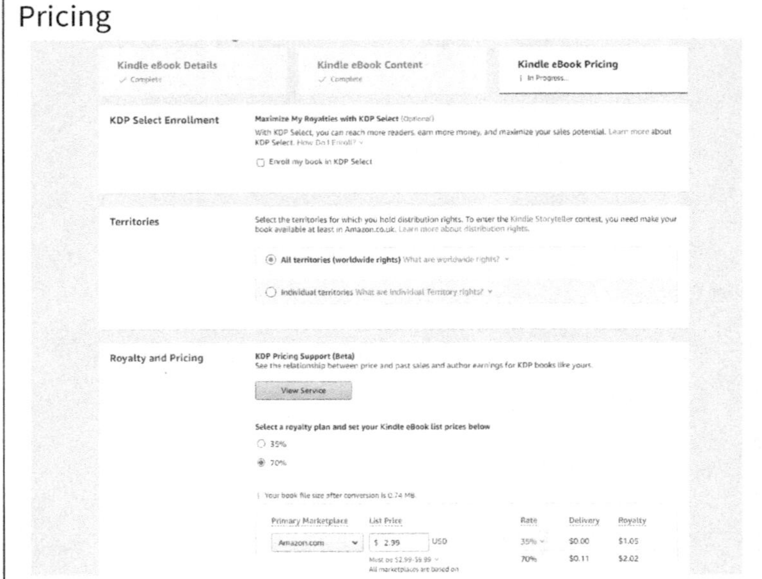

Source: KDP. Screenshot © Albert Griesmayr 2021

- Enroll in KDP select. Find more information here: https://www.youtube.com/watch?v=IVDYO8_V3yI&ab_channel=Kindlepreneur
- Select the territories for which you have distribution rights
- Use the KDP Pricing Support service to see how other books in your niche are priced; it is recommended that you price your books in a similar way to the others.
- If you choose 70% royalty, you must price your book between $2.99 and $9.99. Amazon has calculated that you are most likely to sell your book if you price it within that range, so they give you a higher royalty rate if you follow their advice.
- My recommendation in regards to pricing is that you start with low prices. Price points between $.99 and $2.99 for an e-book are good first month starters that enable you to promote your book with external promotional services easily as well. Paperback prices below $10 or at least below $15 are attractive starting price points for launch offers.
- Change the prices for other regions if required
- Agree to the terms and conditions and publish

Print Book

- Start your print book directly after the eBook as it saves all your data
- The three sections are the same with some additional features specific to print books
- Leave book details the same but tweak the description to suit print books and change the keywords if necessary
- For content, use either your own ISBN or a free one which KDP assigns you
- Choose the type of paper, print size, bleed settings and whether you want a matte or glossy finish.
- Upload your manuscript and cover (PDF recommended for both)
- Launch previewer
- Save and continue
- For pricing, use the same methods as for e-books

Link your e-book and print book

- Make sure that your e-book and print book are linked, so that they create one entry. You can do this right away, when you have published or started with the creation of one format, by creating the other format from the same tab. Alternatively, you link them afterwards (see the options in the screenshots below).

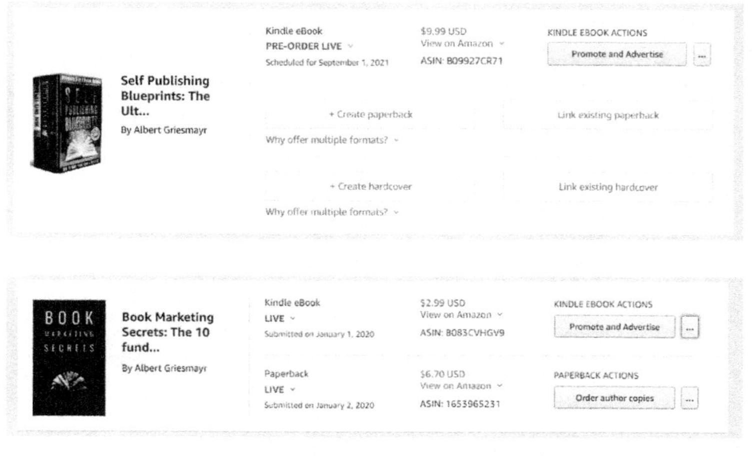

Source: KDP. Screenshot © Albert Griesmayr 2021

In more detail: SEO for Books | Keywords and Categories [Exkurs: SEO For Books]

You have just seen that while publishing your book, you are also filling out seven keywords and selecting two categories for each of your book's editions.

Those activities are important steps in regards to search engine optimization (SEO) for Amazon. Let's take a closer look.

SEO stands for Search Engine Optimization. This is the name given to a wide range of practices you can do to help your book appear higher in the search rankings and therefore be visible to more potential buyers.

SEO does not refer solely to Amazon, but to any search engine on the World Wide Web, such as Kobo, Barnes and Noble, and Blackwell's.

If your book has a high SEO ranking, it means when a potential buyer searches for your book or for a keyword related to it, your book appears higher in the search rankings than your competitors.

If your book appears in the top five results of a search, you have a high SEO Ranking.

It is very important to have a high SEO ranking because 67% of all click throughs occur in the first 5 links. 30% of all clicks on search engines are on the very top link. Failing to appear in the first few search results is very costly as click-throughs decrease rapidly as you go further down the search results.

Amazon SEO refers to all measures taken to improve both visibility and conversion rates in Amazon Search.

SEO has two major aspects:

The first is getting found in search engines.

The second is conversion, i.e., getting people to click on your result and buy your product once they have found it.

Amazon SEO has changed over the years. Traditional SEO (referring to keywords and categories) is certainly not as important as it was a few years ago; however, it pays to do basic SEO right, especially for your main keyword and your title.

Amazon is getting better in looking at conversion and software and AI instead. True performance in regards to sales, conversions, and high customer satisfaction will continue to become more and more important.

There are three main ways to optimize your SEO ranking:

1) Make sure there is demand for your book in keywords and categories
2) Choose a keyword-optimized title, keywords, and categories correctly
3) Make sure your book converts like hell

We shall now examine each of these ways individually, looking at ways to improve on SEO in all three areas.

1) Make sure there is demand for your book in keywords and categories

The first way to optimize your SEO is to check whether potential buyers are actually searching for the keywords and categories you intend to use. No matter how good your book is, no one is going to buy it if no one is searching for your keywords.

Please take what you have learned in step 1 of the Perennial Bestseller Blueprint and work with the keywords and categories that you have researched.

Thankfully, there are ways to check whether your keywords are hot or not. We would recommend three pieces of software to help out:

Publisher Rocket is a program which checks out the rankings for keywords you want to target. By typing in a keyword or set of keywords, Publisher Rocket tells you how many competitors you have, how much money a work using this keyword earns, and how competitive it is. This is the perfect way of foreseeing the popularity of a certain niche before putting your work out there and it is highly recommended to use this before taking the plunge.

You can also use KDPSpy which we have already discussed in chapter 4.

Alternatively, for those of you on a budget and wanting a free option, Book Sales Rank Calculator combined with a common-sense approach by researching on Amazon yourself is your best bet.

2) Choose a keyword-optimized title, keywords, and categories correctly

Once you have successfully assessed the demand, you need to use your selected keywords throughout the description. Ideally, include them in your book title/subtitle as well.

The best scenario is that you use one-two main keywords in the title/subtitle, as well as a couple of times in your book description and once in your backend search terms. This will show Amazon that you want to rank for those keywords. Your book also needs to sell; when a customer types a word into search, finds your book and purchases it, this demonstrates relevancy to Amazon and shows the demand for your book to be related to a particular keyword.

Make sure to have seven keywords entered on the Amazon backend. They must make sense and not be too generic or too competitive.

As an example, you see below the seven keywords I am using on Amazon to market this title (I am using the same keywords for both the e-book and the paperback edition, and I recommend you do the same, unless your book has already some traction and based on sales and visibility it makes sense to expand keywords and choose the best terms for each book edition).

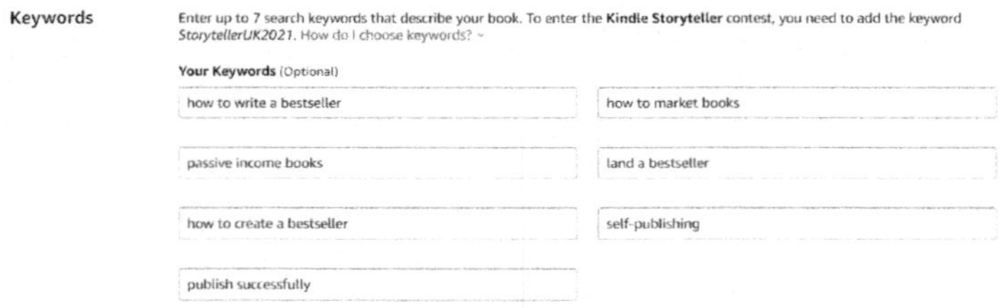

Keywords

Enter up to 7 search keywords that describe your book. To enter the **Kindle Storyteller** contest, you need to add the keyword *StorytellerUK2021*. How do I choose keywords?

Your Keywords (Optional)

how to write a bestseller
how to market books
passive income books
land a bestseller
how to create a bestseller
self-publishing
publish successfully

Source: KDP July, 2021. Screenshot © Albert Griesmayr 2021

In addition, you will select two categories for each book edition, based on Amazon's BISAC system. I recommend that you go through the selection and pick two browse categories that are relevant to your book. It's important to note that once your book is live, we will use a backdoor to get your book editions to appear in more than those categories available for your books in the KDP dashboard. That's why you do not need to invest too much time in your category selection at this point. Pick what is most suitable, and make sure to go as many into niches as possible by clicking the + buttons in Amazon's selection so you see the full picture.

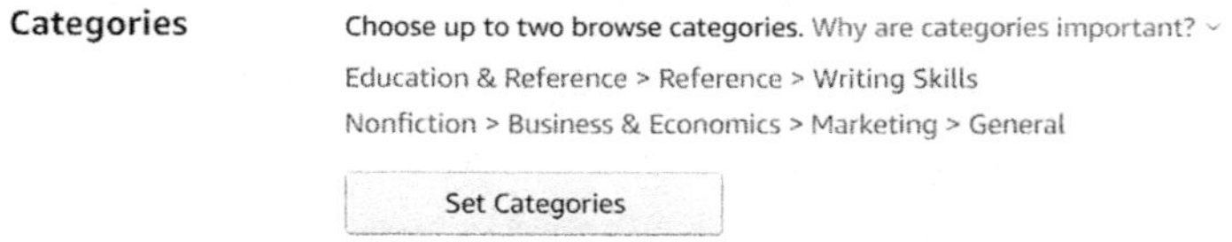

Categories

Choose up to two browse categories. Why are categories important?

Education & Reference > Reference > Writing Skills

Nonfiction > Business & Economics > Marketing > General

Set Categories

Source: KDP July, 2021 Screenshot © Albert Griesmayr 2021

Choosing the right categories determines the amount of competition you will face for becoming an Amazon Bestselling Author. Choosing the right categories is an important Amazon Bestseller Secret.

We want to "stack the cards" in our favor. Right now, the backdoor to Amazon's categories used through Author Central is our way to work this system. However, this might change in the future, and Amazon might allow authors to select all categories on the KDP backend themselves. You must stay updated on those developments and certainly make sure that your books are listed in the best way.

3) Make sure your book converts like hell

As previously mentioned, conversion rates and customer satisfaction are key in modern Amazon SEO. That's why you need a killer book description and excellent book reviews and ratings to convert and to make your readers happy.

In July 2021, Amazon made an existing feature of publishers available to KDP Authors as well: The option of adding A+ content that is directly visible on the Amazon sales page above the editorial review section. That's a huge change and a great opportunity for showcasing your work in a better way. I strongly recommend using this feature. In the screenshot below you see this section in action for the book The YOU Beyond You by my client Ramzi Najjar.

Screenshot of Amazon Sales Page of The YOU Beyond You by Ramzi Najjar: https://www.amazon.com/YOU-beyond-you-Knowledge-Willing/dp/B08KH3S581 Source: Amazon. Screenshot © Albert Griesmayr 2021

The A+ content feature allows you to add images to the more regular text-based book descriptions, which is an excellent expansion of your description ability. It's perfectly suited for showcasing accolades and awards, milestones that have been reached in terms of popularity and sales, and book content such as illustrations, worksheets, and infographics.

You can learn more about the opportunities with A+ content here:
-> https://ericvanderhope.com/kdp-has-added-a-new-marketing-tool-its-called-a-content/
-> https://kdp.amazon.com/en_US/help/topic/G8EP5W6H9CY7T8GS

Make sure to use A+ content to the full to increase conversion rates.

Once you are ready to go and you have filled out all details, hit submit. Within a matter of 24-48 hours your e-book and print book will be published on Amazon (as a pre-order or live right away).

Once you have submitted, it's time to receive the message: Congratulations, your book is published on KDP!

Author Central

An important step that new authors often do not have on their radar is to sign up for Amazon Author Central.

Author Central is an underrated resource that is essential for presenting yourself in the best light as an author on Amazon. When users click your name, they will be directed to your author page with shows all your details, releases, and even your blog feed if you choose to have one. Users can read all about you and choose to follow you.

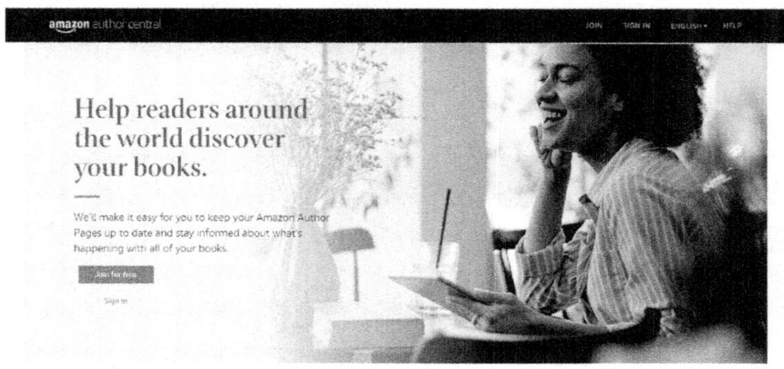

Source: KDP. Screenshot © Albert Griesmayr 2021

So how do you sign up for Author Central?

Visit https://author.amazon.com/ and create your account. I recommend you use the same credentials as you use for KDP, as you keep things simple by doing so. After you sign up and register, Amazon will ask you to confirm the books you have published. They will then check whether those books are yours and may contact your publisher; this process could take up to seven days.

When Amazon has verified your account and your releases, you will then get access to the Author Central dashboard.

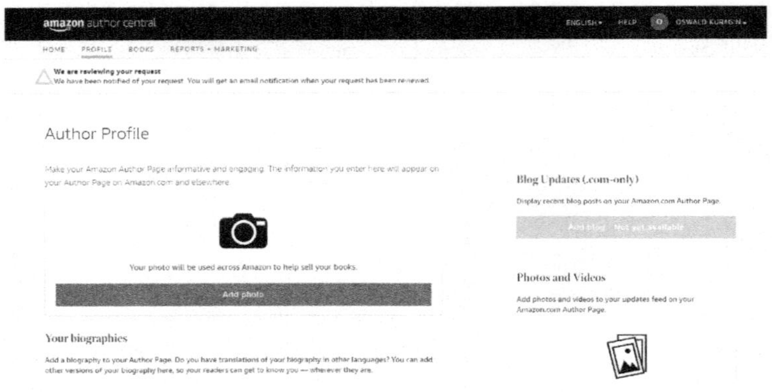

Source: KDP. Screenshot © Albert Griesmayr 2021

On the dashboard, complete all the steps to fill in your profile. A comprehensive tutorial by Kindlepreneur shows you how to do this: https://www.youtube.com/watch?v=I-_MWQrDJQ8&ab_channel=Kindlepreneur

On the books tab, once Amazon has verified your account, you can add editorial reviews. Make sure to make use of the bold and italics font types when adding your reviews.

Using the backdoor for submitting up to 10 additional book categories

As previously discussed, there is a way to submit up to 10 categories for your book through Author Central. Navigate to "Help" and find the relevant path related to "categories and search terms" (see screenshot below).

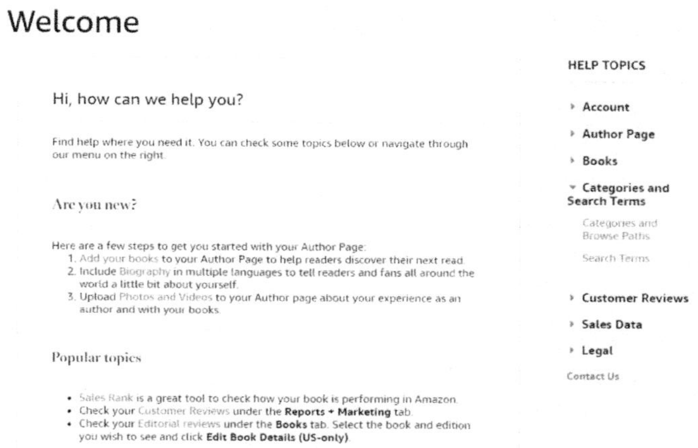

Welcome

Hi, how can we help you?

Find help where you need it. You can check some topics below or navigate through our menu on the right.

Are you new?

Here are a few steps to get you started with your Author Page:

1. Add your books to your Author Page to help readers discover their next read.
2. Include Biography in multiple languages to tell readers and fans all around the world a little bit about yourself.
3. Upload Photos and Videos to your Author page about your experience as an author and with your books.

Popular topics

- Sales Rank is a great tool to check how your book is performing in Amazon.
- Check your Customer Reviews under the **Reports + Marketing** tab.
- Check your Editorial reviews under the **Books** tab. Select the book and edition you wish to see and click **Edit Book Details (US-only)**.

HELP TOPICS

- **Account**
- **Author Page**
- **Books**
- **Categories and Search Terms**
  - Categories and Browse Paths
  - Search Terms
- **Customer Reviews**
- **Sales Data**
- **Legal**

Contact Us

Source: KDP. Screenshot © Albert Griesmayr 2021

Under "categories and browse paths" you'll find a "contact us" option.

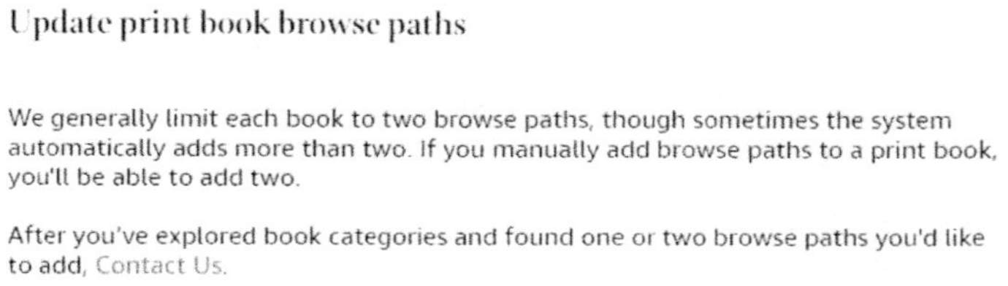

Update print book browse paths

We generally limit each book to two browse paths, though sometimes the system automatically adds more than two. If you manually add browse paths to a print book, you'll be able to add two.

After you've explored book categories and found one or two browse paths you'd like to add, Contact Us.

Source: KDP. Screenshot © Albert Griesmayr 2021

After clicking on "Contact Us" you can submit a message to Amazon, listing your suggested book categories. I suggest copying the browse paths from Publisher Rocket. Make sure to use categories that are not super-competitive but are still relevant. Amazon is getting stricter in approving categories, so relevancy is important. It might also be that Amazon will further limit this "backdoor" and the option to submit categories, as more and more authors are becoming aware of this backdoor, and Amazon has more and more manual work with following the requests submitted.

You can watch the following tutorial by Kindlepreneur about how to add categories as well: https://www.youtube.com/watch?v=PSvQoELQldM

2. Making sure that your book materials are publish-ready for Amazon

Another important pre-launch activity is making sure that your book materials are publish-ready for Amazon.

You can use the Amazon KDP in the previewer both for your paperback and e-book version while/before publishing your books (see step 1 – my recommended method). The good thing is, Amazon will show you right away if there are major flaws with the manuscript/cover, so that you can fix that prior to the launch.

There is also the option to use the desktop version of the Kindle Previewer[112] for testing the e-book version; however, the software is not as effective as the previewer within KDP.

My recommendation from experience is to work with professionals when it comes to your publishing files, in regards to the e-book, paperback, and hardcover files. (Hardcovers are in Amazon Beta as of July 2021 and will likely soon roll out for everyone.) You can find freelance professionals on platforms such as Reedsy and Upwork, saving time and money and still achieving a professional result.

Correctly formatting an e-book or paperback file and making sure that the paperback cover fits in regard to the dimensions is not as trivial as it might seem at first. Even if you have the ability to do it yourself without too much hassle, there's still the question of quality. I advise you not to skimp in this area.

---

112 Download Page for Kindle previewer: https://www.amazon.com/gp/feature.html?ie=UTF8&docId=1000765261

3. Generating reviews/ratings

Another critical pre-launch activity is making sure that you have everything prepared to get reviews and ratings online for your book quickly after launch.

I recommend three core activities:

3a) Leverage your existing network

The best way to get your first 10 reviews is to contact your existing network [launch team, supporters, friends, etc.]. From experience, I know that your close network is usually the most receptive and reliable in terms of providing initial positive reviews.

So do not underestimate the importance of your close network. Amazon has strict guidelines on what is allowed with review generation and what is not (see latest updates for community guidelines[113] and for customer reviews[114] in particular). Most importantly you are not allowed to incentivize reviews in any way, or to get reviews from people that are in a close personal relationship to you.

Technically, that puts you in a moral gray area in terms of asking close friends for reviews. However, in my experience, Amazon doesn't strike those reviews unless the person lives in the same household – for instance, your spouse, children, etc. I don't recommend reviews from those living with you, but in my past experience it's been acceptable to seek reviews from friends, coworkers, and acquaintances. Make sure to tell them that you want unbiased reviews.

113 Community Guidelines: https://www.amazon.com/gp/help/customer/display.html?nodeId=GLHXEX85MENUE4XF

114 Customer Reviews TOS: https://www.amazon.com/gp/help/customer/display.html?nodeId=G3UA5WC5S5UUKB5G

Photo reviews are especially useful (see below). So are reviews with detailed comments. As of 2019, Amazon allows simple star ratings as well. If your network is more comfortable with that, every little bit still helps.

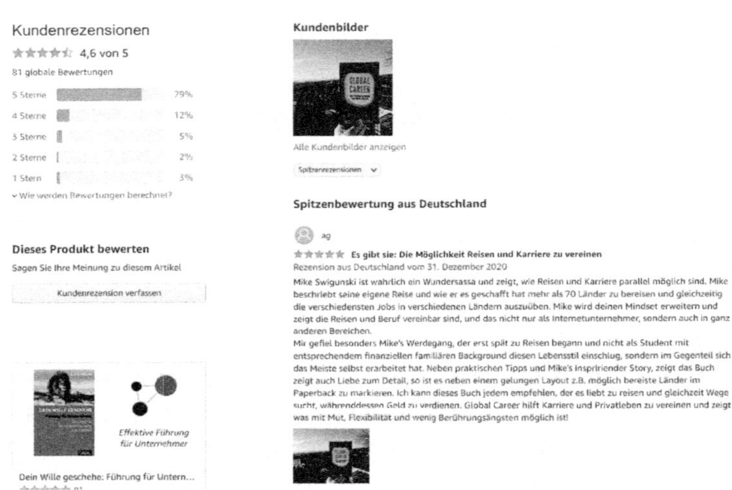

A photo review for Global Career in Germany.
Source: https://www.amazon.de/Global-Career-Anywhere-Travel-Forever/dp/B07Q8SZV7M/ Screenshot © Albert Griesmayr 2021

In general, your review generation should be embedded into your overall launch strategy. I recommend asking persons who are part of your launch team or are close to you for other reasons for reviews. Remember that this comes down to a personal favor, so take the person's attitude toward your work and their willingness to help out into account when choosing who to ask.

My preferred approach for getting reviews is the use of a three-step process. It involves asking for feedback first, reviewing it for helpfulness, and then asking them to post it online if it falls into the "good" category.

Below you find my recommended email sequence, which can be used as a follow-up with your book launch team, as well as outreach to other persons on your network.

DIRECT APPROACH – ONE EMAIL

Subject: My book has just been published 😊

Body:

Hi [first name]!I am happy to let you know that my new book is finally out.Would you like to help me out by posting a review or a rating?

Thank you,

[Your Name]

MORE SOPHISTIACTED APPROACH | EMAIL SEQUENCE OF 3 EMAILS[TARGETING LAUNCH TEAM OR CLOSE CONTACTS]

EMAIL 1 -> Make announcement & give free copy

Subject: My book has just been published 😊

Body:
Hi [first name]!I am excited to let you know that my new book is finally available!To say thanks for your support, I would like to send you a free digital copy. Can I share the book with you by email?

Thank you,

[Your Name]

EMAIL 2 -> Give free copy & ask for feedback

Subject: Here is your free copy -> Feedback would be great

Body:
Hi [first name]!Excellent. Please find attached your free digital copy. I hope you will like it.Could you send me a short feedback regarding the book as well?This would help me to get insight and to improve next editions. Let me know.Thank you,[Your Name]

EMAIL 3 -> Ask for the review | Ask for permission to share the review

Subject: AW: Here is your free copy -> Feedback would be great

Body:
Thank you so much for your feedback. I really appreciate it. That was very helpful! Would it be possible that I use the review on my website? This would help me to show potential readers, that this book is worth reading. And if you have an Amazon account: Would you consider posting the feedback on Amazon as well? Link to Review Page (No pressure of course, but it would be super helpful.)Let me know!Thank you so much,[Your Name]

Please adapt the email outreach to your needs. If you are communicating with friends, you will likely not use my standardized templates, which is perfectly fine. The more personal the correspondence, the more effective the review generation.

Before going to services that you can use to jumpstart your review generation, I'd like to share a power tactic for getting lots of reviews and ratings initially. If you are able to include this tactic into your launch plan, I'd certainly recommend it.

One of my favorite tactics is to enroll the e-book into KDP Select for the first 90 days, and to schedule a free book promo on days 4, 5, 6 after launch day.

At the same time, I do the following:

- Schedule a promotion with Freebooksy for day 5 (or any other recommended service for running discounted e-book alert promotions)
- Inform my launch team and my Magic 100 prior to launch that the e-book will be available free as a thank you on days 4, 5, 6 after launch, and this is the time for them to download the book and post a review/rating. (Make sure that you have told them previously that the book will be available for free to them at some point, rather than promoting or letting them believe that they will need to purchase the book.)
- Look for freelancers via Upwork who are specialized in review/rating generation and can work with you to promote your book through reviewer networks during launch. It's important to notice that you use this step at your own risk. Some freelancers may not operate by Amazon ToS.

By following this tactic, I am usually able to generate 30+ reviews/ratings for books by clients. I can check off the initial review/rating generation after 14 days post-launch, which gives the book strong base credibility. That frees me up to focus on promotions and Amazon ads.

3b) Use Pubby.

In 2019, a new service emerged: Pubby.co. Pubby helps authors get reviews by supporting other authors and earning snaps. Snaps are Pubby's currency, which you can use to post your books and get them reviewed by others.

The advantages of Pubby are as follows:

- You have full control of when and how often to get reviewed.
- You can support other authors and earn snaps to have your books read and reviewed by peers.
- You can get reviews for books within 5-10 days, making book launches or preparations for book promotions far easier.
- You save time and money by reducing efforts to contact book reviewers by email or via social media.

I tested Pubby extensively, and I have been part of publishing groups that have done the same. In today's market, I feel safe in saying that Pubby is truly a helpful service for getting book reviews. You might even call it the secret weapon for authors in 2021. Please note, however, that you need an Amazon.com account with a purchase history of $50 or more in order to be eligible for posting reviews. Additionally, you'll need the time to review books by other authors and collect points in order to make the most of this service.

Also, as a first time author, you can't use Pubby before publishing your book on Amazon. This means you can't collect points pre-launch. If you've already published a book, you can become approved by Pubby and start collecting points prior to the launch of your next book. Learn more about how Pubby works and get a 15% discount by clicking the following link: https://pubby.co/?invite=5101

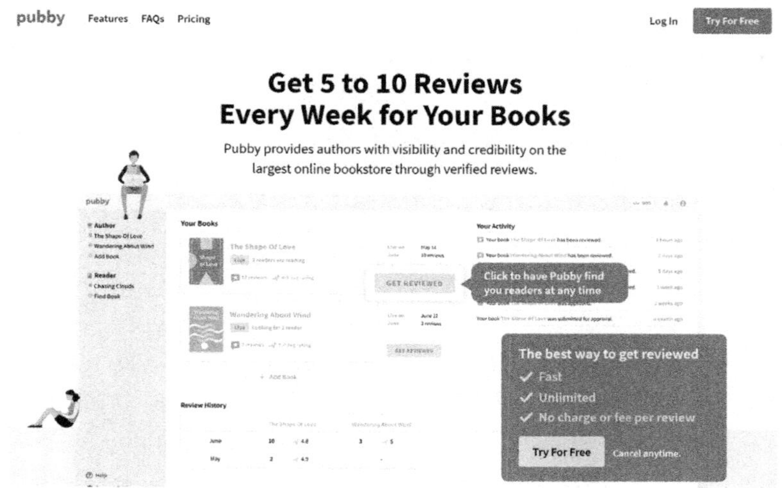

Source: Pubby.co Screenshot © Albert Griesmayr 2021

An alternative to Pubby is a service like the Book Review Targeter [www.getbookreviewsnow.com] or AMZ Discover [https://www.amzdiscover.com/] and to reach out to former reviewers in your niche by email. I personally prefer Pubby, though, as it is much more plannable and reliable. Actual results from email outreach to reviewers tend to be quite disappointing, which is why I don't recommend the step if you're short on resource like time and money.

Once you have organized review generation through your existing network and Pubby, I recommend using one (or more) of the following services which specialize in review generation:

3c) Use dedicated ARC services

Below you find a couple of services that you can use to facilitate review generation through external services. I use these for important book launches:

- Hidden Gems Books [https://www.hiddengemsbooks.com/] | Make sure to book months in advance, as this service is in high demand
- Book Sirens [https://booksirens.com/] | You need to get your book approved, which can take around 7-14 days. Once accepted, you can expect to receive a couple of reviews
- Reedsy Discovery | For $50, you can submit your book to the Reedsy Discovery network. They also have a reviewer pool, and usually you can get one review that is often useful for an editorial review as well. The potential for visibility makes this a solid deal
- Netgalley: Netgalley is one of the most established ARC services and a good choice for fantastic titles. You can book via Xpresso Book Tours at a discount
- Upwork Providers: You might also want to check Upwork for service providers specializing in review and rating generation.

4. Booking launch promotions

The goal is to book at least 3-5 promotions with discounted e-book alert services for your launch phase. You will find a good list of recommended promotions on Reedsy[115].

If you are running a free book promo during launch week, I recommend that you at least book one promotion

115 List of recommended paid book promotion services: https://blog.reedsy.com/book-promotion-services/

through Freebooksy. This is one of my favorite services for free book promotions.

You will be able to book some of those services a few days prior to your campaign; however, some of the services, especially the better ones, are booked out in advance for weeks or even months.

I recommend booking some or all promotions prior to launch (or during launch week, as some services request that the e-book be available on the market before allowing any bookings).

A bit later, I will talk about your bestseller campaign, for which you will book 1-3 promotions as well.

Ultimately, using discounted e-book alerts services is an important part of your book launch for sales, visibility, and bestseller status.

5. Preparing social media & network outreach messages

It's also useful to have your social media and email outreach prepared prior to launch. For social media, you can wait until the book has launched; however, when it comes to email and sending messages to larger subscriber lists, you will want to have your communication prepared in advance. The same is true for PR and the Magic 100 communication.

Phase 3: Launch Phase

After you have successfully completed the pre-launch phase, you are ready to launch your book! Let's talk about the launch phase!

The launch phase duration is usually 1-3 months, though the main focus in on week 1-4. The main goal of the launch phase is to make sure that you generate enough sales and reviews that Amazon recognizes your book for CTR and conversion rate testing. Success in these tests means that you'll be ranked high organically and see ongoing sales from your books. Additionally, of course, you want to ensure that enough people are reading your book to discern true book perception and the potential for word of mouth. As previously mentioned, 250 sales is the minimum; ideally, you'll get more than 1000 within the first three months.

Week One:

a) Right after your book has launched, do a quality check. Order your e-book and paperback and make sure that there is no major flaw that you have missed.

b) Optional: Right after your e-book launches, I recommend that you enroll in KDP Select and schedule three or so promo days, during which your book is available for free during launch week. Only use this tactic if you've already prepared your launch team accordingly; see previous sections.

c) Book 3-10 promotions with discounted e-book alert services that are a match for your book. The best time frame is week two-eight if you're not doing a promo at the very beginning. You can book promos towards the end of week one. Find a recommended list of services at TCK Publishing[116] or Reedsy[117].

---

116 List of paid book promotion services: https://www.tckpublishing.com/book-promotion-sites/

117 List of paid book promotion services by Reedsy: https://blog.reedsy.com/book-promotion-services/

d) Send your prepared email launch sequence to your book launch team and Magic 100.

e) If you have active social media channels, spread the word about your launch. If you followed a pre-order strategy and have good sales from the start, make sure to communicate that your book is a top-selling release

f) Optional: Consider using an Amazon cashback service like massview.com or Amazon gift cards to give 5-25 copies (e-book or paperback) away for free or at a huge discount. This will jumpstart sales and show relevancy to Amazon.

g) Run cross promos or buy single newsletters with your Magic 100 (or 25 at least), with the target of reaching at least 100K subscribers within your niche with your book launch offer [Consider joining the Dream Team Network by Nick Stephenson[118]]

h) Start/Resume the book review generation process via the recommended services, such as Pubby.co and Booksirens, and ongoing activities with your book launch team

i) Create Amazon ad accounts and start your ad campaigns (follow instructions in specific section covering Amazon ads)

j) Make sure that your Author Profile via Author Central looks decent, that your book is connected to your profile, and most importantly, submit your up to 10 prepared categories through Author Central to Amazon

Launch week is busy. I recommend not launching your book when you're busy with other activities. Ideally, you should have the first two days of your book launch

118 Dream Team Network by Nick Stephenson: https://www.yourfirst10kreaders.com/dreamteam

to focus on these action steps and get your book well and truly launched!

During weeks two-four, your job is to keep momentum going by making sure that external promotions are running, Amazon ads are performing, and your email and social media outreach is progressing as planned. In addition, run your bestseller campaign during launch month. Here is all you need to know.

Bestseller Campaign

An essential part of your book launch is the bestseller campaign. While our end goal is to land a perennial bestseller, during launch month our initial goal is to get you on the bestseller lists. That bestseller status will be useful for credibility purposes.

It's essential to note that there are two types of bestseller lists for e-books: the free list and the paid list. For every category, Amazon displays the top 100 paid and 100 free e-books. Each category has a different amount of competition. You can check how many sales you need to get to #1 or #10 by using tools like Publisher Rocket or a sales rank calculator (see step 1 of the Perennial Bestseller Blueprint for details).

Paperback, hardcover[119], and audiobook formats have their own bestseller lists as well. Usually getting a top ranking in a paperback format is more difficult; however, for our long-term aspirations, this is a core goal.

---

119 At the time of writing, hardcovers are in Beta. I assume this will be a standard feature as of next year.

Source: Amazon. Screenshot © Albert Griesmayr 2021

When targeting bestseller status at first during launch month, we focus on e-book bestseller status.

Landing an Amazon Bestseller without running a price promotion is more difficult, but it yields high rewards in terms of credibility ("paid list") monetization and long-term benefits (such as long-term bestseller ranking).

A core question that you need to answer for yourself during launch month is whether you are targeting bestseller status on a free or paid list. Of course, you can do both, e.g. If you enroll into KDP Select initially, run a free promotion, and book external promotions later throughout the month, when your e-book has its introductory price (between $0.99 and $2.99). By following this tactic, you can hit bestseller lists twice.

My recommendation is to start with KDP Select right away and run the "free promo" in order to get as many reviews and ratings as possible. (Remember, this is only achievable in combination with outreach to your book launch team and the Magic 100.) You may be able to reach bestseller status within the launch week. Later that month, you can run more external promotions, and have the chance to get on the list once more.

Let's take a closer look at KDP Select. KDP Select is a program which gives Amazon exclusive rights to sell your eBook. This means by enrolling on this program, you cannot distribute copies of your eBook on other platforms. In return, Amazon gives you several benefits for choosing to go exclusive with them. This program lasts 90 days.

One of the key benefits of using KDP select are the options of using promotional tools, like Countdown Deals and Free Promotions. In addition, customers of Kindle Unlimited can access your e-book for free, which is particular useful for specific genres[120], such as romance, crime, fantasy, or science-fiction.

Kindle Unlimited (KU) is a Netflix-like service for books on Amazon which allows readers to choose an unlimited amount of books for $9.99 a month. When you enroll on KDP select, your book becomes available to those who use their e-readers in a Netflix-style manner.

Right after your enrollment, you will be able to choose a specific promotion. You can either choose a free book promotion (Read all details: https://kdp.amazon.com/help?topicId=A34IQ0W14ZKXM9) or you can choose a countdown deal (Read all details: https://kdp.amazon.com/help?topicId=A3288N75MH14B8).

It's important to note that booking one of the promotions won't definitely be enough for reaching bestseller

120 Source: https://blog.reedsy.com/guide/kdp/kdp-select/

status. Visibility on Amazon will be increased during your promotional period due to being featured in the Kindle Countdown Deals or free e-book sections, but the effect of this is very low.

What really makes a difference is booking one to three promotions with paid promotional services, like Freebooksy/Bargainbooksy, The Fussy Librarian or Robin Reads, within a short time frame of 24-48 hours. You can find an excellent overview of the best paid promotion sites for e-books here: https://blog.reedsy.com/book-promotion-services/

Additionally, follow the SEO recommendations to get listed in up to ten ebook categories (as outlined in step 1 of the Perennial Bestseller Blueprint) that include some relevant but less competitive categories.

So here, in a nutshell, is what you need for the bestseller campaign:

- Free or low-priced e-book (below $2.99) on Amazon
- Book a KDP free book promotion, a countdown deal, or price your e-book below or at $2.99
- Make sure that your e-book is listed in less competitive categories (ideally submitting additional categories via Author Central)
- Book one to three paid promotions with discounted e-book alert services in a time span of 24-48 hours

Let's take a look at the core advantages to either Amazon promotion:

A free book promotion earns you a lot of downloads (usually 1000+ in combination with a promotion through a paid promotion service, such as FreeBooksy). In addition, bestseller ranking is likely if your book is already listed in a less competitive category. (It's important to note that if you run a free promo during week one, you will have to submit your additional categories through Author Central right after your book has been published, otherwise your book will likely not have been added to additional categories).

Although the free offer gives you more visibility and readership, it is important to mention that, based on my experience of running hundreds of paid and free bestseller campaigns, readership for free campaigns is usually much less than the official download numbers. Although we won't know exact numbers of pages that get read outside of KU, I have unfortunately often observed that signups for surprise gifts and additional reviews/ratings tend to be low. This leads me to the assumption that many who download the free book don't ever open it.

If your free e-book doesn't seem to perform well even after 1000+ downloads, this could factor into it. Free deals are unfortunately less useful than they were a few years ago, perhaps because of a glut in the market.

A countdown deal (or similar promotions without a countdown deal during which your e-book is priced below $2.99 so you can submit to most external book promotion sites) has the main advantage that people actually have to pay for your e-book, bringing you royalties, an increase in rankings (as real sales count more for the Amazon algorithm), and true readers.

Nowadays I usually recommend running promotions for paid e-books (often without a countdown deal but based on the introductory e-book price), as results are more meaningful in regards to the performance of your book. Also, there is no need to enroll into KDP Select if you are simply running external promotions based on your e-book at its low introductory price.

If I do a free book promotion, I am really targeting reviews and ratings, and have prepared my campaign with email outreach accordingly.

The decision whether you enroll in KDP Select or not should be based on the following questions:

1) Did you prepare your readers that the e-book will be free during a specific time frame? If yes, and you prepared accordingly, KDP Select together with a free promo makes sense.
2) Is your book in a genre that is used by KU readers? If yes, KDP Select is a good option.
3) Is your e-book exclusively available on Amazon? If yes, you can use KDP Select; if not, you can't use it anyway. Please also note that Amazon checks e-book availability on other retailers automatically, so your e-book will likely get kicked out of KDP Select if uploaded elsewhere[121].
4) Is there a benefit of having your e-book available with other retailers and in other markets? Although Amazon is dominant in most countries, in Germany, Canada and Australia, Kobo, Tolino, and Apple Books perform very well and therefore you would lose sales to these markets if you were to choose KDP select. Likewise, players like Kobo offer specific promotions to authors who publish directly with them, so you would miss out on those opportunities as well.

121 Other penalties, such as a ban from KDP Select for a specific time or other measures, could be the consequence.

At the end of the day, for your bestseller campaign, you need to make a decision on how to do it. My recommended approach is using KDP Select for the first 90 days. Run a free promo towards the end of week one (three free days) and run promotions for the paid e-book later throughout the first one to three months (with your e-book being priced below $2.99). Usually I do not publish wide (upload to other retailers) before I have seen that the book performs well on Amazon during its first three months. For successful titles and for authors with a platform it makes sense to go wide; however, it's usually a good idea to ascertain that you have product-market fit.

Proving Your Amazon Bestseller Status

An important task while you are running your Amazon bestseller campaign is to monitor the lists every hour or at least every couple of hours during your 24-48 hours promotional window, and to take screenshots once your book hits them.

In reality this can be a challenge, because you do not want to be awake for 24 hours or longer and monitor various bestseller lists simultaneously. However, I suggest hiring temporary help from a VA through Upwork, or checking yourself every four hours or so. Once you have your proof screenshots, you can go to bed.

My clients and I do the monitoring ourselves, usually. However, I also have access to software that can monitor the bestseller lists and take screenshots.

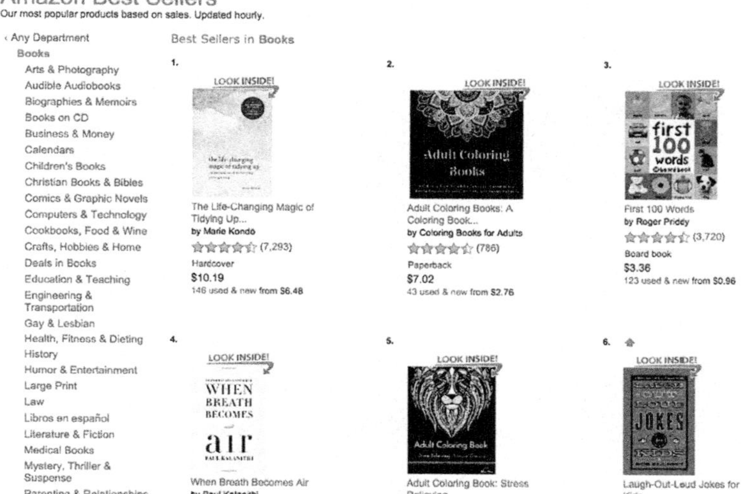

Source: Amazon. Screenshot © Albert Griesmayr 2021

Every hour the software goes through all or the selected target bestseller lists (#1-#100), checks whether your book is included, takes an automated screenshot, and even sends an email with a status report + screenshot every hour. If you are publishing one book only, you likely won't need software like that. But if you are publisher, it is a great help.

The takeaway: Do not miss your book hitting Amazon Bestseller status! The bestseller lists are updated every 60 minutes and in some cases your book might only have the #1 spot for one or a few hours. So don't let it be the hour that you are sleeping.

You can use the screenshots to share on social media and post on your website later.It's useful to have them saved on your hard drive for future purposes as well.

What to Do After Launch Month is Over

Around 30 days after launching your book, it's time to do a proper assessment of your book launch month.

1) Calculate the amount of sales (Above 250: target reached)
2) Calculate the amount of reviews (Above 25: target reached)
3) Check organic rankings for your top 2-3 keywords (In Top 10: target reached)
4) Bestseller status reached during launch month and screenshots taken (target reached)

If you have managed to achieve points 1-4 successfully, you are off to a fantastic start. Congratulations!

Make sure to update your campaigns accordingly, as you have reached bestseller status (update your book description, spread the word via social media, etc.) and continue your journey into launch months two and three. You will learn more about your next steps in the next chapter (step 3 of the Perennial Bestseller Blueprint: Book Sales Automation)

If you did not reach your goals, it's time for you to improve your campaign further and to make sure that you put into place further promotions, so that by the end of month three or earlier you will have reached your launch goals. Check the following section on troubleshooting to learn what to do during months two and three if you fall short of your goals.

Troubleshooting: What to do if your book did not reach goals 1-4?

For each of the launch goals, do the following if you fall short:

1) You did not reach 250+ sales:
Keep your e-book introductory price at the lowest level ($0.99) for another month, and book 2-5 additional promotions with discounted e-book alert services for the upcoming weeks.

In addition, continue with your email outreach to your Magic 100 and book launch team. Inform them about your achieved success and give them a last chance to get the discounted book price and bonuses.

You might also want to consider getting sales through a cashback campaign, a cross-promotion, or an increase in your Amazon advertising budget.

2) You did not get 25+ reviews/ratings (with an average rating of at least 4.5):
If quantity is a problem, simply order more reviews via Pubby. If you are not using Pubby, reach out to your early reviewers, especially the ones that have confirmed with you that they will leave a review. There is also the option to post a job on Upwork "looking for reviews/ratings." There are a couple of providers who are offering the organization of ratings if you are doing a free book promotion, so you could use your remaining two free days for doing that. Important: Some service providers might operate in conflict with Amazon ToS, so I can't recommend using their service. Please do your background check before hiring.

If review ratings are a problem, you need to assess the exact problem (e.g. manuscript quality, market-fit, etc.,), and take appropriate action quickly. A lack of customer satisfaction is the biggest risk in regards to long-term book success.

3) Your book is not ranking well (or not at all) organically: Sometimes, you need to wait 6-12 weeks for organic ranks to kick in. However, if you notice that Amazon tested conversion rates (so your book ranked high already, but dropped, or Amazon ad campaigns were delivering but dried out), you know that you have a problem that needs a response. Locate the area where the problem is most likely to be (e.g. weak book description, weak bonus offer, etc.) and increase the quality of the affected area. Continue to book promotions and run ads to get Amazon to test conversion rates again.

4) You did not reach bestseller status:Make sure that you did the steps outlined for running a bestseller campaign in this chapter. If the campaign has failed, it could be that your book is listed in too competitive categories or that your external promotion did not bring (sufficient) sales. I suggest doing a re-run (book two promotions on one day and make sure that you are listed in at least one less competitive category).

Usually it is quite easy to get a top ranking on a free bestseller list; on paid lists it is more difficult, as you might run into troubles if competition is too high or sales too low. The sales that come from paid promotional services have slowly dwindled over the years as well, so overall the importance of promotion through your own channels has increased.

SPECIAL TOPIC: RUN A FREE OR DISCOUNTED BOOK GIVEAWAY THAT PUSHES BOOK RANKINGS VIA A CASHBACK CAMPAIGN

A rather unconventional approach for making sure that your book gets a healthy amount of sales during the launch month is to organize a cashback campaign. There is one service I used for both e-books and paperbacks with success in Q1 and Q2 of 2021: Massview by Snagshout: https://go.massview.com

The service allows you to present your books in front of their userbase (500K at the time of writing in July 2021) and to offer your book for free or at a big discount. Interested people go to Amazon then to purchase your book at the real/full price, and get the money back at Massview/Snagshout.

Of course, the costs you have for using Massview include the price that your readers have to pay, so basically you are purchasing the books for them.

The major advantage is that this shows Amazon that your book sells, which pushes it up the rankings.

Important: I can't guarantee that the service will still support e-books by the time you read this. I tried many other services, and Massview was the only one supporting e-books, so this might be discontinued. Check before counting on it in your campaign. In addition, although the service says to be 100% compliant with Amazon Policies (ToS), this might not be true at a later point or may be based on Snagshout's interpretation. It's true that there are many cashback services on the market; however, from my understanding using a service like this has to be at least regarded as operating in the "gray zone." That's why using a cashback service is not part of my program and not an official recommendation. However, some of you might be up for it, so I wanted to make sure to include it as an option.

Now it's time to put everything together and to start your chapter exercise. You've learned the tactics for launching your book strongly and for reaching bestseller status; now it's time to sustain this energy over the next months, and turn your book into a long-term success.

Chapter Exercises

This is what you will learn in step 3 of the Bestseller Blueprint: automate your book sales.

Before you dive into that, please take pen and paper and set up your book launch by doing the exercise below. You will also find a handy checklist for your book launch phase at the end of this chapter.

Exercise Box [Launching with a bang]
After you have learned about how to launch your book with a bang, it's important that you decide on the action steps that you want to use: Preparation time: I will dedicate a launch preparation phase of X months, before being ready to start the launch/relaunch warm-up phase ______________________________ (amount of months and exact timespan) SEO: I am focusing on the following three main keywords and book categories ______________________________ (list main keywords and categories) Outreach (Pre-Launch): [Regular duration: 3 months] I will use the following outreach tactics during the launch warm-up phase ______________________________ (list outreach tactics + duration/timespan) Outreach (Post-Launch): [Regular duration: 3 months] I will use the following outreach tactics during the book launch phase ______________________________ (list outreach tactics + duration/timespan)

STEP 2: LAUNCH WITH A BANG – B: BOOK LAUNCH PHASE (1-3 MONTHS FROM LAUNCH DATE)	
Signing up for Pubby, submitting your book, and starting to collect points	
Getting reviews for your book via your Pubby account (Alternatively: You might want to hire professionals to generate reviews via Pubby or other services)	
Optional: Booking review services (Booksirens, Hidden Gems Books, Netgalley)	
Optional: If you are using KDP Select, enroll your e-book when publishing and book your free promo days during launch week, so that you can inform your reviewers and subscribers about the free promo	
Booking 2-10 launch promotions (e-book launch promotions with third party services that will run during your launch month)	
Submitting up to 10 browse categories for your book via Author Central	
Immediately after launch: Signing up for Amazon advertising, filling out payment and tax details and starting ads for your books in the US, the UK, and Canada	
Optional: Starting your PR campaign (sending out your outreach)	
Spreading the word about your launch via social media	
Initiating your launch email outreach to subscribers	
Initiating your launch email outreach to influencers/ Magic 100	
Initiating your launch email outreach to your book launch team	
Right after launch: Ordering your e-book and other book formats and make a quality check	

Amazon Ads: Running your Amazon ads launch campaign for 1-3 months and making adjustments on an ongoing basis	
After 14 days: First check point in regards to sales and reviews (adjust measures if needed)	
During launch month: Running your Amazon bestseller campaign	
During launch month: Taking screenshots of your Amazon bestseller status	
One month after launch: Updating your book description and author bio and making sure to include credibility factors such as bestseller status, top reviews, etc.	

6

BOOK SALES AUTOMATION [STEP 3]

"Traffic, traffic, traffic.
It all starts with traffic online."
Albert Griesmayr, February 15, 2021

After having completed step 2 of the bestseller blueprint, you should have had a strong book launch and should be one to three months post-launch, having achieved the core milestones of at least 25 reviews/ratings and 250+ book sales. Ideally the Amazon ads that you are running are performing in profits (unlikely for book launch campaigns, however), at break-even (or below 100%), and you are getting ongoing sales.

What's next is to make sure that sales do not dry out. Instead, you will establish a system that runs on autopilot to bring you sales in a profitable way. That's where true success with books is at.

Step 3 of the Blueprint looks in detail at the action steps needed to establish an automated book sales system and helps you to do so for your book.

According to Russell Brunson, founder of ClickFunnels and author of *Traffic Secrets*, the number one reason online businesses fail is that they are not able to generate enough traffic. I could not agree more with this statement when it comes to book publishing.

The main reason why book projects fail is that they simply do not get enough attention—they don't get enough eyeballs or visibility. Of course, a kick-ass product is the core of everything; however, if you are not able to ensure ongoing visibility at affordable cost, it will likely not have a big chance to succeed in the market.

That's why you have to make sure that you are getting traffic to your book. Not only for the book launch, by running launch promotions and engaging your network, but continuously in the long run.

What's interesting is that many authors and publishers do not realize that a lack of traffic is the core problem behind their lack of book sales. There is still the assumption in the market that if you upload your book to Amazon and have a good book launch, it will automatically become successful in the long run as well.

Often, publishers underestimate how much attention their books actually need to achieve a perennial bestseller. Even with a strong book launch, running promotions, and engaging subscriber lists, the traffic will often not be enough to give your book a true chance for long-term success.

And the story continues. Let's assume that you were able to do a solid book launch. Amazon noticed your book and calculated conversion rates, and you have been able to drive a good amount of traffic to your book.

However, sales stayed modest. The Amazon ads you're running show that ACOS is high, and Amazon is giving you fewer and fewer impressions as a result. In this case, you likely have a problem with conversion rates, and you will have to fix this in order to make your book sales system work.

Even if you were able to fix conversion rates and generated sales for a couple of months, it might be that suddenly your sales dwindle and are slowly drying out. What could have happened?

In this case, you likely ran into troubles with your retention rates. People bought your book, but reading did not spark sufficient word-of-mouth. You may not have a reader email signup system in place, either.

It's simple enough: you need traffic to your book on an ongoing basis. Traffic which converts at or below break-even costs and a healthy level of retention, meaning that your readers purchase more than one book from you over time, spread the word, and bring further readers to your book.

In order to get sales running on an ongoing basis, you need three phases for your book.

In the following pages, we will discuss all three phases in detail, and at the end of the chapter you will set up your own automated book sales system.

BOOK SALES SYSTEM

[BASED ON PERENNIAL BESTSELLER BLUEPRINT]

ATTRACTION	CONVERSION	RETENTION
Organic Traffic (own channels)	Track traffic* + royalty dashboard	*Mostly your ability to drive traffic from one book to another (or word of mouth) -> difficult to track and figure out which channels produce the best results*
Organic Traffic/Sales (Amazon vs. paid)	Compare ad to royalty dashboard	
Organic Traffic (ext. channels)	Track traffic* + royalty dashboard	
Paid Ads (Amazon)	See ad dashboard	
Promotions (ebook promos)	See royalty dashboard	

*Eg. Amazon Affiliate Links or Google Tracking

Book Sales System. Source: © Albert Griesmayr, July 2021

The Book Sales System Overview

Think of the book sales system in three elements: attraction, conversion, and retention.

The attraction part is based on each of the individual channels that drive traffic to your book, such as your own organic channels (e.g. your website, email lists, Facebook, YouTube), external organic channels (e.g. Magic 100, incoming links from highly trafficked sites), paid ads and promotions, and organic traffic coming through Amazon.

In regards to conversion rates, you need to know how well your core traffic channels are converting visitors to book buyers. With Amazon ads it's quite easy to assess conversion rates (e.g. ACOS); for most other channels, it's difficult. But don't start overanalyzing or thinking you need to be a math wizard. Some simple observations will give you strong clues.

Here are some examples.

- If almost all sales come through Amazon ads, there is likely very low organic traffic both through Amazon and driven externally (compare your Amazon Ads dashboard with your sales dashboard, and look at the difference in sales)
- For assessing external promotions, book each promotion or newsletter campaign on a separate day or widen the gap between campaigns, and check your sales dashboard (Is there a jump in sales in close date proximity to your promotion? The promotion will likely be the cause)

Of course, when running external promotions, you will still need to calculate if specific expenses are economical. However, by following the steps above you will likely not only be able to assess which attraction channels are working well, but also if they are economically.

Once you have a good overview of attraction and conversion of your current book sales system, it is time to look at the third phase: Retention.

Retention is all about your ability to earn more per reader (above the book sale) and to get growth from your reader base (through word-of-mouth, reviews, etc.)

Interestingly, retention is usually one of the most overlooked phases, even though there is big potential in focusing on this one. Your job as an author is not to make the sale. Your job as an author is to keep your readers happy. And happy readers are the ideal prerequisite for healthy retention rates. In addition, when combined with tactics that you learned in this book (built-in-virality, surprise gifts, email campaigns for readers, etc.), retention can become the main reason why your book sales system works.

In the following pages, let's take a close look at the action steps that you can take once you have laid out your book sales system in order to make it more profitable and successful. Please find below an example of an automated book sales system for this book, *Bestseller*. As I can't share real results at the time of publishing, my plan is to update this information in a later edition, so that you see the real-world results for this title.

EXAMPLE OF AUTOMATED BOOK SALES SYSTEM

Example of automated book sales system [Book: Bestseller, Published in 2021]

Attraction	Conversion	Retention
-> Scribando.com (Funnel) -> AlbertGriesmayr.com (Blog & Funnel) -> Facebook Ads (To Scrib & AlbG) -> Amazon Ads (To Book)	-> Amazon Sales Page -> Scribando Membership -> AG Funnel	-> Email Follow Up (Surprise Gift) -> Upsells: other books, Scribando membership, Bestseller Program
Tolerated Aquis. Cost: $5 Average Royalty: $5	Tol. Conv. Rate: 5% (0.25$)	Lifetime Value: $25+

Example of Book Sales System for my book *Book Marketing Secrets*
Source: © Albert Griesmayr 2021

To understand the effectiveness of your system, you will also need to project and calculate important metrics.

The five metrics below will help you to calculate the effectiveness of your book sales system.

Tolerated acquisition cost per new reader: How much you are willing to spend on advertising and campaigns per new reader.

Average royalty & royalty per format: The average amount you are making from all your book formats together plus each type of format your book is in.

Net profit book: The amount of profit you are making per sale. Here, you are basically deducting your costs for winning a new reader from your average royalty per title. (Please note that any taxes will still need to be deducted, so you real profit will be lower)

Lifetime value per reader: The total value you are getting per one of your readers. Are they buying all your books or just one of them? Do you have upsells that increase revenue?

Net profit from life time value: The profit you are making if you are not deducting from your book royalty but your reader's lifetime value instead

Let's take a look at the example for an automated book sales system with the book *Bestseller*, including important metrics.

For the attraction phase, the book is included in my existing website funnels on both Scribando.com and Albertgriesmayr.com[122]. On Scribando, the e-book is included free of charge to all new members, and I hope to generate some paperback sales on top. On AlbertGriesmayr.com the book is part two of my welcome funnel, and readers can purchase the book via Amazon. For both funnels, I am running Facebook ads

122 All information is valid at the time of writing in July 2021. Data and information will likely change over time.

in order to get fresh traffic. In addition, both websites have existing traffic (which is quite modest, so I don't expect to sell a lot based on organic traffic right now).

An important pillar of my attraction phase is Amazon Ads. I am running those in the US, the UK, and Canada and am confident in spending $5 per book sale. This tolerated acquisition cost is higher in regards to Facebook Ads, as both Scribando and AlbertGriesmayr.com have upsell products that allow for higher acquisition costs.

In regards to conversion rates, I am focusing on three sales pages. The Amazon sales page, the Scribando membership sales page, and the Albert Griesmayr Funnel. I will have to optimize all three sales pages over time to increase conversion rates.

Finally, for retention, I am working with the surprise gift system that I was already using with my two existing books, *Book Marketing Secrets* and *Book Sales Explosion*. Each reader is presented at the beginning and/or the end of the book with an invitation to access a surprise gift for free by signing up via email on my website[123].

My website.
Source: Screenshot © Albert Griesmayr 2021

After signup, readers get a useful surprise gift that helps them with their book marketing. Once readers are on my autoresponder, I invite them to give feedback for my books and post reviews, and can potentially inform them about future opportunities.

123 Source: https://www.albertgriesmayr.com/thank-you/

Upsell products are another important element for retention. I have two existing books, plus the Scribando membership, the bestseller program (and soon will presenting books via Novelify as well), so I have valuable offers for my readers. In total, my expected lifetime value per new reader is $25 at the moment. This allows me to invest significantly more in ads, if I believe it is useful, even if I am netting losses on the promotion of *Bestseller*. The key is that historically some of my readers became Scribando members or booked consulting with me, and I expect this to stay the same in the near future as well.

Before it is time for you to illustrate your own system yourself, I want to show you the necessary action steps to take in order to improve the effectiveness of your book sales system.

Increasing Conversion/Adding Channels/ Adding Upsells

In the end, there are three important action steps to make your book sales system more profitable and actionable.

1) **Adding traffic channels:** This is quite self-explanatory. Follow-up with your Magic 100, run a PR campaign to get featured on highly trafficked sites, start Facebook ads, etc. A new traffic channel has the power to bring fresh traffic. My recommendation is to stick with your main activities discussed in step 2 (e.g., Amazon Ads, Magic 100), as the true opportunity lies in mastering what you already do and perfecting it.

2) **Increase your conversions:** Both the quality of your channels and the power of your book sales page have a profound effect on your conversion rates. By paying close attention to the quality of all your channels and your sales page, you will see improvement points, such as:
   - Improving the credibility on your book sales page by adding customer reviews
   - Improving your Facebook ad creative
   - Formatting your book description in the best way
   - Updating your website
   - Updating your author picture on an external website

3) **Raise your profit margins:** A very important aspect for making book sales systems work economically is raising profits. The main ways you should consider are:
   - Add new formats such as a hardcover or audiobook version
   - Consider translating and publishing your book in a different market
   - Add an upsell to your book (e.g., a course, book bundle, etc.)
   - Include information about your other books at the end of your book
   - Raise your book prices

In the end, you'll see that book sales automation is a gradual process. However, if you have a clear structure in mind, keep an eye on your finances, and continuously work on your book sales system (attraction, conversion, retention), you will increase your profitability over time.

Here's a powerful secret conversion booster that may be much easier to implement than you might think.

Increasing Conversions: Secret Weapon – Awards & Accolades

One of the best conversion boosters is to win a book award and to include this in your book description and author bio right away. Take a look at the following books on Amazon to see the power of awards in action:

- *Sam and Dave Dig a Hole*, by Mac Barnett: https://www.amazon.com/James-Excellence-Childrens-Literature-Awards/dp/0763662291
- *The Dreams of the Dying* by Nicolas Lietzau: https://www.amazon.com/Dreams-Dying-Enderal-Book-1-ebook/dp/B08CL355Y9

The truth is that winning a prestigious award is extremely difficult and often out of reach for self-publishers. However, there are award opportunities available that are much less competitive, as well as honorable mentions, shortlists, and other forms of approval that you can use to boost your credibility.

You might not win the Pulitzer Prize, but getting shortlisted or receiving an honorable mention that is less well known is much easier than you might think. I'm talking from experience, as I've helped dozens of authors to gain award-winning status.

Usually, you need to calculate with an investment between $100-$1000 in order to submit your book to award organizations that your book might suit. It takes a few months before this happens, but the chances are promising if you have a strong product and choose the right awards to submit to.

So how do you find the best book award opportunities for your book? There is a service called bookawardspro.com that matches your book with award opportunities. Alternatively, you can do the research yourself. I personally had good experiences with services like Literary Titan[124] and Author's Circle Awards[125].

From my experience, it's certainly worth the effort trying to get at least one award or accolade for your book. This is one of the best markers of credibility, which makes it an excellent conversion booster.

To sum up Step 3 of the Perennial Bestseller Blueprint, your job is to make sure that you're driving traffic that converts in a profitable way when looking at your business as a whole. Ideally, you should be able to let this system run on autopilot.

Please find below the sales numbers for one of my client's books.

Amazon KDP sales dashboard Source: Amazon.
Screenshot © Albert Griesmayr, 2021

This is what healthy, consistent book sales look like. This particular client is solely relying on organic traffic through his own websites and channels (e.g. YouTube),

124 Literary Titan: https://literarytitan.com/bookawards/

125 Authors Circle Awards: https://www.authorscircleawards.com/

making his system very profitable, as he is not even running ads.

I recommend, based on the Perennial Bestseller Blueprint, that you use the following attraction channels and analyze system optimization over time:

- Amazon Ads
- Traffic through your existing channels
- Traffic opportunities with the Magic 100 (cross promos, features, etc.)

As far as conversions, I recommend that you optimize your Amazon sales page and author profile over time. Make sure to power up your profiles with as much credibility and excitement as possible, and that your content looks top-notch at all times.

When it comes to retention my core recommendations are as follows:

- Include a surprise gift invitation in your book, in order to collect your reader's email addresses
- Make your book the best it can be and improve it over time
- Have at least one upsell product in order to improve your profit margins

Chapter Exercises

Now it is time that you outline your own book sales system. Please take pen and paper and start the book sales automation exercise.

Exercise Box [Book Sales Automation]

After you have learned about the core tactics for automating your book sales, it's important that you create your own book sales system and decide on the action steps that you want to initiate for your book in order to increase profitability.

STEP 1: Please take an extra sheet of paper, and outline your book sales system. Divide the sheet into three sections (attraction, conversion, retention) and note the following:
-> What are the current traffic channels?
-> What are the conversion rates per core channel?
-> What are your core activities in regards to retention and what is your customer (reader) lifetime value?

____

____

____

STEP 2: In order to increase my traffic, I will do the following:

____

____

____

(please include current traffic and new traffic tactics)

STEP 3: In order to increase my conversion rates, I will do the following:

____

____

____

(please write down action steps for increasing your conversion rates)

STEP 4: In order to increase retention, I will do the following:

____

____

____

(please write down action steps for improving your retention)

STEP 5: Estimate numbers for your core metrics (or if you already have data, use your current numbers)

____

____

____

Tolerated acquisition cost per new reader: ____________

Average royalty & royalty per format: ________________

Net profit book: ___________________________________

Lifetime value per reader: _________________________

Net profit from lifetime value: ______________________

7

STRATEGY CREATION

As you now know all three steps of the Perennial Bestseller Blueprint, it's time for you to put it all together and create a more complete strategy.

So far, we've talked a lot about the Blueprint itself, the best ways to implement it, best practices, and the theories and tactics behind landing a perennial bestseller on Amazon.

I am confident that you are now equipped with the knowledge needed to land a perennial bestseller.

As a very quick reminder, the Perennial Bestseller Blueprint is summed up in three steps as follows:

1) Create an Irresistible Book Offer:
   - Create an outstanding book which people want to read; make sure it is well-crafted, original, and gives value to your reader.
   - Make sure there is demand for your book. Your book may be immaculately written and well presented, but if there is no demand for your subject or are already hundreds of books written on your chosen subject, not a lot of people are

going to want to read it, even if it is as well-written as Byron or Shakespeare.
- People love offers and readers are no different. Make your offer as attractive as possible, offer discounts on the price, promotions, and deals to entice potential readers.

2) Launch with a Bang
    - The launch of your book is almost as important as the actual book you are marketing, so make sure people know about your launch so Amazon can see conversion rates for your book. Within your first three months (ideally in month one):
    - At least 25 ratings/reviews for the book
    - At least 250 sales (all editions combined)

3) Automate Book Sales
    - Make sure to create a process that brings you consistent sales over time (traffic, conversion, retention)
    - Understand where your readers come from, what your best channels are, and optimize your channels, offers and tactics consistently.
    - Rinse and repeat. Go over the blueprint several times to make sure you have covered all the bases.

This chapter will be all about YOU. In chapter 3 you formulated your goals, and it's now time to actually create your complete Amazon bestseller book marketing strategy.

As a first step, please revisit your goals so that you have them in mind again.Next, please take a look at the Perennial Bestseller Blueprint in chapter 4 and the book summaries (including your exercises) from the three steps for landing a perennial bestseller again, so that you have the big picture and core action steps in mind.

Are you ready?
I hope so. Let's take pen and paper and create your strategy for landing a perennial bestseller!

My book title (+subtitle) is ________________ and I want the book to be a perennial bestseller from ________________ (include your date).

For launching/relaunching the book, I choose a preparation time of __ months, a pre-launch phase of __ months, and a launch phase of ___ months. I am starting the preparation time on ______.

The main characteristics of my irresistible offer for readers are: ________________________________.

The main characteristics of my irresistible offer for enablers are: ________________________________.

My main keywords are ____________________ and my main book categories are ____________________.

I will do the following action steps during preparation phase:

____

I will do the following action steps during pre-launch phase:

____

I will do the following action steps during post-launch phase:

____

Regarding book sales automation, my main action steps are the following:

____

scriBando

MY PERSONAL AMAZON BESTSELLER STRATEGY

I WANT TO BECOME AN AMAZON BESTSELLING AUTHOR

MY BOOK TITLE (+SUBTITLE) IS ______________________________ AND I WANT THE BOOK TO BE A PERENNIAL BESTSELLER FROM __________________ (INCLUDE YOUR DATE).

FOR LAUNCHING/RELAUNCHING THE BOOK, I CHOOSE A PREPARATION TIME OF ___ MONTHS, A PRE-LAUNCH PHASE OF ___ MONTHS, AND A LAUNCH PHASE OF ___ MONTHS. I AM STARTING THE PREPARATION TIME ON ______.

THE MAIN CHARACTERISTICS OF MY IRRESISTIBLE OFFER FOR READERS ARE: ______________________________.

THE MAIN CHARACTERISTICS OF MY IRRESISTIBLE OFFER FOR ENABLERS ARE: ______________________________.

MY MAIN KEYWORDS ARE ______________________________ AND MY MAIN BOOK CATEGORIES ARE ______________________________.

I WILL DO THE FOLLOWING ACTION STEPS DURING PREPARATION PHASE:

____

I WILL DO THE FOLLOWING ACTION STEPS DURING PRE-LAUNCH PHASE:

____

I WILL DO THE FOLLOWING ACTION STEPS DURING POST-LAUNCH PHASE:

____

REGARDING BOOK SALES AUTOMATION, MY MAIN ACTION STEPS ARE THE FOLLOWING:

____

8

CONCLUSION

Let me tell you something – I'm pretty psyched up right about now. Do you know why?

Because now you hold in your hands a book marketing plan that's not only proven and effective but also fits on one sheet of paper, so it is actually actionable.

I am convinced that if you follow the steps from your plan, your book launch will be a success and you will achieve bestseller status on Amazon.

A successful book launch means to achieve credibility (25+ ratings/reviews), make enough sales to let the Amazon algorithms work (250+ sales) and to make sure that you are proud of your book and that it has product-market fit, giving it a good outlook for the future.

And here we come to the critical point: Time!

The purpose of the book and the blueprint is that you not only have a successful book launch and land a bestseller on Amazon, but that your book is successful long-term and generates consistent sales over time. Ideally it will stay in the bestseller ranks (between Rank 1-100 in a suited category) for a long time. I've seen this with some of my clients, like Patrick McKeown (consistent Top 10 Bestseller with *Close Your Mouth*), Dave Todaro (consistent Top 25 bestseller with *The Epic Guide to Agile*) or Mike Swigunski (Consistent Top 20 bestseller with *Global Career*).

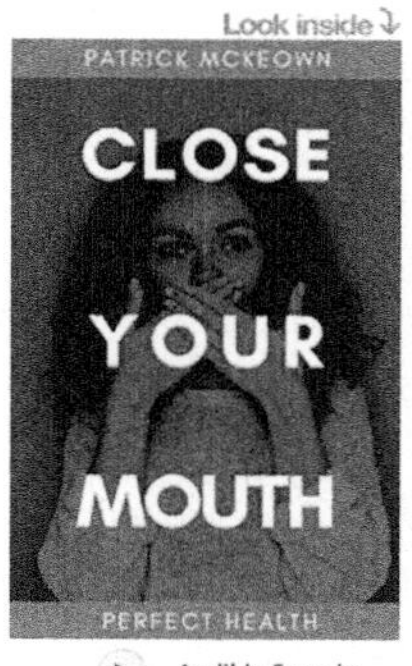

Look inside
PATRICK MCKEOWN
CLOSE
YOUR
MOUTH
PERFECT HEALTH

Close Your Mouth:
Kindle Edition
by Patrick McKeown (Author)
86 ratings
See all formats and editions
Kindle $7.75
Read with Our Free App
3 Used from $56.19
6 New from $49.95
Audio $0.00
Close Your Mouth is a self-help boc
Method for asthma, coughing, whe
publication *Close Your Mouth* is in
The **Buteyko Method** can be learned
Read more
Audible Sample

Best Sellers Rank: #104,412 in Kindle Store (See Top 100 in Kindle Store)
#8 in Respiratory Diseases (Kindle Store)
#24 in Respiratory Diseases (Books)
#25 in Lung & Respiratory Diseases
Customer Reviews: 86 ratings

Source: Amazon. Screenshot © Albert Griesmayr 2021

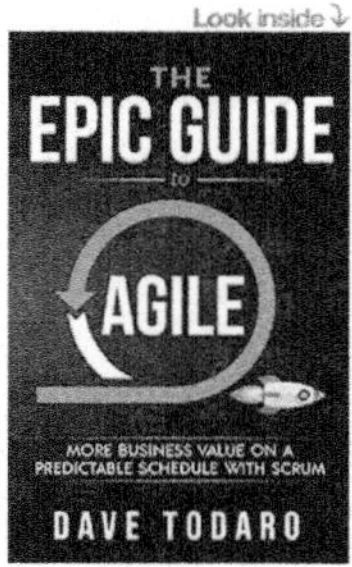

Look inside
THE
EPIC GUIDE
to
AGILE
MORE BUSINESS VALUE ON A PREDICTABLE SCHEDULE WITH SCRUM
DAVE TODARO

The Epic Guide to Agile:
Schedule with Scrum Kir
by Dave Todaro (Author) Format: Kindle E
74 ratings

Most executives, managers, and team members
expectations. This book has the answers to the t
includes all the content we teach in our six-figure

Best Sellers Rank: #129,140 in Kindle Store (See Top 100 in Kindle Store)
#17 in Software Project Management
#17 in IT Project Management
#38 in Business Project Management (Kindle Store)
Customer Reviews: 74 ratings

Source: Amazon. Screenshot © Albert Griesmayr 2021

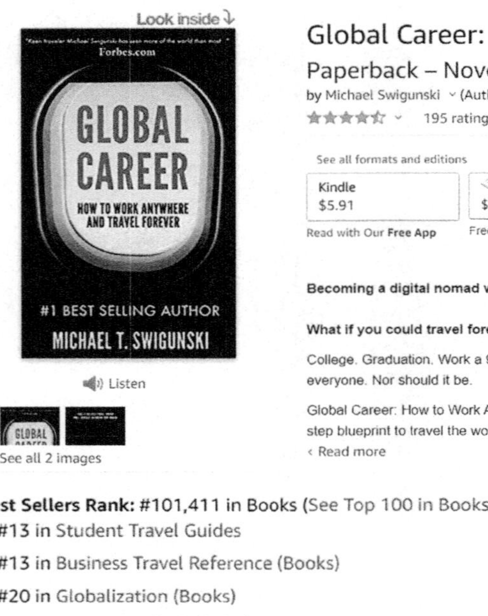

Source: Amazon. Screenshot © Albert Griesmayr 2021

The most decisive point for achieving the result of a perennial bestseller is mastering step 1 of the blueprint. Why? Because in the end, even after doing steps 2 and step 3 correctly, you will always fall back to your core offer.

- Is it strong enough to outperform competition, so that Amazon chooses to display your book vs. your competitor's?
- Is your book strong enough to make your readers rave and tell their friends and colleagues about your book after they've purchased it?
- Does your book provide true value to your readers?

If your answers are YES and the market sees it the same way, Amazon and other book retailers will reward you with consistent book sales. And that's what we are looking for.

Before I start with the next chapter, which describes how you can profit from your bestseller status in the best way, I want to provide answers to one more important question:

What if you did all the steps of the blueprint correctly and your book is still not selling well?

In this case, one thing is true for sure: There is at least one element in your book sales process that is not performing as it should. I recommend going to step 3 of the blueprint and examining the graphic that shows a book sales system. Ask yourself the following questions:

1) Is my book getting enough traffic? And if yes, from where? If no, run more promotions to get traffic. (Attraction)
2) How well is my book converting? What are detailed numbers? [e.g. Provided in your Amazon ads dashboard] What are needed action steps to increase conversions? (Conversion)
3) Is Word of Mouth working for my book? Do readers truly love my book? Did I implement all recommended systems? (email signup for readers, review generation, surprise gift, free copy for a friend, etc.) What can I do to increase reader satisfaction?

Usually after analyzing the book sales system, some homework will become evident which has the power to improve your book's performance in the market. I know from experience that fixing just one or two aspects of your marketing can have a profound effect.

BOOK SALES SYSTEM

[BASED ON PERENNIAL BESTSELLER BLUEPRINT]

ATTRACTION	CONVERSION	RETENTION
Organic Traffic (own channels)	Track traffic* + royalty dashboard	Mostly your ability to drive traffic from one book to another (or word of mouth) -> difficult to track and figure out which channels produce the best results
Organic Traffic/Sales (Amazon vs. paid)	Compare ad to royalty dashboard	
Organic Traffic (ext. channels)	Track traffic* + royalty dashboard	
Paid Ads (Amazon)	See ad dashboard	
Promotions (ebook promos)	See royalty dashboard	

*Eg. Amazon Affiliate Links or Google Tracking

Book Sales System© Albert Griesmayr, July 2021

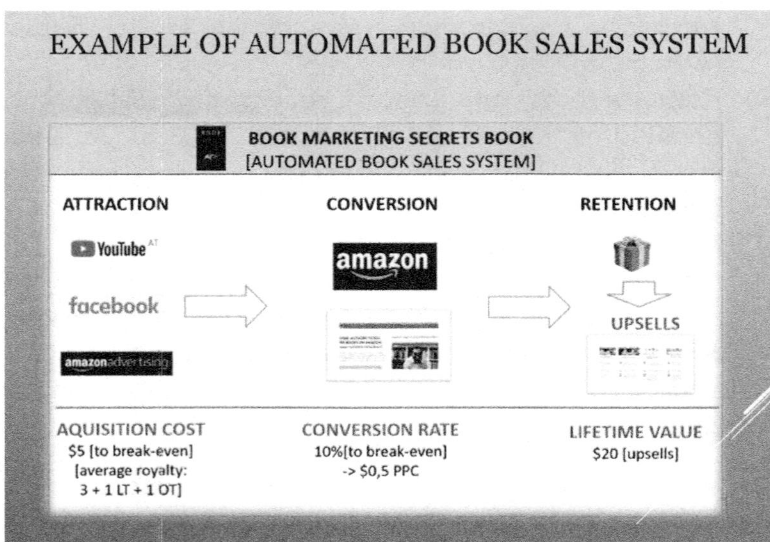

Example Book Sales System © Albert Griesmayr, July 2021

This happened with a client of mine. All he did was change his book cover, and suddenly his system began to work. For another client, we fixed the book description, re-edited the book, and added a bonus chapter. This improved the system over time, making the title sell consistently.

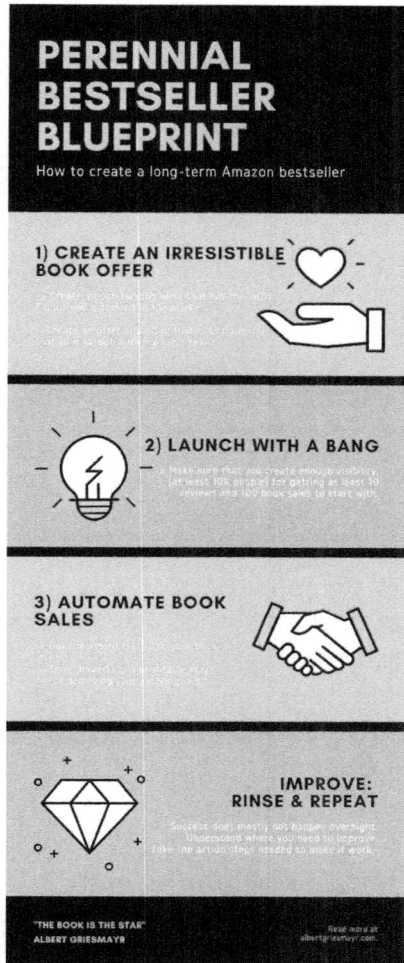

PERENNIAL BESTSELLER BLUEPRINT

How to create a long-term Amazon bestseller

1) CREATE AN IRRESISTIBLE BOOK OFFER

2) LAUNCH WITH A BANG

3) AUTOMATE BOOK SALES

IMPROVE: RINSE & REPEAT

"THE BOOK IS THE STAR"
ALBERT GRIESMAYR

Perennial Bestseller Blueprint © Albert Griesmayr, July 2021

Finally, I want to add one word of caution. And I want to be as honest as possible with you in this.

The question is: Does the bestseller blueprint work for everyone? Are all of my clients successful?

The clear answer is NO. The system does not work for everyone; however, this is mainly not because the system is flawed, but because implementation is critical and difficult.

I am not saying that this is the magic pill and that success is easy. On the contrary, it likely *won't* be easy. But if you stick to the project and improve your system over time, the odds that it will eventually work are high.

Nevertheless, there will always be books for which there is a ceiling. This might be a ceiling that's there because of the demand, some element in the offer like the cover, the title, or the author, or something else in the system that is not performing and is not overcome because it is either not identifiable or worth fixing.

It's totally fair to accept at some point that there is a ceiling, an offer that is not perfect, that there is a lack of resources to improve a certain element, or an alternative project that is more promising.

And then the right decision may be not to invest more resources into a specific title, but instead to move on to a different book or project.

In the end I'd like to briefly address fiction books in particular. You might have noticed that a lot of my client projects are works of non-fiction and most tactics in this book apply best to non-fiction books as well. What does that mean? Does that mean that other rules apply if you are a fiction author? Will this book not work for you?

The answer is that the Blueprint works for fiction as well. I've worked with award-wining and bestselling fiction authors, such as B.C. Schiller (thriller), Nicolas Lietzau (suspense) and Elizabeth Lennox (romance), and have seen that the same rules apply to their game.

The manuscript (story, language, writing) is even more important and there is a limit to throwing bonuses on top of those titles; however, most aspects work in the same way. What you need to be more careful with, though, is that critical market reception is usually more difficult to overcome than with non-fiction titles.

If readers are not amazed by the story, it will be difficult to fix. In this case, you need to be very critical with yourself and ask whether it's really worthwhile to continue to put resources into that title, or whether it's smarter to just move on. Sometimes the latter is the better option for your long-term career.

9

PROFITING FROM BESTSELLER STATUS

You made it! Your book became a bestseller, it looks strong on the market due to the favorable reception (reviews/ratings), and it is generating sales.

How do you make sure that you get the most out of your bestseller status?

That's what this chapter is all about!

first of all, let's take a moment to celebrate together.

Lean back, enjoy a glass of sparkling wine and get comfortable with the thought that from now on, you are an **Amazon Bestselling Author**!

That is an awesome achievement, and you deserve congratulations.

Here is what I recommend to get the most out of your Amazon bestseller status. The most important thing to remember is that no one will find out about it unless you tell them. There will be multiple opportunities and occasions to profit from this status, and I'm about to tell you some of the best. One word of caution before you scream it to the world, though:

- Make sure that your book has achieved product-market fit (not only in regards to the reviews/ratings you have, but also in regards to your confidence due to significant reader feedback).

My recommendation is to wait until you have at least 25+ ratings/reviews visible on Amazon, ongoing sales, and confidence in the book before you communicate your status, as it can be bad for your credibility to oversell your achievements.

During your launch month, it's likely that you reached bestseller status (e.g. During the free promotion week on a free bestseller list, or on a paid list during later launch promotions). Often you will get a "new release" badge as well. Communicating that your book is tagged as "#1 new release" or "top new release" is fine and recommended from the start; however, wait on selling your bestseller status until the book really looks good in the market.

Below are the best opportunities for communicating and profiting from your bestseller status:

1. **Update your Amazon book description, author page, online profiles, etc.**

Step 1 is to update your Amazon book description, your Amazon author page, and online profiles, and include that you have landed an Amazon bestseller. The more specific you are, and the more successful your book appears in the market, the more credible you'll be.

Below find a couple of screenshots from authors and books who are doing a good job with that.

Source: Amazon. Screenshot © Albert Griesmayr 2021

2. Write personal thank you notes to your supporters

Landing a bestseller is a good occasion to thank all of your supporters. This means that you should not only thank your closest supporters but also your Magic 100, newsletter subscribers, etc. Let everyone know about your success and that you appreciate their support.

Think about how many messages you received from friends or colleagues with thank you notes within the last year. These were probably not too many. Unfortunately, thank you notes have become quite rare. People ask for favors and then they simply move on. It's unusual for those who see success to stop and reflect on everyone who helped them along the way.

Choose to be different. Go through your supporters and write thank you notes. The more personal the letter, the better.

I prepared a "thank you letter" template for you as an inspiration. It's short and sweet but does the job. Feel free to adapt the letter to your needs and make every letter as personal as possible.

Template 1

Subject: Thank You

Body: Dear [name],

I want you to know how much I appreciate your support during my book launch. On [date] I became an Amazon Bestselling Author. I am so happy to have reached this goal! This would not have been possible without your support.

Thank you!

[Affectionately, Fondly, Much love, Take care, Warm regards, etc.…] [your signature]

3. Share the news on social media and your website

Your website, online profiles, and social media channels such as LinkedIn, Goodreads, or Facebook provide a fertile ground not only for displaying your achievement in static sections, but also in news feeds.

Be sure that you share the good news on your social media channels and your website as well. You will be surprised by the good engagement rates (likes, comments, etc.) you can get by spreading positive news and saying thank you to your fans. Ideally, include screenshots of your book on the bestseller list (proof) and a link to your book on Amazon. Many authors I've consulted for reported an increase of sales during this news-spreading as well, so don't underestimate the sales potential of this tactic. Here are some screenshots that show how you could do so:

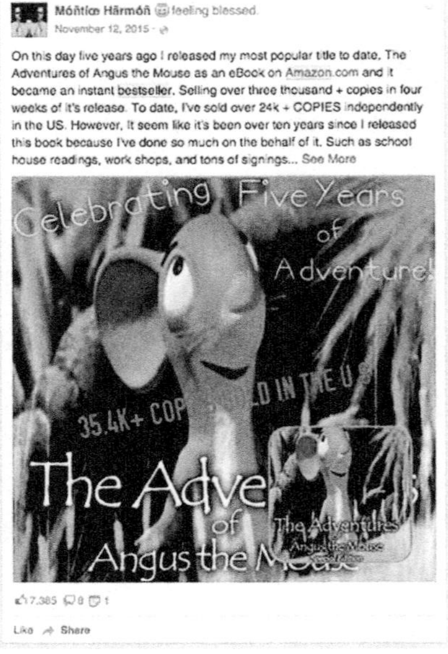

Source: Facebook. Screenshot © Albert Griesmayr 2021

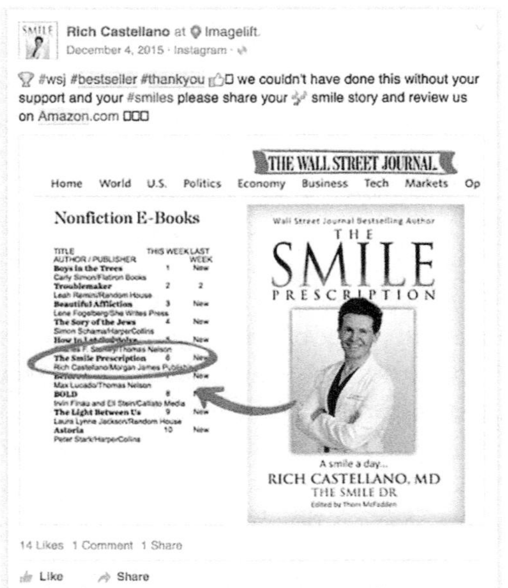

Source: Facebook. Screenshot © Albert Griesmayr 2021

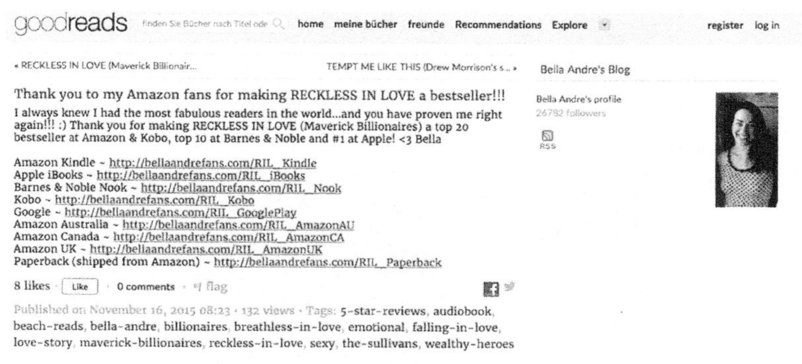

goodreads
home meine bücher freunde Recommendations Explore
register log in
« RECKLESS IN LOVE (Maverick Billionair...
TEMPT ME LIKE THIS (Drew Morrison's s... »
Bella Andre's Blog
Bella Andre's profile
RSS
Thank you to my Amazon fans for making RECKLESS IN LOVE a bestseller!!!
I always knew I had the most fabulous readers in the world...and you have proven me right again!!! :) Thank you for making RECKLESS IN LOVE (Maverick Billionaires) a top 20 bestseller at Amazon & Kobo, top 10 at Barnes & Noble and #1 at Apple! <3 Bella
Amazon Kindle ~ http://bellaandrefans.com/RIL_Kindle
Apple iBooks ~ http://bellaandrefans.com/RIL_iBooks
Barnes & Noble Nook ~ http://bellaandrefans.com/RIL_Nook
Kobo ~ http://bellaandrefans.com/RIL_Kobo
Google ~ http://bellaandrefans.com/RIL_GooglePlay
Amazon Australia ~ http://bellaandrefans.com/RIL_AmazonAU
Amazon Canada ~ http://bellaandrefans.com/RIL_AmazonCA
Amazon UK ~ http://bellaandrefans.com/RIL_AmazonUK
Paperback (shipped from Amazon) ~ http://bellaandrefans.com/RIL_Paperback
8 likes · Like · 0 comments · flag
Published on November 16, 2015 08:23 · 132 views · Tags: 5-star-reviews, audiobook, beach-reads, bella-andre, billionaires, breathless-in-love, emotional, falling-in-love, love-story, maverick-billionaires, reckless-in-love, sexy, the-sullivans, wealthy-heroes

Source: Goodreads. Screenshot © Albert Griesmayr 2021

Take a look at some examples of writers who spread news about their promotions on social media during their bestseller list campaigns:

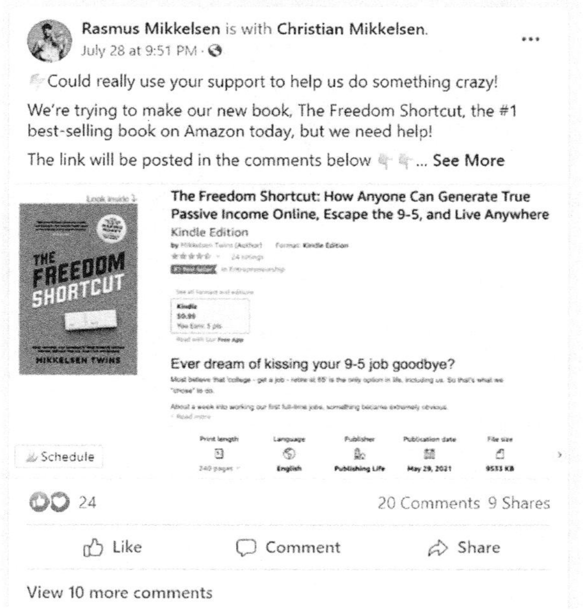

Rasmus Mikkelsen is with Christian Mikkelsen.
July 28 at 9:51 PM
Could really use your support to help us do something crazy!
We're trying to make our new book, The Freedom Shortcut, the #1 best-selling book on Amazon today, but we need help!
The link will be posted in the comments below ... See More
THE FREEDOM SHORTCUT
MIKKELSEN TWINS
The Freedom Shortcut: How Anyone Can Generate True Passive Income Online, Escape the 9-5, and Live Anywhere
Kindle Edition
Ever dream of kissing your 9-5 job goodbye?
Schedule
24
20 Comments 9 Shares
Like
Comment
Share
View 10 more comments

Screenshot of Facebook page for Rasmus Mikkelsen
Source: https://www.facebook.com/rasmus.mikkelsen.336
Screenshot © Albert Griesmayr 2021

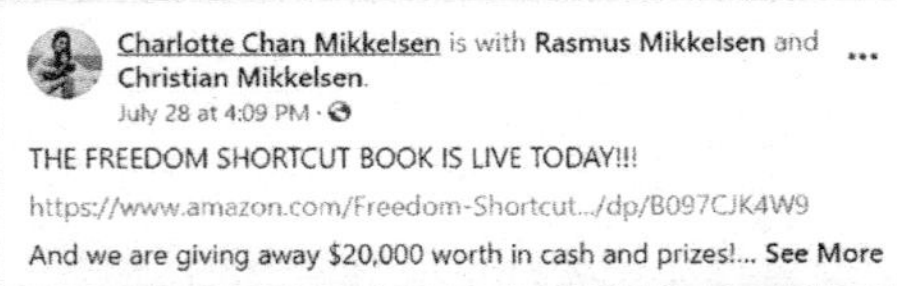

Screenshot of Facebook page for Christian Mikkelsen
Source: https://www.facebook.com/christian.mikkelsen.900
Screenshot © Albert Griesmayr 2021

You can use text to include the information, but remember that visuals work wonders. The guys from Adazing have created visually appealing badges that you can use on your website and marketing materials. Read more and download them on Adazing: http://www.adazing.com/amazon-best-seller-logos/

[According to Adazing you have full and complete rights to use these logos/badges without giving Adazing credit. But please check the latest update and make sure to download any badges from their website. — January 10, 2021]

Below are screenshots of bestselling authors who communicate their bestseller status prominently:

Source: Julia-Butler.com. Screenshot © Albert Griesmayr 2021

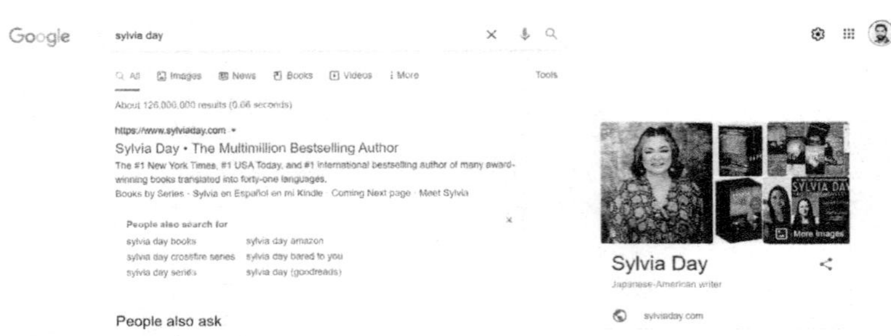

Source: Google. Screenshot © Albert Griesmayr 2021

Source: BC Schiller, 2018 Screenshot © Albert Griesmayr 2021

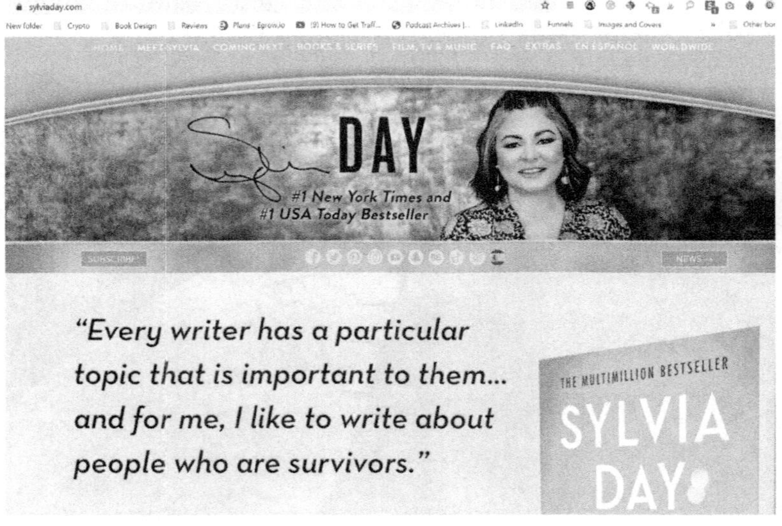

Source: https://www.sylviaday.com/ Screenshot © Albert Griesmayr 2021

4. Offer speaking engagements | Land a TedX Talk

Once your book has reached true credibility in the market (e.g. 100+ reviews/ratings and healthy ongoing sales) you might want to consider offering speaking engagements, keynotes, and lectures.

Your topic will most likely not be your book, but the topic in which you are an expert. Your bestseller gives you the credibility needed to land speaking engagements or to charge higher fees.

According to *Forbes Magazine* (2013), New York Times bestselling authors can command $40,000 and up per speech. Bestselling authors in general can ask between $2,500 and $40,000 per speech according to the New York Times.

Fees will likely have dwindled in recent years, partly due to the rise of self-published books and partly due to the shift to online events as well (not only because of COVID-19); however, there are still great opportunities available.

Make sure to check out these resources by Chandler Bolt, founder of Self-Publishing School, on landing speaking engagements and becoming a TEDx Speaker, if you have an interest in this opportunity:

TEDx Talk: https://podcasts.apple.com/tr/podcast/tedx-speaker-chandler-bolt/id1485819324?i=1000478182742

Become a motivational speaker: https://self-publishingschool.com/become-motivational-speaker-authors/

See Chandler Bolt's speaking landing page in action: https://selfpublishingschool.lpages.co/sps-speaking-landing-page/

Being a bestselling author boosts your credibility enormously. Of course, it will be easier for you to land speaking engagements with non-fiction (e.g. business, medicine, etc.) but you can get them as a fiction author as well. Think about the target audience for your book and where it would make sense that you speak. Then make a list of events and contact them personally. Be clear about what you offer, communicate good references, and start to see extra income from speaking engagements.

5. Publish a success story/Share your experience

Success attracts people. People want to learn more about how an individual achieved success, usually in the hopes that they can do the same. That's why I recommend that authors share the stories behind their books and their rise to success. The media is also interested in bestselling authors, so if your story has true substance, you can offer them a scoop.

You don't necessarily need to reach out to journalists and online magazines. You can share your story on your blog as well. Just a simple search for "How I became a bestselling author" will reveal dozens of stories on blogs as well as popular newspapers and magazines.

A highly ranked article in Google can bring you fresh traffic every month, which you can convert into sales in the long run. Don't underestimate the power of your bestseller story.

6. Increase your salary / Charge higher fees

Unless you already sell thousands of books every month, you will very likely still have a job, speaking engagements, etc. along with your writing career. Whenever you apply for a job, supply a profile or a resume. I recommend that you update your profiles to include your book and that the book has achieved Amazon Bestseller status. Your increased credibility might lead to a promotion, new job opportunities, or a pay raise down the line.

If you are a business owner, consultant, or in any independent business role, I recommend that you use your increased credibility to charge more for your services. The global market is full of providers who are able to charge less for your services that you do, so competing in price will get you nowhere, unless you are living in a country with low living costs.

If you are located in the western world and working in the knowledge industry, then your expertise is your true capital. Having written a successful book supports your expertise and gives you and your clients another argument for booking your services, even at higher prices.

From experience, I personally recommend positioning yourself in the premium segment in the knowledge economy, as the quality of your work will improve as well.

7. Approach agents and publishing houses

As a bestselling author you have achieved a certain level of proof that your book is able to sell. That is what agents and publishing houses are looking for.

Being able to achieve a milestone creates proof of concept, something that venture capitalists in business always want to see. Self-publishing gives every author the opportunity to get this proof of concept nowadays. My advice is, even if you are happily self-published, keep your eyes open for opportunities with publishing houses. The fact is that the big houses are still largely controlling physical bookstores and are gatekeepers to many attractive PoS opportunities. I recommend that you create a list of publishing agents and publishing houses that you would love to work with. Contact them with a compelling "book kit" that makes it highly visible that your book already is an "Amazon Bestseller" and has achieved proof with reviews/ratings, book sales, awards, or any other form of proof.

Many successful writers, such as Jack Canfield, Amanda Hocking, BC Schiller, E. L. James, and many more originally self-published before one or all of their works were acquired by publishing houses. Some of my clients are also self-publishing certain books, while going with respected publishers for other titles at the same time. In today's world, flexibility is paramount.

8. Create a book series/Sell further books

Having a bestseller that sells consistently is one of the best prerequisites for creating a series or sequel. The most successful movies and books have been part of a series, such as Harry Potter, James Bond, the Hunger Games, Twilight, and many more.

The biggest advantages of installments are that you can promote further books within the ones that are already selling, that you're building on a brand or characters that your readers know and love, and that you add proof to your new book in the reader's mind, since they loved your first books.

If you don't want to write more books, you can also think about dividing your existing book into parts or creating smaller installments, such as alternative endings, bonus books, or background insights.

A great example for creating a powerful book series is British writer Mark Dawson. His crime thriller series sold a hundred thousand copies and you can look at how phenomenally he markets his books by checking out his website: www.markjdawson.com

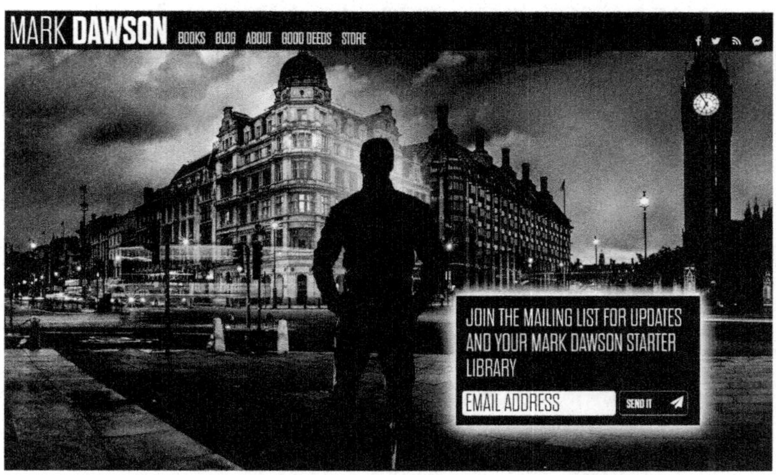

Source: Mark Dawson. Screenshot © Albert Griesmayr 2021

In addition, you do not always need to create new titles in order to create more revenue. Instead, consider translating your top sellers into different languages or adding another edition, such as an audiobook or hardcover version.

The audiobook market especially has been booming over the last couple of years. The market is getting crowded. However, if you already have a bestselling book which lends itself to an audiobook version, I recommend considering this option. Amazon's ACX platform is an excellent publishing choice for audiobooks. The edition will be available through Audible and also show up on your Amazon sales page.

9. Create additional revenue streams (courses, consulting, etc.)

One problem with a book is the comparably low price and profit margin compared to other products and services. Let's say that your e-book costs $2. You get 50 percent royalty, resulting in a profit of $1. In order to earn $1000, you need to sell 1000 books. That's a lot, and in truth, it's a number that is reached by only a small percentile within the top 1 percent on Amazon. And that doesn't even include your marketing costs.

The point that I want to make is that it is very difficult to earn a lot of money with books alone, unless you have a big platform and audience. On the other hand, there are services connected to your book that you can offer, which have far bigger profit margins. Take a look at the following table:

	Amazon Ebook	Course	Consulting Fee	Speaking Eng.
sales price	$2	$100	$1000	$2500
est. profit	$0,50	$50	$500	$1000
items needed	2,000	20	2	1
revenue target	$1,000	$1,000	$1,000	$1,000

The table shows how many items you need to sell with an e-book, a course, consulting, or speaking in order to reach an income of $1,000. As you can see, products like digital courses, consulting, and speaking are a lot more profitable.

That's why I recommend that you sit down and think about whether you can introduce one of these revenue streams in order to benefit even more from your Amazon bestseller status.

Check out the websites of BJ Fogg (author of *Tiny Habits*) or Marie Kondo (author of *The Life-Changing Magic of Tidying*) to see the additional revenue streams that they have in place along with their books.

Learn the Tiny Habits Method
Free, 5-day Program

Tiny Habits for Coronavirus Challenges

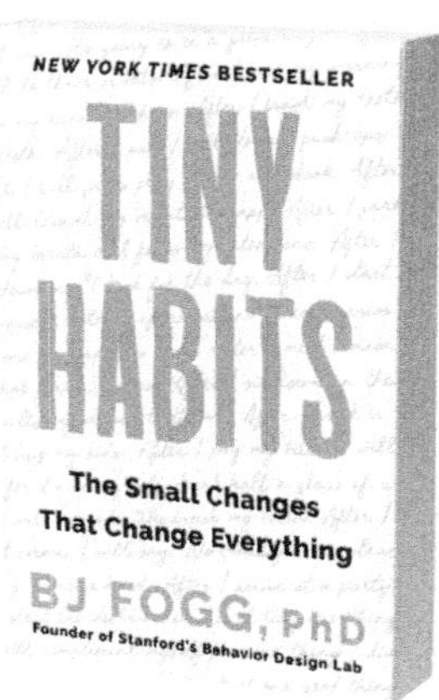

Source: tinyhabits.com Screenshot © Albert Griesmayr 2021

Source: konmari.com Screenshot © Albert Griesmayr 2021

10. Amazon Affiliate and affiliate programs in general

A final recommendation is to consider joining affiliate programs. This recommendation is only valid for authors and publishers with existing audiences, as you need a certain amount of traffic and/or leverage (for cross promotions and affiliate services).

If you have a big audience, you are promoting your books through your own channels, or are active in marketing and cross-promoting with other authors, I recommend signing up for the Amazon Affiliate service. Replace your book links with affiliate links that contain a unique tag, showing Amazon that you deserve a small commission if someone came to Amazon and purchased your book via your link.

It still surprises me to see how many high-selling books I'm referred to without an affiliate code. It's relatively easy money. However, as mentioned, you do need a good amount of traffic to make sure that registration, installation, and financial management pay off in the end.

If you are an established writer and/or established website owner, head over to the Amazon Affiliate program[126] and add Amazon affiliate links to your book and other Amazon items you promote.

The more books you sell and the bigger your own platform (e.g. an email list with 1000+ subscribers or successful social media profiles with a good following), you can also start to think about adding your books and services to other affiliate systems, in order to motivate

126 Amazon Affiliate Program: https://affiliate-program.amazon.com/

other people to promote your book. For cross-promo opportunities via email newsletter subscriber lists, you might want to take a look at *The Dream Team Network* by Nick Stephenson[127].

Think about which of my ten recommendations is the best option for you to help you benefit from your bestseller status. You may want to implement more than one. In the end, the point is to make the most of your bestselling book.

127 *Dream Team Network* by Nick Stephenson: https://www.yourfirst10kreaders.com/dreamteam

EPILOGUE:

BOOK SUCCESS IN 2030

> *"The best way to predict the future is to create it."*
>
> Abraham Lincoln

I want to finish this book by taking a look into the future. Let's see what creating sustainable successful book projects might look like in 5-10 years. What will change? Are there things that you can already do today to improve your success in the future?

As digital publishing and globalization are moving so quickly, I learned that it is vital to look ahead and be among the first to catch major new waves and trends. That's why I decided to focus my epilogue on this topic. My goal is to make you fit for the future and to show you what major trends are in play that will have profound outcomes over the next decade. Join me on this journey into the future for ideas and inspirations about what you can do today to be leading the race in five to ten years.

There are three underlying forces that will have significant outcomes on book publishing over the next five-ten years. The forces are:

a) Artificial Intelligence & NLP
b) Big Data
c) Voice User Interfaces

I believe that these three forces will result in the strengthening of the following characteristics becoming vital for success with book publishing:

1) Reader satisfaction as the Holy Grail

AI and big data will further increase the effectiveness of achieving and measuring true reader satisfaction. This will start with computer systems that can better analyze search intent, make suitable book recommendations, and calculate reader satisfaction scores, greatly influencing book rankings and customer decisions at the PoS.

I see a future that is bright for publishers focusing on creating fantastic books and on true reader satisfaction. It's bit like going back to our roots. On the other hand, I see a decrease of necessary investments into old-school SEO, book review allocation, and paid advertising.

Reducing paid advertising might sound counterintuitive at the moment; however, the change is already happening if you look at Amazon now. I have clients who want to spend money on ad campaigns, but their ads simply do not get shown, as Amazon compares competing ads with each other in terms of click-through rates (and later sales) and simply does not display low-performing ads. Why is that? It's because Amazon's primary purpose is of course to make money. The best way for them to make money is to deliver to their customers the best products. That's why they are favoring high-converting books, displaying their ads and suppressing lower-performing ones. And I am confident that this trend will continue with the further sophistication of auction-based advertising systems in combination with the relentless customer focus of tech giants like Amazon, Google, and Facebook.

Search engine optimization, as least as we know it, will also decrease in importance, and make the shift to customer satisfaction and user behavior metrics more important for getting found. And finally, reviews as we know them today will become less important. Tech giants will supplement the review systems of today with "satisfaction scores" that are calculated based on user behavior such as the amount of pages read and anonymous ratings.

2) Computer calculated "reader satisfaction scores" as the primary customer satisfaction metric

Computer calculated "reader satisfaction scores" will become an important purchase factor, maybe even becoming the leading customer satisfaction metric for books, as far as book shopping at online retailers is concerned. Although Amazon's search algorithms are not displayed publicly, Amazon very likely already weighs factors such as seller performance, sales data, CTRs, amount of orders, purchase likelihood, anonymous ratings, etc. into their product listings, and I assume this trend will continue.

The intelligence of systems will lead to higher accuracy in favoring books with high customer satisfaction, as well as reducing the publisher's need for generating customer reviews on a consistent basis. Amazon's system of customer reviews is flawed at its heart anyway, with studies claiming that more than 50% of customer ratings are not genuine or are manufactured in some form.[128] That's why Amazon is fighting hard against fake reviews and taking steps to reduce incentivization. The system can only be repaired by adding a metric that is based on true purchase data. And I am confident that data around customer satisfaction will not only be used "invisibly" by Amazon and other big retailers, but also in the form of an important metric displayed at the front-end, visible to customers, informing them of the books rating, largely independent of the existing customer review systems that are in place today.

3) Books that support voice user interfaces will have an advantage

Audiobooks will continue to play a big role; however, the main change will come from voice interfaces. Not only on devices like Alexa, but also on smartphones and computers in general. Did you ever try to talk to your smartphone to find out what the weather will be or to open specific webpages? If so, you already know that the ease of communicating with our devices has increased significantly over the last years. And the next step is the transformation from a one-way communication to two-way communication, in which you can truly interact with your devices.

What has this to do with books? A look at popular toys being used by kids today gives us clear clues. Germany has seen a major rise of two toys called the Tonie Box[129] and "magic pen" over the last few years. The Tonie Box is a device on which you put a figure in the shape of a popular story to play an audiobook. The "magic pen" is a pen that you point to characters and shapes in the books,

128 Source: https://marketingland.com/study-finds-61-percent-of-electronics-reviews-on-amazon-are-fake-254055

129 Source: https://tonies.de/

to display audio portions, ask questions, play music, etc. Recently they introduced a feature called "create" that allows kids to record their own audio portions and upload that to specific characters and shapes in the books. For both toys, the future direction is clear: to enable content that allows kids to interact with their toys by talking to them. And technology is improving rapidly.

I am confident that over the next couple of years "interactive" audiobooks, paperbacks, e-books will grow significantly, allowing listeners to communicate with the products by voice, opening up for alternative endings, background information, quizzes, riddles, and more.

4) AI supported book writing, editing, proofreading and quality assurance

The rise of Artificial Intelligence (AI) and Natural Language Processing (NLP) will also bring about a number of widely used services supporting writers with writing, editing and proofreading. While many of those solutions are already on the market today, such as Amazon's software-supported quality assurance for Kindle books, Grammarly, Talk-to Transformer[130], Quill, and Wordsmith[131], many more services will emerge. But most importantly, it is likely that software will reach a level in which it will play a big role in book editing, proofreading, and eve writing as well. Simply visit the job board of Amazon and you will see dozens of job postings looking for "quality assurance engineers"[132].

130 Source: https://www.theverge.com/tldr/2019/5/13/18617449/ai-text-generator-openai-gpt-2-small-model-talktotransformer

131 Source: https://staenz.com/content-automation-ai-tools/

132 Source: https://amazon.jobs/en/search?base_query=quality+assurance+books&loc_query=&latitude=&longitude=&loc_group_id=&invalid_location=false&country=&city=®ion=&county=

The first AI-written novels are already on the market. When we look at the advancements in technology over the last decades, it is only reasonable to assume that computers will be able to not only write non-fiction, but commercially successful fiction as well.

My realistic assumption for 2025-2030 is that the magic will happen in the intersection of human-computer interaction, as far as book writing is concerned. I expect companies to offer services where writers can enter book details, such as the storyline, the setting, ambience, characters, etc., with software then generating books based on the core details. Also, editing services like Grammarly will reach a level where the need for human editing and proofreading will have reduced substantially.

The future for books is certainly bright. We didn't need the COVID-19 pandemic to show us that people still read books. Paperback books survived when everyone was saying that they will go down with the rise of e-books. The book publishing industry is still holding strong against its closest competition, video. Books have shown that they are strong, both as a "kulturgut" and as an important form of entertainment and education.

I do believe that the future for books is strong. It is fantastic to be in this industry. Now it is time for you go out into the world, and apply the Perennial Bestseller Blueprint in order to create long-term success with your book projects.

I wish you the best on your endeavor. Do not hesitate to contact me with questions, remarks, and feedback.

Best wishes,

Albert Griesmayr
August 1, 2021

BONUS

BOOK LAUNCH CHECKLISTS

[Based on the Perennial Bestseller Blueprint]

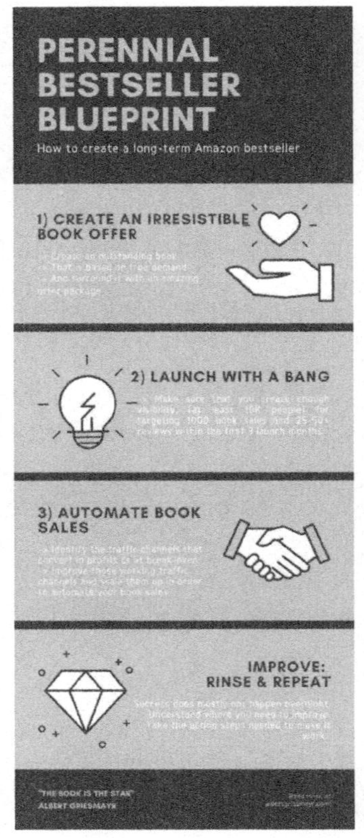

PERENNIAL
BESTSELLER
BLUEPRINT
How to create a long-term Amazon bestseller
1) CREATE AN IRRESISTIBLE BOOK OFFER
2) LAUNCH WITH A BANG
3) AUTOMATE BOOK SALES
IMPROVE: RINSE & REPEAT
"THE BOOK IS THE STAR"
ALBERT GRIESMAYR

As a reminder, please find below the 3 steps of the Perennial Bestseller Blueprint. This book launch checklist compiles the core items to consider at each phase of the implementation.

Step 1: Create an irresistible offer

- Create an outstanding book
- Based on true demand
- Supplement it with an amazing offer package

Step 2: Launch with a bang

- Get enough visibility to give your book a true chance for success (Amazon algorithm and reader WoM)

- Ideally, achieve at least 25+ ratings and 250+ book sales during launch month

Step 3: Automate book sales

- Create a system that encompasses attraction (traffic), conversions, and retention in a profitable way
- Rinse and repeat until your book sales automation is working

STEP 1: CREATE AN IRRESISTIBLE BOOK OFFER	
Book Manuscript Finished	
Book Manuscript Edited by Professional	
Book Manuscript Proofread by Target Audience	
Book Manuscript Formatted by Professional (for all targeted book formats, such as e-book [Mobi, Epub], paperback [PDF])	
Book Cover Created by Professional (for all targeted book formats, such as e-book, paperback and audiobook)	
Book Description for Amazon Sales Page (Formatted in HTML as well)	
Book Blurb for Book Back Cover	
Editorial Review for Book Back Cover	
Rights for Book Cover, Visuals Used in Manuscript/Cover and other parts of the book and marketing checked	
Author Bio written for Book Back Cover, Inside Flap, Amazon Author bio and other relevant places	
If suited: Publisher Bio prepared, Book Series Description Prepared	
Book Title for all book formats	

Book Subtitle for all book formats	
Price Defined for major book formats	
Optional: Additional publishing channels apart from Amazon defined	
3 Main Target Keywords for Amazon search defined	
7 Backend Search Term keywords for KDP defined	
2 Book Categories for Amazon KDP defined	
Optional: Up to 10 target book categories via Publisher Rocket Defined	
Offer Package for Readers defined (bonuses, etc.)	
Special Launch Offer Package for readers defined (bonuses, introductory price, etc.)	
Special Offer Package for Influencers, Magic 100, and Launch Team Defined (e.g. cross promotion, thank you gift, etc.)	
Built-In Virality Elements and Cialdini Principles respected in offer and book?	
Goal Setting: Target Book Sales and Expectations from Launch and Ongoing Book Appearance Defined	
Book Marketing Plan: Basic book marketing plan including launch dates and main promotional activities defined	
Final Question: Does my book offer have the WOW effect and am I truly confident in it?	

STEP 2: LAUNCH WITH A BANG – A: LAUNCH PREPARATION (12-1 MONTH PRIOR TO LAUNCH)	
Making sure that book materials (covers, manuscripts, etc.) are ready at least 14 days prior to launch [Hiring professionals early if necessary]	
Making sure that all marketing materials (website, funnel, author bio, book descriptions, email outreach to subscriber and influencer, etc.) are ready at least 14 days prior to pre-launch phase (or launch if you have no pre-launch phase) [Hiring professionals early if necessary]	
Website and Funnel	
Author Bio	
Book blurb	
Book Description	
Email Outreach (Sequence) to Subscribers	
Email Outreach (Sequence) to Magic 100/ Influencers	
Email Outreach (Sequence) to Book Launch Team	
Email Outreach to Reviewers (People you request a review from)	
Optional: Surprise Gift (within book, on website, plus email sequence)	
Optional: Preparing social media messages for your book launch phase	
Magic 100 List created (100 Targets)	
Book Launch Team Email List Created (10+ Targets)	

List of Reviewers (people you ask for a review) from your network created	
Optional: If you do PR, outreach message and media kit for journalists created	
Optional: 1 month prior to launch, signing up for Reedsy Discovery and submitting your book for launch (launch date must be one month in the future)	
Optional: If you put your e-book up for pre-order on Amazon: Signing up for KDP, filling out payment and tax details and creating an e-book entry for your pre-order (Note: You don't need a manuscript, just an e-book cover, a publishing data and a core book description for the pre-order)	
Optional: If you already have at least one book published, signing up for Pubby.co, submitting a prior book, and collecting points (Ideally you launch your book when you have 20.000+ points on Pubby)	
Optional: Organize cross promos via Magic 100/influencers	
1 Month prior to launch: Signing up for KDP (and checking out required fields for publishing, making sure you have all info to fill out)	
1 Month prior to launch: Signing up for Amazon Author Central (and starting your author bio and claiming your prior books if available)	
1 Month prior to launch: Checking within KDP that your book files will be approved by Amazon (Previewer for Kindle, Paperback which is available when you upload your book)	

1 week prior to launch: Making sure that you have a professional hired for Amazon ads, so that you have keyword lists and categories to target the moment your book launches	

STEP 2: LAUNCH WITH A BANG – B: BOOK LAUNCH PHASE (1-3 MONTHS FROM LAUNCH DATE)	
Signing up for Pubby, submitting your book, and starting to collect points	
Getting reviews for your book via your Pubby account (Alternatively: You might want to hire professionals to generate reviews via Pubby or other services)	
Optional: Booking review services (Booksirens, Hidden Gems Books, Netgalley)	
Optional: If you are using KDP Select, enroll your e-book when publishing and book your free promo days during launch week, so that you can inform your reviewers and subscribers about the free promo	
Booking 2-10 launch promotions (e-book launch promotions with third party services that will run during your launch month)	
Submitting up to 10 browse categories for your book via Author Central	
Immediately after launch: Signing up for Amazon advertising, filling out payment and tax details and starting ads for your books in the US, the UK, and Canada	
Optional: Starting your PR campaign (sending out your outreach)	

Spreading the word about your launch via social media	
Initiating your launch email outreach to subscribers	
Initiating your launch email outreach to influencers/Magic 100	
Initiating your launch email outreach to your book launch team	
Right after launch: Ordering your e-book and other book formats and make a quality check	
Amazon Ads: Running your Amazon ads launch campaign for 1-3 months and making adjustments on an ongoing basis	
After 14 days: First check point in regards to sales and reviews (adjust measures if needed)	
During launch month: Running your Amazon bestseller campaign	
During launch month: Taking screenshots of your Amazon bestseller status	
One month after launch: Updating your book description and author bio and making sure to include credibility factors such as bestseller status, top reviews, etc.	

STEP 3: BOOK SALES AUTOMATION	
14 days prior to launch: Making sure that you have your book sales automation system outlined and expectations for your core metrics ready	
1 month after launch: Analysis of your book sales system and calculate your true metrics	

1 month after launch: Deep analysis of your Amazon ads and sales via Amazon (and other retailers)	
1 month after launch: Making sure to update sales pages, author bios, book descriptions, etc., to increase conversion rates	
1 month after launch: Considering adding upsell products or new traffic channels	
Optional: Booking further promotions throughout the launch year	
Optional: Booking further review services throughout the launch year	
Optional: Continuing and adapting email outreach, ad campaigns, and social media messages throughout the launch year	

BOOK 3

BOOK SALES EXPLOSION

HOW TO 3X YOUR BOOK SALES USING THE 32 HOTTEST BOOK MARKETING TACTICS OF 2021

1

INTRODUCTION

A few weeks ago, I was chatting with the founder of one of Germany's fastest-growing Kindle book publishing businesses at the Frankfurt Book Fair. We were animatedly discussing the latest industry developments, such as audio-enabled conversations on Alexa and the impact AI will have on book writing. The conversation turned to the latest book marketing tactics on Amazon. Suddenly, we were exploring the seedy underworld of publishing.

This guy was giving me a deeper glimpse into the dark side of the industry, things I'd heard about but preferred not to contemplate: bots, advanced SEO, black-hat tactics, lawsuits, and much more. These things do not match the respectable, even glamorous, image of the publishing world, and I wish I were not aware of them—but sadly, they do exist.

Sitting at the Frankfurt Book Fair, surrounded by the most prestigious publishing houses and authors anywhere, it felt surreal to conjure up this dark world. But as we talked, it dawned on me that there's no escaping from this parallel world. It's part of the new reality. Welcome to digital book publishing!

Walking home that day, I reflected deeply on three questions:

1) Is my knowledge about book marketing tactics equally beneficial to all authors?
2) Is it okay to "help" authors or publishers with books when they're primarily looking to make a quick buck?

And lastly...

3) Where are we headed? Will there be a clash between traditional publishers and new players like Kindle or Audible, with their innovative and non-traditional methods?

Do not get the wrong idea. This book is essentially about helping you sell more books; it will not be a deep exploration of questions like these. But I am raising these issues because they have a direct bearing on what your book can achieve. The sections that follow introduce you to strategies that are guaranteed to benefit your book, whether it is something you have thrown your heart and soul into or a ghost written, profit-driven project meant to bring in cash.

So here is my take on the questions above:

1) Your book is the star. This is rule #1 of my Book Marketing Secrets. A good book can be a winner without good marketing, but a bad book cannot. Simple as that. But the flipside is that a bad book with good marketing can still get far. I have seen this numerous times in the market, not only in the digital world but also in the realm of print. Good marketing still moves products far and fast. Simply enter a popular term—for example, "Keto Diet"—into your Amazon search bar, and you will find dozens of high-ranking books with the same basic

content, the same look, and lots of reviews (many of them written, interestingly, in short timeframes). But many of those books do not add value. They were written by publishers more interested in keyword rankings than in creating a good read for their customers. And yes, it is all part of the game. But sooner or later, customers, as well as Amazon, will figure out which books deserve their attention and which ones do not. I am convinced that you can only "play the system" to a limited extent with a product that is not superior. And that is a good thing. Also, although there is still a long way to go and some people will always find ways to play the system, Amazon is becoming better and better at detecting and prioritizing truly valuable books.

That leads me to the second question:

2) As a book marketing consultant, I work with authors and publishers from around the world, and I do not always get to choose who I work with. I have often been confronted with books that lacked the quality I was hoping for. But over the years I have improved at sharing my honest perspective. Today, when an author or publisher hands me a book that does not provide additional value, I tell them so point-blank. Then I try to work with the client to improve the basics, primarily focusing on the book's quality. So, is it okay to help someone achieve best-selling status on Amazon when they might not deserve it? In general, yes—but first I always try to improve the book and help my clients develop and grow long-term in their craft. My approach is the same in the book you are reading now. I cannot control how you will use the tips that follow, but I can control what I communicate and teach. So, let me be clear at the

outset: success is ultimately about having a book you can be proud of, one that adds value to your target audience. This is what creates true satisfaction and makes every author happy at the end of the day. That sense of loving and taking pride in what you have created, in the impact you have achieved, is worth more than turning a quick buck anytime.

Regarding question number 3, I want to share my personal perspective with you. I have always felt more connected to the outliers in the publishing world than to traditional publishing houses. It all began when I launched my own start-up company, Scribando, around 10 years ago and reached out to traditional publishing houses to explain my concept. Quite honestly—and it happened more than once—some people made it clear they were not impressed.

You know that skeptical look, that feeling you sometimes get from an expert in your field, when you describe what you do? You can read it in their eyes: "You're not good enough. You're not part of the crowd." I still get this impression from time to time, even after having achieved some success and gained a little respect in the market.

Maybe I've been making the wrong connections, or maybe my impressions are off. In any case, I feel happier talking to outliers in the market, such as start-up founders, self-published authors, and service providers.

My sense is that there is still a substantial gap between these two groups that will not be easy to bridge in the near future. However, I hope that both communities will learn from each other—traditionalists from digital marketers about how to promote their books, and

Kindle publishers from the traditional houses about how to create wonderful book projects.

* * *

To sum it all up, in my role as a book marketing consultant and CEO of the publishing start-up Scribando | Novelify, my main job is to help authors and publishing houses sell more books.

Achieving this goal requires not only a deep understanding of basic book marketing strategies but also an ability to stay on top of the latest insights and time-sensitive tactics in the market.

Staying current in both areas is difficult, even for people who do this full-time, because the market is extremely fast-paced—especially in digital book publishing.

One of the main reasons it is hard to keep up with the rate of change is that the digital world is not confined to specific sectors or industries. A change in the digital landscape has immediate effects on many industries, including traditionally slower-moving markets like the book industry. There is no escape from this trend. "Safe harbors" are increasingly rare in the book publishing business today.

Being able to succeed requires being alert and continuously up to date on the latest developments and strategies. With my start-up Scribando | Novelify, I focus on exactly that: keeping authors and publishers at the cutting edge of marketing.

As I mentioned earlier, my book *Book Marketing Secrets* offers timeless advice about how to sell more books.

The one you are reading, however, includes the latest knowledge, the newest opportunities, and the most current and effective ways to market your book.

Here I share with you the 32 best book marketing tactics.

Most of these tactics are simple to understand, and if applied correctly, can have a huge impact on your book's performance. Do not try to add all the tactics to your marketing mix, though. Instead, focus on the ones that promise the best results for your specific setup and situation.

Based on my experience in digital book marketing, it is better to master 1–3 tactics and excel in your implementation than to apply 10 of the tactics poorly. In today's market, so many book marketers are screaming for attention that it is wiser not to scream louder but instead to scream differently, or to find alternative routes to reach your target audience.

* * *

My goal is for the tactics I share in this book to become as valuable to you as they have been to me and to hundreds of my clients around the world over the past several years. I am quite certain that each of the tactics in this book has the power to double your book sales, and that all of them combined have the power to triple them at the very least.

One way for me to measure the success of this book is if you get at least a 100% return on investment from purchasing it. In other words, if you spent $10 on it, I want you to make at least $20. Would you kindly send me an email or post a review letting me know if you hit that mark? I would love to hear about your experience of applying my tactics. Few things in life make me happier than seeing how my work helps authors and publishers and learning from their constructive feedback how to improve.

So, press forward—use the strategies in this book—and be a bold book marketer. Prove the effectiveness of these tactics in your own publishing journey.

Then my job with this book will have been a job well done.

2

TACTICS LIST OVERVIEW

Tactic	Summary	Hotness Factor
#1. Book Sales Funnel	Taking your visitors on a powerful marketing-oriented customer journey, from first contact to book purchase and potential upsells—quickly and effectively.	Fire!
#2. Look Inside / Reading Samples + Bonus Content	Including a visual in your book's first 10 pages that links to bonus content available on your webpage to get traffic.	Fire!
#3. The Truly Free Print Book	Offering a free print book and also covering shipping costs (targeted at limited editions & exclusive launches).	Super Hot
#4. Alexa Skills Book Promotion	Promoting books by creating related Alexa skills.	Super Hot

Tactic	Summary	Hotness Factor
#5. Affiliate Marketing	Using Amazon and Audible affiliate programs (Audible Bounty & Amazon Affiliate) to increase book royalties.	Hot
#6. Translation & New Format Tactic	Increasing revenue and visibility by translating existing books and/or creating new formats.	Hot
#7. Kickstarter Book Funding	Funding books on Kickstarter and applying pre-order strategies in general.	Super Hot
#8. Cialdinify Your Book	Spicing up your book marketing by applying Cialdini's principles from psychology to your approach.	Hot
#9. Permafree Ebook	Driving traffic to your author/publisher webpage from a permafree ebook from online retailers.	Hot
#10. Cover/Genre/Title Match Tactic	Matching book covers with the genre, title, and theme of books.	Hot
#11. Irresistible Bonus Offers	Spicing up the offer you make with your book by adding bonuses and creating irresistible packages and book offers.	Super Hot
#12. Pre-Order Tactic	Taking advantage of Amazon's expanded pre-order phase and BookBub's new release promo to give your book a powerful start.	Super Hot

Tactic	Summary	Hotness Factor
#13. Amazon Bestseller Badge Tactic	Landing bestsellers on Amazon by focusing on short time spikes in non-competitive categories.	Hot
#14. Pinterest Traffic Generation	Getting traffic to your author webpage or Amazon sales page by leveraging Pinterest together with Tailwind Tribes.	Hot
#15. Building an Author Platform with Email Marketing	Focusing on building a base of dedicated subscribers through email. (Get to 1,000!)	Hot
#16. Collaborative Book Promotion	Teaming up with other authors through legitimate review swapping, newsletter swapping, guest blogging, and Pinterest + Tailwind.	Hot
#17. Video Marketing on YouTube, Amazon & Beyond	Using video to tell your story to readers on YouTube, Amazon, Facebook, and other platforms.	Hot
#18. Amazon Select Price Promo + Discounted Book Service	Using discounted ebook alert services with a price promotion through Amazon KDP Select.	Hot
#19. Authority Book Publishing	Publishing a book with the primary goal of establishing authority and helping you reach higher-level business or career goals.	Hot

Tactic	Summary	Hotness Factor
#20. Powerful Amazon SEO	Focusing on your top 1-3 keywords and rankings on Amazon and other major book retailers.	Hot
#21. Running Amazon Ads	Running ongoing Amazon Ads with a focus on book categories and/or keywords that you'll improve over time for maximum profitability.	Fire!
#22. Audiobook Creation and Audiobook Giveaways	Releasing your book in an additional, fast-growing medium (audio) and supporting it with audiobook giveaways by using ACX, Findaway Voices, Audiobook Boom, and other services.	Super Hot
#23. Retargeting with Facebook Advertising + Messenger Marketing	Retargeting warm audiences to them engaged through Facebook ads and using Messenger marketing for viral campaigns or direct contact with fans.	Hot
#24. Kobo Publishing Tactic	Offering promotions through the smaller book retailer Kobo, where there's less competition and big sales opportunities.	Hot
#25. The Upsell Product Tactic (Infinite Selling Loops)	Getting profitable by always having another upsell product ready for your readers, like a companion course, personal coaching, or a book bundle/series.	Fire!

Tactic	Summary	Hotness Factor
#26. Book Review Automation	Automating your book review process by offering a special bonus for feedback.	Super Hot
#27. Review Gathering with Pubby.co	Getting reviews with the help of Pubby.co	Fire!
#28. Using Librarybub	Reaching out to libraries with the help of Librarybub.	Hot
#29. Using Patreon	Patreon allows creators to build their userbases while getting paid at the same time	Hot
#30. The Magic 100	Growing traffic and an influential network with The Magic 100	Fire!
#31. Running Cashback Campaigns	Running cashback campaigns in order to increase book rankings and to jumpstart sales algorithms.	Super Hot
#32. Google Play Promo Codes	Using promo code campaigns via Google Play.	Hot

Index Hotness Factor:

- Fire: 5x Potential
- Super Hot: 3x Potential
- Hot: 2x Potential

The Hotness Factor is primarily based on the potential return (80% relevance). The second factor it acknowledges is the cost of implementation in terms of time and money (20% relevance).

3

TACTIC DETAILS

TACTIC 1
BOOK SALES FUNNEL

Description

A book sales funnel is a powerful marketing-oriented customer journey that quickly and effectively takes your visitors from first contact to book purchase and potential upsells.

Book sales funnels can range from simple to complicated. To create the simplest type of funnel, you must have the right mindset about what a funnel is, why it is beneficial, and how to design it effectively. A complicated funnel requires a comprehensive business visualisation with a clear understanding of the channels that bring traffic, the points of sale that convert traffic into paying customers, and systems of customer retention and activation.

Online sales funnels are especially important for selling books, since books are extremely competitive and do not have high profit margins. That is why it is critical to be able to convert traffic at healthy and profitable rates if you want your book business to work.

Examples of Success

Look at the following three main types of book funnels showcasing economically profitable book funnels. Consider how you could apply a book funnel to your own book business.

1. Free Print Book Funnels

Free print book funnels offer a free print copy; readers only pay for shipping.

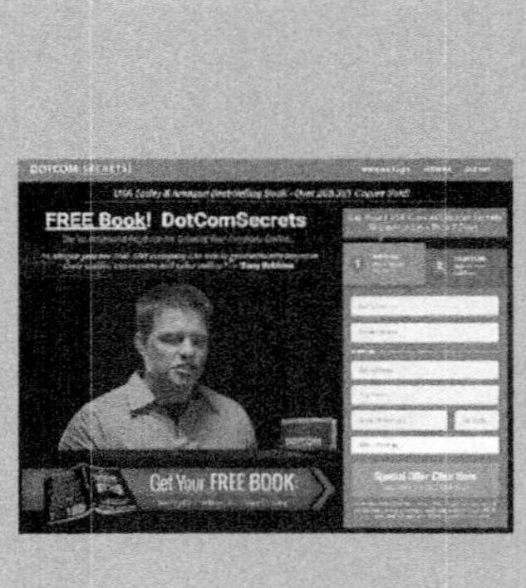

Example: Russell Brunson—DotComSecrets

Russell Brunson (Founder of Clickfunnels) has reported multiple times that his book funnels were profitable, as he was able to pay for traffic with book sales at break-even, while being able to make profits from upsell products.

Thumbnail (January 31, 2019): https://dotcomsecrets.com

Example: Sabri Suby—Sell Like Crazy

Although we do not have reports directly from Sabri Suby about the profitability of his funnel, I suspect it works well based on the number of Amazon reviews and the ads running to the funnel for many months already.

Thumbnail (January 31, 2019): https://selllikecrazybook.com/

Example: Rob Kosberg—Publish, Promote, Profit

Rob Kosberg shares interesting insights on the performance of his funnel here: http://bestsellerpublishing.org/the-ins-outs-of-a-book-funnel/

Thumbnail (January 31, 2019): https://www.publishpromoteprofit.com/freebook

2. Paid eBook Funnels

Paid ebook funnels charge for an eBook directly at the point of sale and normally include upsells as well.

Example: Robert Neckelius—2 Hour Agency

Robert Neckelius sold an ebook for $4.95 upfront and had high-ticket coaching later. He was able to make the funnel profitable and cover most of his advertising costs with the book.

Thumbnail (January 31, 2019): https://2houragency.com/book/ +Insights: https://www.facebook.com/rneckelius/videos/721728171664333/

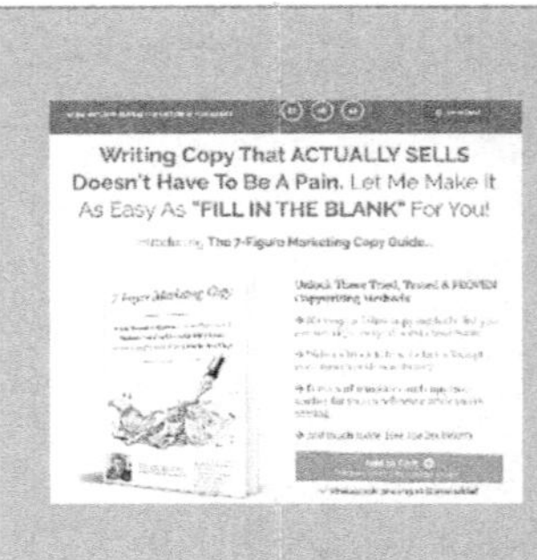

Example: Sean Vossler—7 Figure Marketing Copy

Sean Vossler successfully sold a package including an ebook for $37 total, as this campaign was running for a long time.

Thumbnail (January 31, 2019): https://app.increase.academy/most-important-skill-guide

3. Traffic-Oriented Book Funnels

Traffic-oriented book funnels have the primary target of driving traffic from online retailers, social media, or websites to other paid products, such as further books, digital courses, or affiliate products.

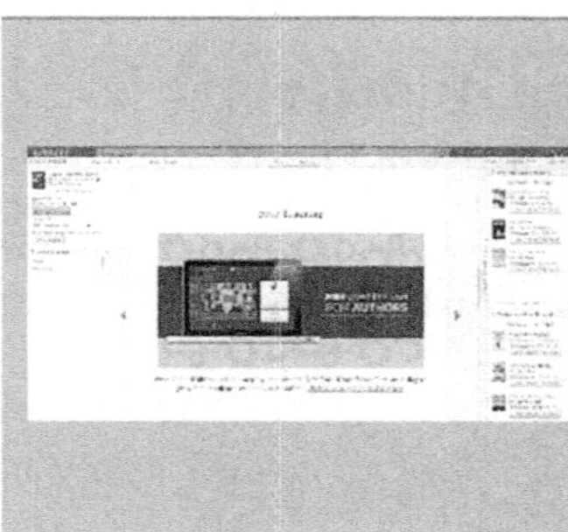

Example: Nick Stephenson—Reader Magnets

Nick Stephenson used a permafree book on Amazon to drive traffic to his webpage.

Thumbnail (January 31, 2019): https://amzn.to/2MBKZU3

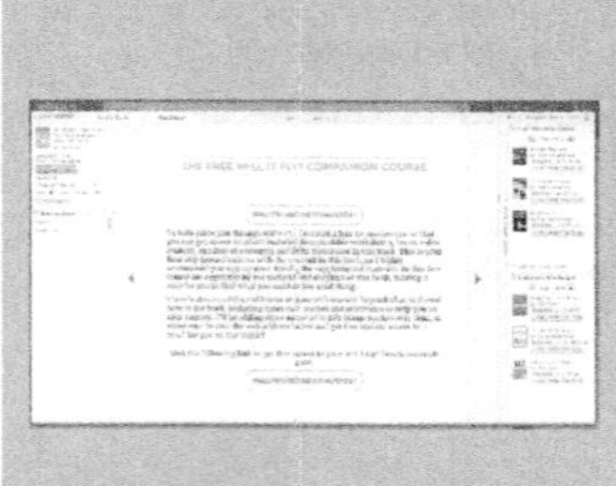

Example: Pat Flynn—Will It Fly?

Pat Flynn also used a permafree book on Amazon to drive traffic to his own products. According to Dave Chesson of Kindlepreneur, 30% of Pat's book buyers go on to access his Smart Passive Income course.

Thumbnail (January 31, 2019): https://amzn.to/3692D9I

Application

The first step in applying the funnel tactic is to keep the concept of a "funnel" itself at the front of your mind. It will change your mindset and enable you to make the right decisions. The easiest application is to add links from your book description or author bio to your webpage and to start thinking about upsells for your book.

The funnel strategy kicks in by creating a powerful, marketing-oriented book sales mechanism that quickly and effectively brings your visitors from first contact to book purchase and potential upsells. Equally important as the definition of the funnel steps and the funnel design (lead magnet, sign up, sale 1, sale 2, retention, etc.) is the choice of appropriate software.

Choosing the right software for your funnel is vitally important. You can design an incredible funnel on paper, but when it comes to execution, you will be largely dependent on your software capabilities and how quickly and effectively you can execute.

I recommend exploring Clickfunnels and Thrive Themes (the latter especially if you are using Wordpress), as well as Thrivecart, if you're primarily looking to integrate a powerful checkout process. When it comes to book fulfilment, and shipping free print books, look at Ship Your Books (shipyourbooks.com), Woocommerce (woocommerce.com), Amazon FBA, or local fulfilment providers.

Resources

- The Book Funnel: How to Go From Zero Audience to 6-Figure Business in One Book: https://fizzle.co/sparkline/book-funnel-zero-audience-to-6-figure-business
- Sales Funnel Strategy - 7 Simple Hacks To Get Your Sales Funnel To Convert: https://www.youtube.com/watch?v=Ip59Qbv6J_w
- Should I sell my book on Amazon or in a sales funnel? https://marketingsecrets.com/sell-book-amazon-sales-funnel/
- The Coaching/Consulting Book Sales Funnel: https://www.crazyeyemarketing.com/blog/the-coaching-consulting-book-sales-funnel-clickfunnels/
- The Ins and Outs of a Book Funnel: http://bestsellerpublishing.org/the-ins-outs-of-a-book-funnel/
- Mechanics behind free plus shipping funnels: https://www.clickfunnels.com/blog/mechanics-behind-free-plus-shipping-funnel/

TACTIC 2
USING AMAZON'S "LOOK INSIDE" AND READING SAMPLES TO COMMUNICATE BONUS CONTENT

Description

This tactic is all about creating enticing book intros and offers that can be included in a book's first couple of pages. Not only do these present the book favorably, but they also drive traffic by linking to bonus content available on external webpages.

Features like "look inside," "peek inside," or "reading samples" for download are a staple of most major online book retailers, often available for both ebooks and print books. In fact, it is a feature that readers have come to expect, and they use it frequently. It is natural for people to want to preview the content they're thinking of purchasing.

Optimizing and improving this content is a great tactic, and it can often be done easily by just working on a couple of pages and uploading a new version.

Examples of Success

Example: Barnes & Noble—Look Inside / Reading Sample Feature

Look at Barnes & Noble's reading sample feature. It's highly used, so make sure your first 10 pages are enticing and, ideally, communicate value.

Thumbnail (January 8, 2020): https://bit.ly/2Frpt0y

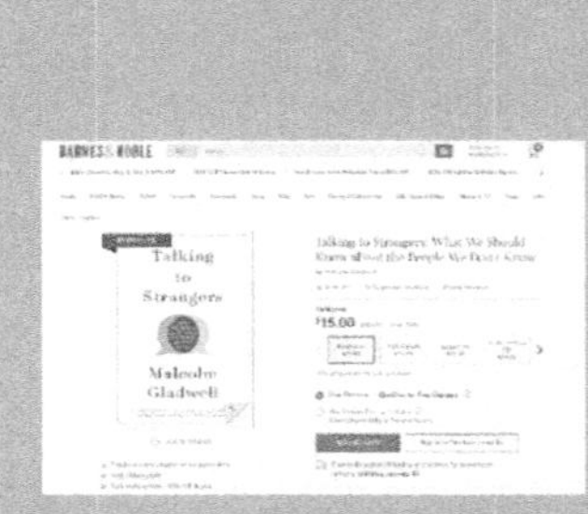

Example: Malcolm Gladwell—Talking to Strangers

Open the reading sample to see how the publisher is using the preview to advertise his book giveaways, sneak peeks, and other benefits by visiting his website.

Thumbnail (January 8, 2020): https://bit.ly/39OvGl8

Example: Nick Stephenson—Reader Magnets

Nick Stephenson's Reader Magnets is another good example of using Amazon's "Look Inside" feature to show readers bonus content and drive traffic to a webpage.

Thumbnail (January 31, 2019): https://amzn.to/2MBKZU3

Application

Below you will find some low-hanging fruit, easy ways to work on your first couple of pages and your reading samples in order to optimize them (for higher conversion rates with book buyers) and drive traffic to your websites (for building email lists, selling further book titles and companion books, or presenting upsells).

Here are simple tips for optimizing:

- Copyright information and disclaimers: Reduce and/or move to the end of the book.
- Table of Contents: Design it neatly and attractively.
- Bonus content feature: Add a visual that catches the reader's attention, and include a big-font link to your webpage.
- Foreword / Note from the Author: Make it stand out. This section should still be promoting your book by listing benefits, or if it is a fiction book, by drawing readers into your story.
- Testimonials: Add them at the beginning to increase credibility.

If you're driving traffic to your webpage, you'll need to have enticing bonus content. Regardless of your specific niche, that content should add value. It could be a worksheet that complements the book, a market-specific report or analysis, a training video, or a free booklet or audiobook. Many authors also give away free ebooks of previous or upcoming releases.

Resources

- How to build an email list through Amazon: https://www.crazyegg.com/blog/build-list-through-amazon/

- Proven traffic strategies (Including getting traffic through Amazon): https://neilpatel.com/blog/7-proven-strategies-to-increase-your-blogs-traffic-by-206/#trafficstrategy1

TACTIC 3
THE TOTALLY FREE PRINT BOOK FUNNEL

Description

We have already discussed book funnels in Tactic #1. By now you are familiar with free print book funnels, which offer a print book for free, apart from shipping costs. This is a great tactic; not only are print books perceived as more valuable than ebooks because they are a physical item, but there are still loads of readers who prefer holding a good old-fashioned book in their hands and turning its pages. However, Tactic #3 goes one step further by offering a totally free print book that covers shipping as well.

How is this possible? How can you make it work financially?

This tactic relies on two ideas. First, you need to see the totally free print book as a marketing tactic aimed at generating buzz by making an exclusive offer to key target groups, such as influencers, journalists, or important beta readers. The goal is not to get a profit from the funnel itself, but to offer a limited number of copies for free (e.g., between 50 and 1,000) in exchange for something more valuable down the road—media attention, social media mentions, or a strong launch team built from enthusiastic readers.

Second, think of the funnel step as a way of bringing in leads who will purchase upsell products later, which will make the funnel profitable in the long run. This tactic is rarely used today, but it can be highly effective.

If you can master these two concepts and keep in mind the long-term benefits of offering a totally free print book, you'll have a very high chance of success.

Examples of Success

Example: Goodreads Giveaways

(Core idea: Giving away a limited number of free ARCs to create buzz and to secure feedback and reviews)

Thumbnail (January 10, 2020): https://www.goodreads.com/giveaway

Example: Cynthia L. Copeland—Win a copy of CUB

(Core idea: Giving away a limited number of free ARCs to create buzz and to secure feedback and reviews)

Thumbnail (January 10, 2020): https://bit.ly/2tInz8V

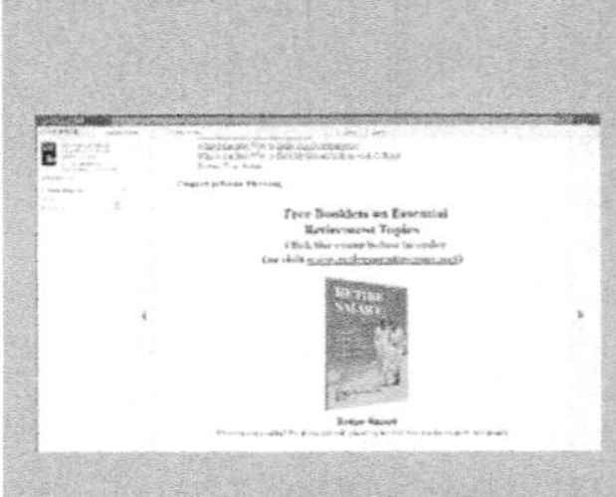

Example: Retirement Investing

(Core idea: Driving traffic from Amazon to landing pages, where you will offer a truly free print book, since lifetime value of customers is higher than print book + shipping costs)

Thumbnail (January 10, 2020): https://amzn.to/2Qzxxm5

Application

You can apply the "totally free print book" tactic either by limiting the offer in some way (normally by time, by number of copies, or to an exclusive audience) or by creating a totally free print book funnel with upsells. Find the most common applications below:

1) **Pre-Launch/Pre-Order Package:** The main goal is to generate interest among a target audience early. This could be achieved by creating a "secret landing page" that you only show to beta-readers, journalists, and influencers, where they can get a free copy shipped to them in exchange for signing up by email and joining a launch team.

2) **Exclusive Audience Offer:** Companies and authors in the industry with high-ticket clients apply this tactic to gain targeted readers, strengthen loyalty with existing customers, and build audiences. The free print book serves as a lead magnet, making it a profitable marketing tactic, since income from upsell products exceeds what you will spend on giving away the books for free.

3) **Book Launch & Readings:** Book launches, book giveaways, and readings are also a good practical application, provided there are upsell products available to compensate for the upfront expense.

Resources

- How to Maximize Goodreads Giveaways for Better Engagement: https://www.amarketingexpert.com/maximize-goodreads-giveaways/
- How to Use Boost Book Sales With Advanced Reader Copies (ARCs): https://www.authormedia.com/155/
- How to Get Books Before They're Published: https://bookriot.com/2018/08/17/how-to-get-books-before-theyre-published/

TACTIC 4
ALEXA SKILLS BOOK PROMOTION

Description

The main idea behind Tactic #4 is to use Amazon Alexa-enabled devices as a channel for promoting books and related services. Amazon Alexa is a colossal investment by the company. By November 2018, Amazon had more than 10,000 employees working on Alexa and related products. As of January 2019, Amazon's devices team announced that they had sold over 100 million Alexa-enabled devices. It's one of the fastest-growing market phenomena, closely related to audiobooks because of its voice technology and to the purchase of other products on Amazon, such as books, due to its integration with the company's ecommerce business.

The Alexa Skill Book Promotion Tactic certainly launches you into a fresh field, but one that offers high rewards for publishers with existing audiences to tap—especially if you are willing to put a little energy into creating an amazing Alexa skill and marketing it effectively.

Examples of Success

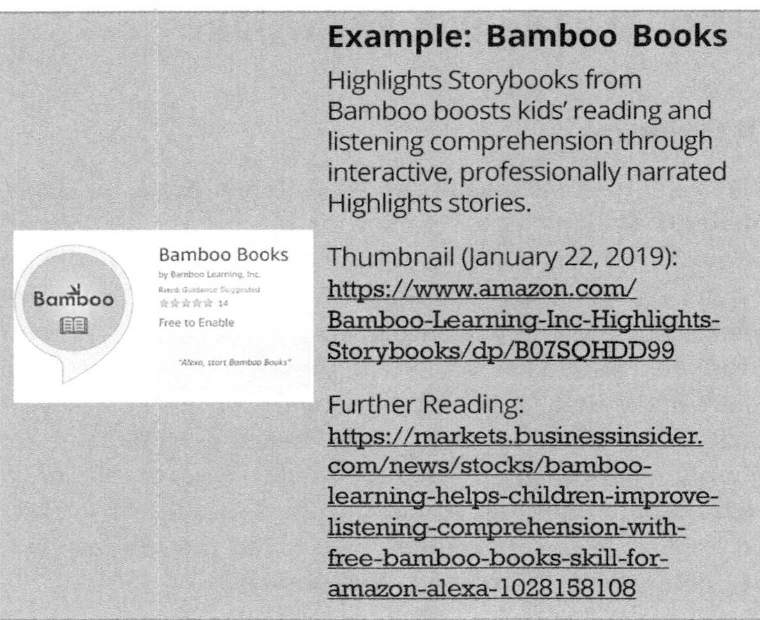

Example: Bamboo Books

Highlights Storybooks from Bamboo boosts kids' reading and listening comprehension through interactive, professionally narrated Highlights stories.

Thumbnail (January 22, 2019): https://www.amazon.com/Bamboo-Learning-Inc-Highlights-Storybooks/dp/B07SQHDD99

Further Reading: https://markets.businessinsider.com/news/stocks/bamboo-learning-helps-children-improve-listening-comprehension-with-free-bamboo-books-skill-for-amazon-alexa-1028158108

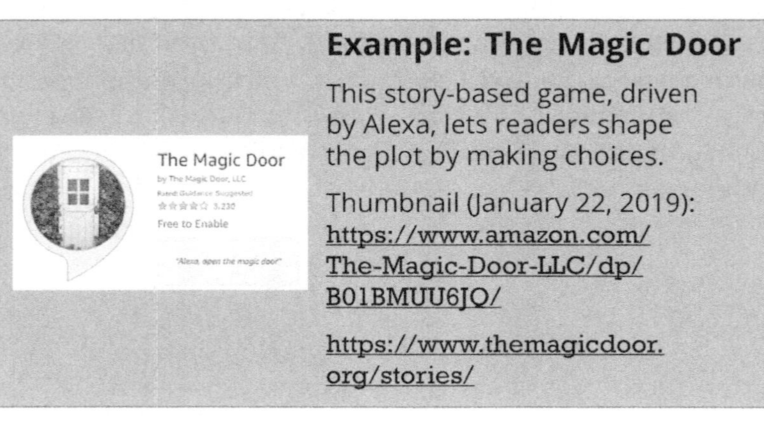

Example: The Magic Door

This story-based game, driven by Alexa, lets readers shape the plot by making choices.

Thumbnail (January 22, 2019): https://www.amazon.com/The-Magic-Door-LLC/dp/B01BMUU6JQ/

https://www.themagicdoor.org/stories/

Alexa Skills are not limited to particular books. The examples above are just a glimpse of what is possible in fiction by bringing stories to Alexa in an engaging, interactive way.

Application

There are numerous practical applications when it comes to promoting your book on Alexa. Amazon Alexa makes it easy to create a skill for non-developers as well, by using Alexa Skill Blueprints (https://blueprints.amazon.com/). You can create quizzes, games, stories, and much more. Developers can even work with in-app purchases that allow customers to buy your ebook on Amazon Kindle through Alexa.

Another very promising, largely untapped field is the re-use of existing audiobooks (and podcasts) on Alexa. Opportunities are rapidly expanding! To get started, I suggest visiting Alexa Skill Blueprints and exploring the options. Make sure you also read up on the latest developments and best practices. One example of low-hanging fruit is to simply take advantage of what Alexa can already do with Kindle books: read your book aloud.

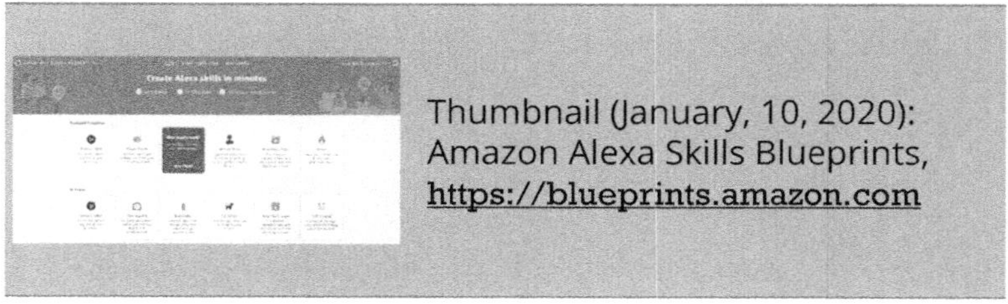

Thumbnail (January, 10, 2020): Amazon Alexa Skills Blueprints, https://blueprints.amazon.com

The most critical step in using Alexa Skills is being proactive about promotion. Unfortunately, if you publish a skill today without any marketing, the chances of someone finding it are slim. Like any other product on the internet, it needs to be promoted. If you are going to publish an Alexa skill to promote your book, make sure you already have an audience or marketing steps in place. If your skill becomes popular, the rewards can be high.

Resources

- How to market Alexa Skills: https://blog.hubspot.com/marketing/alexa-skills-marketing
- Ways to increase your Amazon Alexa audience: https://medium.com/effct-voice/7-awesome-ways-to-increase-your-amazon-alexa-audience-right-now-fb22040ba20d
- How to promote your Alexa skill: https://onlim.com/en/how-to-promote-your-amazon-alexa-skill/
- The 60 most useful Alexa skills of 2020: https://www.lifewire.com/alexa-skills-4126799
- Publisher Capstone to bring children's book bundles to Alexa subscribers: https://www.publishersweekly.com/pw/by-topic/childrens/childrens-industry-news/article/79505-capstone-brings-children-s-book-bundles-to-alexa-subscribers.html

TACTIC 5
AFFILIATE MARKETING

Description

Affiliate Marketing starts with a mindset—a mindset of looking further than your own nose (and your products) and imagining things from the client's perspective. How can your clients get the best possible value?

This mindset changes your whole approach. You automatically start noticing the best products of other marketers and thinking about how to incorporate them when offering your own products, giving advice, or interacting with other people.

Luckily, the internet has made it relatively easy to get little financial rewards for recommending others' products and making referrals. That is what affiliate marketing is all about.

For authors and publishers, affiliate marketing starts with Amazon. When you become an Amazon affiliate, you add links on your personal website that will lead your audience to useful products on Amazon. You can, of course, promote others' products, but you can also link to your own books! When someone follows a link and makes a purchase, you make money.

But if you are a business-minded author, affiliate marketing does not need to stop with Amazon. Audible also has a fantastic affiliate program and skilled marketers.

One caveat: This tactic works best for authors and publishers with an established audience since affiliate marketing requires substantial site traffic to really become profitable. So, make sure you have already built an audience before investing too much time in an affiliate marketing strategy.

Examples of Success

Example: A. D. Starrling

Author A. D. Starrling uses Amazon affiliate links to send readers from her webpage to her books. The string of text at the end of the URL (right image, highlighted for illustration) shows that an affiliate tag has been placed.

See affiliate links to her popular book series: https://www.adstarrling.com/division-eight/

Thumbnail (February 20, 2020): https://www.adstarrling.com/division-eight/

Debbie Drum Made $4,154 with a single Promotion!

"My subscribers are loving Dave's Tool! It is one of the best Kindle research tools on the market because Dave uses his expert SEO knowledge and brings it to books. Highly recommended to promote for sure!!"

Example: Debbie Drum

Debbie Drum, the face behind the popular review software Book Review Targeter and bestselling author of Read Better, Faster, is also a power affiliate marketer. She regularly shares others' products in her newsletter. Sometimes a single newsletter brings her thousands of dollars in affiliate commissions.

Thumbnail (January 21, 2020): https://publisherrocket.com/affiliate-program/

Application

- There is a simple first step if you currently do not have much traffic: sign up for Amazon Affiliates and use the affiliate link to send readers to your own book. You will begin earning a little commission.
- Next, use the Amazon affiliate link whenever you are promoting others' products on your website. Visit https://affiliate-program.amazon.com/ to get started.
- If you have an audiobook on Audible published through ACX, make sure you look at their Bounty Referral Program. You can make as much as $75 every time someone gets an Audible membership because they bought your audiobook through your referral link.
- Tips for pro marketers:
- Check out popular affiliate networks like Clickbank, which enable you to do even more.
- Reach out to related businesses and strike a deal—see if they are willing to collaborate through newsletter swapping, social media mentions, or direct promotion of your books and products.

Resources

- How To Guide: Affiliate Marketing: https://www.youtube.com/watch?v=eJkqtLPymQs
- Amazon Affiliate Marketing for Beginners: https://www.youtube.com/watch?v=kMZ92_jzhO0
- Why You Should Be an Amazon Affiliate If You Are an Author: https://justpublishingadvice.com/why-you-need-to-be-an-amazon-affiliate-if-you-are-an-author/

TACTIC 6
TRANSLATIONS AND NEW FORMATS

Description

So, you have published a book that sells. Congratulations! Now what is your next target?

Selling it as often as possible, no doubt. You want to double down on sales and get an edge in the market. But what is the best strategy?

Oftentimes it is creating new formats and translations. Compared to the labor involved in creating totally new books and products, it is easy to make a new iteration of something you have already had success with. Some examples would be turning a paperback book into an ebook, a print book into an audiobook, or an English bestseller into Spanish, German, or French. These are low-hanging fruit.

Moreover, if you use a freelancer platform like Upwork or Fiverr, you can keep your costs down by working with freelancers or agencies that offer more competitive pricing. Some will create translations or new formats of your book for only a few hundred dollars.

Examples of Success

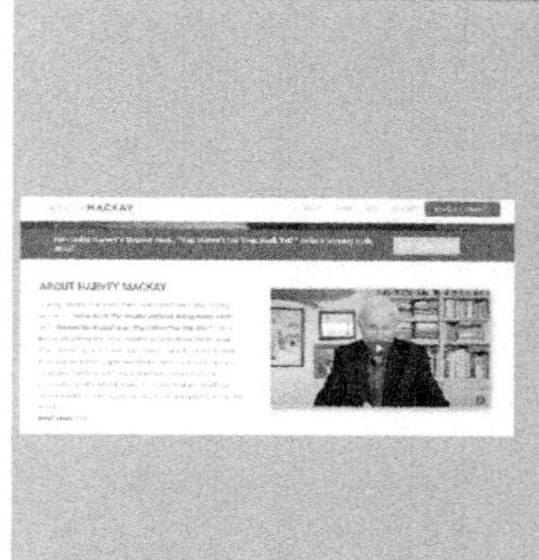

Example: Harvey Mackay

Bestselling authors like Harvey Mackay have made huge profits from translations. According to Mackay's website, "Harvey's books have sold 10 million copies worldwide, been translated into 46 languages and have sold in 80 countries."

Thumbnail (January 21, 2020): https://harveymackay.com/

Example: Patrick McKeown

Successful Irish writer and medical practitioner Patrick McKeown turned his bestseller Close Your Mouth into an audiobook. The new version immediately opened a powerful income stream, attracting customers who preferred an audio format to reading.

Thumbnail (January 21, 2020): Audible https://www.audible.com/author/Patrick-McKeown/B006X1OD3U

Application

Creating a new format for your book—e.g., audiobook, hardcover, paperback, or ebook—is remarkably easy through Amazon's self-publishing services. Translating your book into another popular language can also tap into an untapped audience, bringing in new profits (see below for resources on translation).

Resources

- How to Get Your Book Translated: https://kindlepreneur.com/book-translation/
- How to Make an Audiobook Step-by-Step: https://self-publishingschool.com/creating-audiobook-every-author-know/

TACTIC 7
KICKSTARTER BOOK FUNDING

Description

Kickstarter is a crowdfunding platform with enormous potential for authors and publishers—but it is often overlooked. Use Kickstarter's publishing section to create amazing projects, pre-fund your book, and implement a smart pre-order strategy.

Kickstarter provides a great model of "lean publishing," or publishing that does not require huge capital or a lengthy, complicated process to get your book into the hands of readers. It also offers significant advantages over the traditional publishing model. For example, you can share your ideas with followers, build a fanbase early, plan a promotional campaign, and get feedback on the development of your book before you even write a single chapter. The examples in the section below became publishing sensations on Kickstarter, raising hundreds of thousands of dollars from tens of thousands of supporters.

Check out kickstarter.com and browse other book projects to see what is possible. The support you get while writing your masterpiece could be priceless.

Examples of Success

Example: Hello Ruby

Hello Ruby is a children's book that teaches the basics of programming in a fun and engaging way. As the screenshot above shows, author Linda Liukas raised far more than her stated funding goal from enthusiastic backers

Thumbnail (January 24, 2020): Linda Liukas, Hello Ruby, https://www.kickstarter.com/projects/lindaliukas/hello-ruby

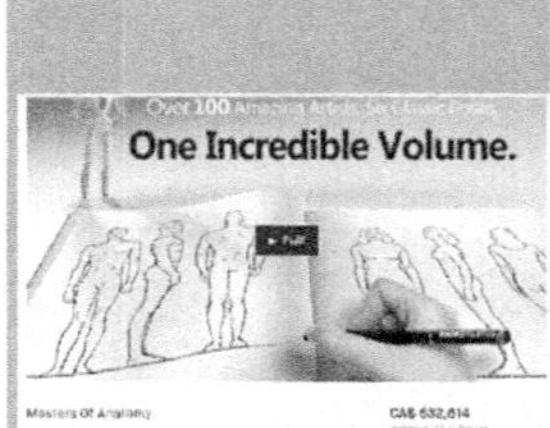

Example: Masters of Anatomy

Masters of Anatomy is
a collaborative book by dozens of artists, designed to be a reference work for modern illustrators and comic book artists. As you can see from the funding bar (above), the idea was wildly popular.

Thumbnail (January 24, 2020): Masters of Anatomy, Master of Anatomy: The Ideal Male and Female, https://www.kickstarter.com/projects/1302528630/masters-of-anatomy

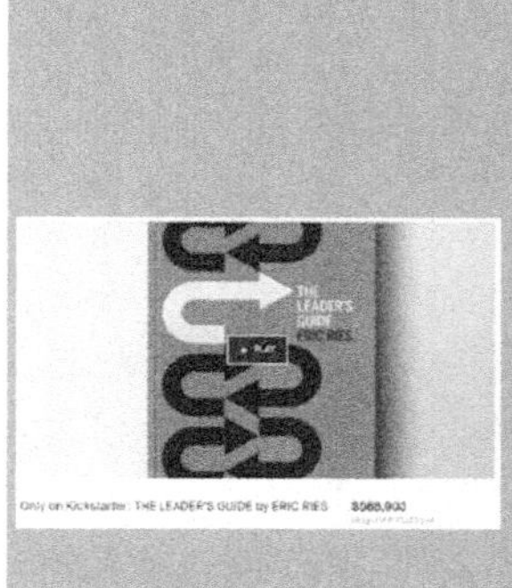

Example: The Leader's Guide

Entrepreneur and author Eric Ries built on his successful "Lean Startup" principles to launch a book project on Kickstarter. The pitch was well received by thousands of business leaders who had benefited from Ries's ideas.

Thumbnail (January 24, 2020): Eric Ries, The Leader's Guide, https://www.kickstarter.com/projects/881308232/only-on-kickstarter-the-leaders-guide-by-eric-ries

Application

Publishing on Kickstarter can save you lots of time, money, and energy. Publish the lean way and find out early if your target audience is interested in your book (or not). They will let you know through their funding support. Similarly, use Kickstarter to test your marketing approach and identify what resonates with your prospective readers. Build an audience early so you can hit the ground running with your book release.

Resources

- 8 Lessons for Launching Your Book with Kickstarter: https://scribewriting.com/8-lessons-for-launching-your-book-with-a-kickstarter-and-raising-25000/
- Creator Handbook: https://www.kickstarter.com/help/handbook. How does my project become a Project We Love?: https://help.kickstarter.com/hc/en-us/articles/115005135214-How-does-my-project-become-a-Project-We-Love-

TACTIC 8
CIALDINIFY YOUR BOOK

Description

When it comes to attracting and converting potential readers, few things matter more than your book offers or book descriptions. They need to be awesome. Every word adds spice to the "dish," making the content appealing to prospective buyers.

I take my ingredients for spicing up offers and book descriptions from well-known psychologist Robert Cialdini. His classic book on persuasion and influence describes 6 principles: reciprocity, consistency, social proof, liking, authority, and scarcity. (A seventh principle, "unity," was added in 2016.) I personally use these principles like salt and pepper in my own marketing. Taken together, they are a powerful arsenal for any marketer.

Check out the examples of Cialdini principles in action below and read my tips for how you can season your own marketing with these powerful persuasion tactics.

Examples of Success

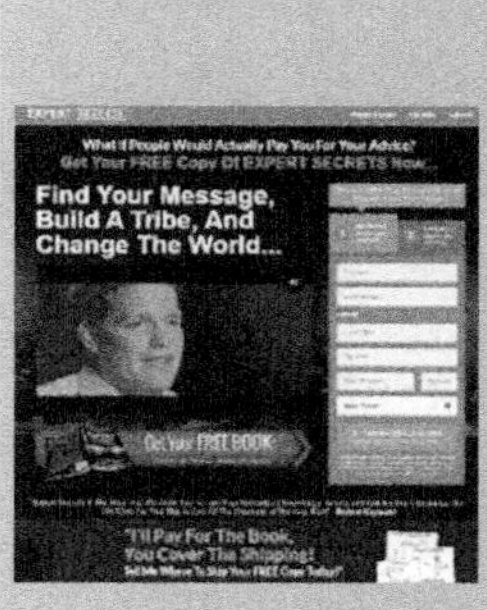

Example (plus a quick exercise):

The book sales page of Expert Secrets by Russell Brunson: How many of Cialdini's principles can you find?

Thumbnail (January 30, 2020): https://expertsecrets.com/freebook

Solution: If you look over the whole sales page, you'll see that Russell actually uses all of Cialdini's principles. In the screenshot above, he uses reciprocity (offering a free book), social proof (providing a testimonial), and authority and liking (with a video).

Example: Bad Blood: *Secrets and Lies in a Silicon Valley Startup* by John Carreyrou

This Amazon sales page uses credibility (listing awards) and authority ("prize-winning journalist") heavily to create a compelling book description and subsequent offer.

Thumbnail (January 30, 2020): Amazon, https://www.amazon.com/Bad-Blood-Secrets-Silicon-Startup-ebook/dp/B078VW3VM7

Application

Find my concrete applications for each Cialdini principle below.

Principle	Application
Reciprocity	◆ Give your readers something valuable (for free) first to trigger "reciprocity" in return (this can even be used in descriptions by sharing a valuable insight or quote early on in your book description or offer). ◆ Before making your offer, tell your readers what you've already done for them (this works well if you've already provided value, e.g., with the delivery of a lead magnet).
Consistency	◆ Get your readers to commit by signing up or reading part 1 of your series. ◆ Remind your readers of the specific goals your book can help them with ("You want to reach X, so read the book").
Social Proof	◆ Use testimonials and reviews to highlight what other readers liked about your book.
Liking	◆ Present yourself, as the author, in the best possible light. Use pictures/videos on Author Central where you're on a stage. Share audience numbers, like number of YouTube subscribers. Show reviews of your work by popular, respected figures.

Principle	Application
Authority	• Make sure your offers, book descriptions, and author biography include details that establish your credentials, experience, and recognition. What makes you qualified to write this book?
Scarcity	• Give your readers a sense of urgency and priority. Limit your offer in some way to incentivize engagement—for example, through an early-bird bonus for the first 100 readers.
Unity	• Connect with your readers on a deeper level by creating a shared identity around your book and subject—e.g., based on location, traits, personal interests, or challenges.

Resources

- Robert Cialdini. Influence: The Psychology of Persuasion (1984): https://www.amazon.com/Influence-Psychology-Persuasion-Robert-Cialdini/dp/006124189X
- Cialdini's 7th Persuasion Principle: Using Unity in Online Marketing: https://cxl.com/blog/cialdini-unity/
- How to Use Cialdini's 6 Principles of Persuasion to Boost Conversions: https://cxl.com/blog/cialdinis-principles-persuasion/
- Dr. Robert Cialdini: The Psychology Powering Influence and Persuasion [podcast]: https://guykawasaki.com/dr-robert-cialdini-the-godfather-of-influence/

TACTIC 9
PERMAFREE EBOOK

Description

Driving traffic from a book to a webpage is a potent way to grow your audience. Tactic #9 uses a related tool: offering a free ebook as a magnet for readers.

Free ebooks are not a new concept in and of themselves. But as with so many things, it is all about context. When you offer a free ebook on a platform where content is not usually free—e.g., through a book retailer like Amazon, or as an exclusive download on a file-sharing website—perceived value for readers increases. If you can lead them from an ebook to your webpage, you will boost site traffic and ultimately your sales.

The examples below show several ways you can leverage this tactic.

Examples of Success

The core idea in examples 1 and 2, below, is offering a free ebook / print book, or a "Look Inside" bonus (often an exclusive or limited time offer), in order to drive traffic to the author's website, combined with upsells in the back.

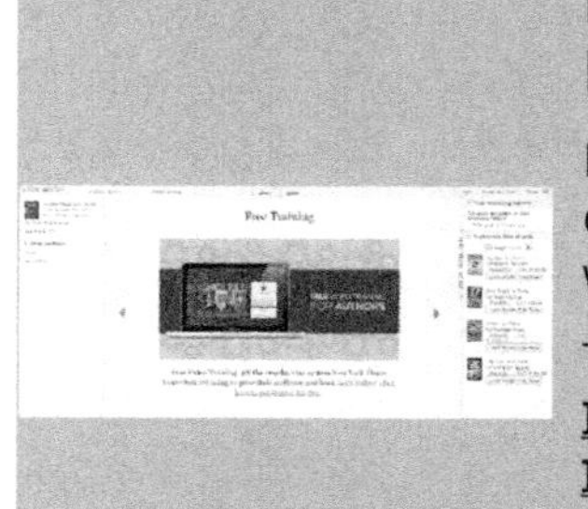

Example: Nick Stephenson, Reader Magnets

Drive traffic from a permafree ebook on Amazon to your website.

Thumbnail (February 20, 2020): https://www.amazon.com/Reader-Magnets-Platform-Marketing-Authors-ebook/dp/B00PCKIJ4C

Example: Tim Ferriss, "4-Hour Chef"

Use BitTorrent to generate interest in a special pre-release package.

Thumbnail (February 20, 2020): https://now.bt.co/bundles/651c-d5ae832b9607eb35b394708b-f8c5c5245f5a0573a64e93c4e-b87364eeeae

Example: Russell Brunson, The Marketing Secrets Blackbook

Brunson uses a free ebook to build authority and drive traffic to ClickFunnels, his software company and upsell service.

Thumbnail (February 20, 2020): https://marketingsecrets.com/blackbook

Application

- Offer readers a free ebook by distributing it free of cost to online book retailers. Stores like Apple and Kobo accept permafree ebooks. Although Amazon does not accept permafree ebooks at the moment, until recently it supported price matching, meaning that if your book is set to $0.00 on another major bookseller's website, Amazon will set its price to $0.00 to match.

- Alternatively, make Permafree ebooks a key part of your funnel strategy, to draw readers from the ebook to your personal webpage. Another way to do this is to bypass online book retailers. Instead, simply upload your ebook as a PDF to your webpage. Google search engines favor PDFs, and you might be surprised at how many hits your book gets through basic Google searches. Of course, it helps if you already have a core audience, and your book should have an SEO-smart title.

- If you create an exclusive limited time offer, prospective readers are even more likely to visit your webpage to take advantage of the free ebook.

- If you use the popular Kindle Direct Publishing (KDP) on Amazon, you can also enroll in KDP Select and run a "Free Book Promotion" for up to 5 days to make your book available to readers at no cost during that period.

Resources

- Get more insights from my presentation "Book Sales Funnels," available through the link below: https://docs.google.com/presentation/d/e/2PACX-1vTrL-nmehyAlIMK-w92wR-GHKDuzJQ272UJNAwtMFqb6nAwWeohA24OmfgkuUoP0S3Afg-z0KGTSrGV/pub?start=false&loop=false&delayms=3000
- Making my Book Free on Amazon and Other Book Stores: https://loganbrookfield.com/2019/03/making-my-book-free-on-amazon-and-other-book-stores/
- How to Build Your Marketing List Through the Amazon Kindle Store: https://www.crazyegg.com/blog/build-list-through-amazon/

TACTIC 10
THE KILLER BOOK COVER TACTIC

Description

Even though we all know the old saying, we cannot help judging books by their covers. Typography, title, and design send a powerful message to our brain, quickly telling us whether a book is worth our time—or not. For us authors and publishers, it is crucial to design a cover that will make readers want to see what is inside and ultimately buy the book. Designing a good cover can be hard, but you can succeed by applying the "magic book cover formula" to create a killer book cover.

Magic Book Cover Formula:
Genre Match + Title/Visual Match + Benefits + Unique Twists = Resulting Wow Effect

---

The four things you need to keep in mind are "genre matching," "title matching," "communicating benefits," and "uniqueness to stand out." I will explain each of these through examples below.

In the end, your cover should survive the test question, "Is my cover a killer book cover? Is my cover truly awesome?" If you can answer yes, you have done a great job.

Examples of Success

Example: Classic Business Book Designs (Cover/Genre Matching + Benefits)

Note the large title fonts and the sparing use of background images in these business covers. There's also a heavy focus on communicating the benefits of the book, something that's super important for non-fiction books

Thumbnail (February 20, 2020): https://www.amazon.com/Best-Sellers-Kindle-Store-Business-Investing/zgbs/digital-text/154821011/ref=zg_bs_nav_kstore_2_154606011

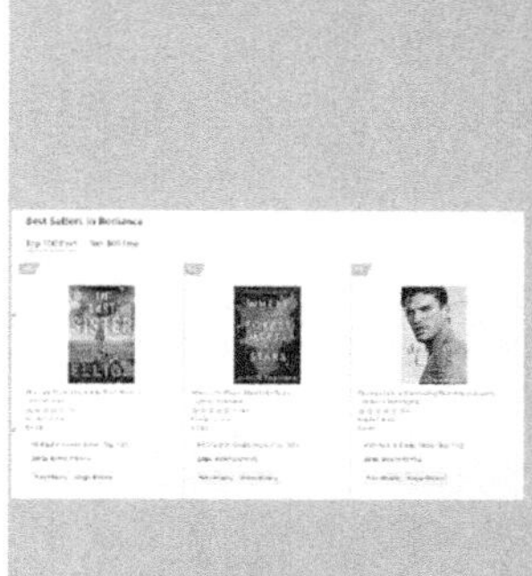

Example: Classic Romance Book Designs (Cover/Genre/Title Matching)

These romance covers all use subtle, warm imagery. Glendy Vanderah's Where the Forest Meets the Stars, especially, shows brilliant title/cover matching. The cover stands out. It's unique.

Thumbnail (February 20, 2020): https://www.amazon.com/Best-Sellers-Kindle-Store-Romance/zgbs/digital-text/158566011/ref=zg_bs_nav_kstore_2_154606011

Example: Classic Mystery, Thriller & Suspense Book Designs (Cover/Genre Matching)

A pattern in the Mystery, Thriller & Suspense bestseller covers above is big-font author names and mysterious imagery. Dean Koontz's In the Heart of the Fire also shows magnificent title/ cover matching—there's no mistaking what kind of book it is, and the cover itself isn't like to be confused with others. It has a unique twist.

Thumbnail (February 20, 2020): https://www.amazon.com/Best-Sellers-Kindle-Store-Mystery-Thriller-Suspense/zgbs/digital-text/157305011

Finally, see below two examples of covers with a unique twist.

Phil Knight's *Shoe Dog* clearly stands out by using the iconic Nike sign on the cover.

Thumbnail (February 20, 2020): https://www.amazon.com/Shoe-Dog-Memoir-Creator-Nike-ebook/dp/B0176M1A44

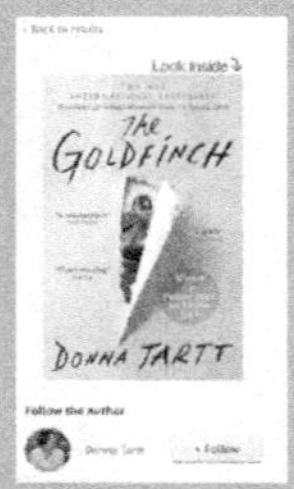

Donna Tartt's *The Goldfinch* jumps out by adding a 3-D element to the cover.

Thumbnail (February 20, 2020): https://www.amazon.com/Goldfinch-Donna-Tartt-ebook/dp/B00C74SHRK

Application

Apply the magic book cover formula to your book. Make sure it has the following four qualities:

1. Genre Match. First, a book's cover should clearly communicate the genre it belongs to. If you browse bestsellers in your genre, you'll notice consistent aesthetic trends. Your book should follow suit. By matching the main design elements of the genre—like trim size, fonts, and visuals—you not only accurately meet readers' expectations but also align with proven selling indicators for your type of book. Bestselling how-to books always look crisp, current, and straightforward. Bestselling romance novels always look dreamy, intimate, and inviting. If you want readers to open your book, it is wise to match the cover with the genre.

2. Visual/Title Match. You will want to carefully match your visuals with your title. Authors know that the title should reflect the book's contents, but equally important is to make sure the title and the cover design are in harmony. Take this book, for example: Book Sales Explosion. If I had used an image of something calm or peaceful, not something explosive, it would have miscommunicated the idea behind the title. That kind of mismatch can be jarring, ultimately turning away prospective readers. So, when you are designing your cover, consider whether your title and your visuals are really saying the same thing.

3. Communicating Benefits. Make sure your book communicates what is in it for readers. Title and subtitle matter the most in this, but the overall book design also plays an important role. Adding credibility to covers also conveys the benefits to readers. You can do this by adding powerful testimonials from established authors and professionals, and by displaying on the cover the awards and achievements your book can already claim.

4. Uniqueness. Outstanding covers have one element that makes them unique. Find the one element that will make your cover unique and add it. Often this one unique element has a profound impact on your book's performance.

A final tip is to check out the bestsellers in your genre on Amazon. Pay attention to trends in the covers, such as color scheme, fonts and font size, visuals, how the author's name appears, and the interplay between text and image. Now go back to your cover draft: how does it compare to the bestsellers? Consider the design elements as well as the title. Make sure everything matches!

In the end, you need to be able to look at your book cover and say it is awesome. It is a simple but effective test!

Resources

- The Impact a Book Cover Has on Sales: https://en.99designs.at/blog/tips/impact-book-cover-design-on-sales/
- How to Design a Book Cover Based on Its Genre: https://blog.flipsnack.com/how-to-design-a-book-cover-based-on-its-genre/
- The Complete Guide to Choosing Your Book Cover Font with Examples: https://blog.publishdrive.com/book-cover-font-guide/

TACTIC 11
IRRESISTIBLE BONUS OFFERS

Description

Every pro marketer knows that one of the best things you can do to sell your book is make an irresistible offer.

Ideally your book will already be irresistible—but competition is fierce. You might be up against dozens or even hundreds of books in your category, and it can be difficult to stand out and show the value your book offers.

That is where the irresistible bonus offer comes in, adding value to the book purchase for prospective buyers and giving you a competitive edge. Classic examples of irresistible bonus offers are companion courses, included memberships, and bonus ebooks.

It is important not only to have an irresistible bonus offer but also to feature this prominently in your first few pages and in your book descriptions at online retailers like Amazon.

Examples of Success

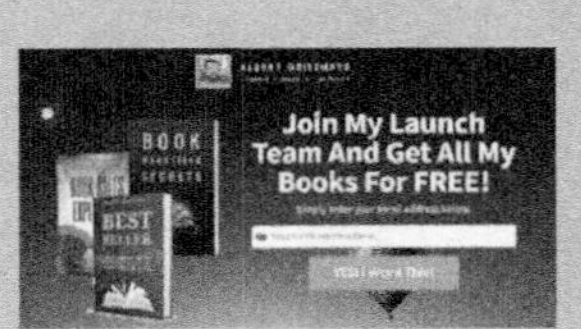

Example: Albert Griesmayr landing page

You can use a landing page to create an enticing offer. I did this by offering a free read of my books to the first 1,000 persons who joined my book launch team.

Thumbnail (February 10, 2020): https://www.albertgriesmayr.com/launch-team

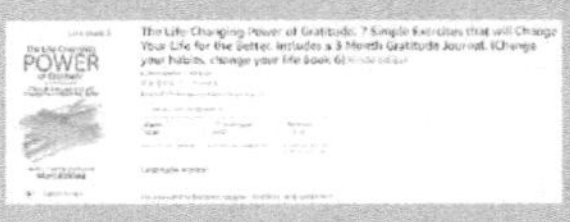

Example: Amazon sales page for The Life-Changing Power of Gratitude

Notice how the line "Includes a 3 Month Gratitude Journal" appears in the subtitle on the sales page, instantly attracting prospective buyers.

Thumbnail (February 10, 2020): https://www.amazon.com/Life-Changing-Power-Gratitude-Exercises-Journal-ebook/dp/B07KW132ZL

Example: Amazon sales page for Hacking Sleep Apnea

Again, this sales page shrewdly advertises the bonus in the subtitle: "Includes Bonus 100+ CPAP Comfort Hacks."

Thumbnail (February 10, 2020): https://www.amazon.com/Hacking-Sleep-Apnea-CPAP-Hacks-ebook/dp/B01BU9U6OE

Application

- Brainstorm ways to create an irresistible bonus offer with your book. Also, consider whether it will be sustainable and scalable—for example, you would not be able to offer free coaching calls for every reader, as this would quickly become too time-consuming and quite unprofitable.
- Some commonly used bonus offers you can use are companion courses, additional ebooks, website memberships, and adding purchasers to an exclusive email list.
- The perceived value of your bonus offer also matters. I recommend creating a bonus worth at least twice the price of the book. Companion courses become highly attractive for readers when you can offer content with a theoretical value of $37 or more.
- Finally, make sure your readers pay attention to your bonus offer. The best way to do this is to include it in your book description. Another good place to add it is in the first few pages of the book, since potential buyers will see this when they click Amazon's "Look Inside" preview.

Resources

- How to Sell Anything to Anyone with an Irresistible Offer: https://www.youtube.com/watch?v=AbDMNSfOY6c
- How to Craft an Irresistible Offer: https://www.digitalmarketer.com/blog/how-to-craft-an-irresistible-offer/
- How to Sell A Product — Sell Anything to Anyone with The 4 S's Method: https://www.youtube.com/watch?v=jsPYqsnJgf4

TACTIC 12
PRE-ORDER TACTIC

Description

If you want your book to hit the ground running, you should make the most of the pre-launch phase. This is the time to generate buzz, get feedback, recruit beta readers, and secure potential reviews. You can even monetize the process by getting pre-orders through online retailers like Barnes & Noble or Amazon.

This tactic has proven increasingly effective over the last few years, and with new developments at the start of 2020, it is going to become even more valuable. The two big trends are (1) Amazon extending its pre-order phase up to one year and (2) BookBub offering submissions for featured new release promotion (which have less competition than the featured discounted book deals).

Amazon's new allowance means that you can not only "claim" a future release one year in advance but also rack up pre-orders far ahead of the launch. If used correctly, it can also act as pre-funding. A good approach is to offer special pre-order packages exclusively for readers who pre-order the book.

Examples of Success

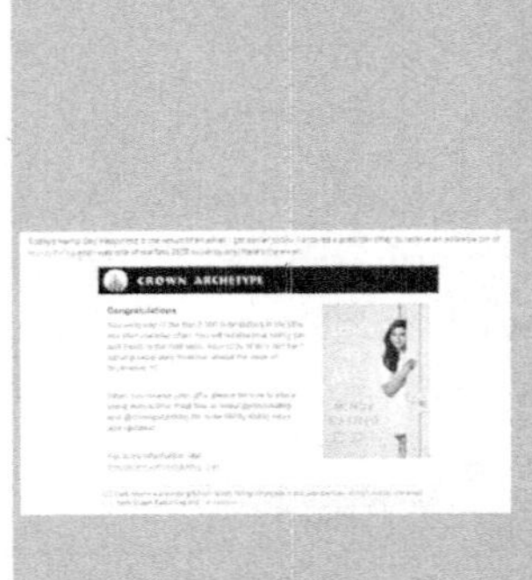

Example: Why Not Me?

Mindy Kaling's second book, Why Not Me?, was launched at #1 on the New York Times bestseller list. The pre-publication phase included a gift-with-pre-order promotion consisting of her favorite licorice and a Why Not Me? pin to readers who pre-ordered the book.

Thumbnail (February 10, 2020): Emerald City Glow, http://www.emeraldcityglow.com/2015/08/19/hump-day-happiness-preorder-gift-from-mindy-kaling/

Example: Julia Ember giveaway

Julia Ember invited readers to forward pre-order receipts by email in exchange for a simple pre-order giveaway.

Thumbnail (February 10, 2020): A Marketing Expert, https://www.amarketingexpert.com/the-13-pre-order-strategies-that-increase-book-sales/

Example: BookBub pre-order alert and campaign by author Kathryn Le Veque

Kathryn Le Veque used BookBub to get publicity and pre-orders for the first book in her popular Warwolfe series.

Thumbnail (February 10, 2020): BookBub, https://insights.bookbub.com/promoted-preorder-launch-bestselling-book/

Application

- Make your book available for pre-order on your own sales page or through online retailers (like Amazon and Barnes & Noble) long before the release date.
- Create an enticing pre-order package that will clearly reward readers who pre-order rather than waiting until the release date. You can do this by giving value right away—for example, you can send a bonus ebook, add readers to a special email list, or give them an early-bird version of the book.
- Make sure to tap the ecosystem around pre-order tactics, such as using ARC services for securing reviews or submitting your title for a BookBub new release feature.

Resources

- All about Pre-Orders: http://authornews.penguinrandomhouse.com/all-about-pre-orders/
- The 13 Pre-Order Strategies That Increase Book Sales: https://www.amarketingexpert.com/the-13-pre-order-strategies-that-increase-book-sales/
- How I Promoted a Preorder to Launch a Bestselling Book: https://insights.bookbub.com/promoted-preorder-launch-bestselling-book/

TACTIC 13
AMAZON BESTSELLER BADGE TACTIC

Description

Did you know that even though the "bestseller" label has been overused, it is still an instant credibility booster for authors and books? Why is that?

Let us admit that people use the word "bestseller" too freely. Also, Amazon's ranking algorithms and multiple Bestseller lists have created numerous "bestselling" authors. But the fact remains that most people who are not in the book selling world have no idea how this label gets applied, so they see "bestseller" status simply as a badge of success. That why "landing a bestseller" is still a superb tactic—it increases your credibility and your book's.

Now I am not advocating applying this label loosely and irrespective of your book's actual success. You still need to use it appropriately, which means writing a solid book and promoting it in the relevant categories. But used correctly on Amazon, the bestseller tactic can be a powerful one.

Amazon is still the best retailer for achieving bestseller status. The smartest approach is to enroll in Amazon's KDP Select program and reserve a free promotion period of up to 5 days. Alternatively, you can target paid lists by going for a Countdown deal. Landing a bestseller this way is more difficult, but on the other hand, you can not only make a campaign profitable but also increase your ranking on Amazon much more sustainably than with a free promotion. During the

Amazon promotion time you book 1–3 promotions with discounted ebook alert services, such as BookGorilla, Booksends, or Freebooksy. Be sure to monitor the Kindle bestseller list for free (or paid) books in your categories every couple of hours during your promotion days. If you follow these steps, you have a particularly good chance of landing a bestseller.

Examples of Success

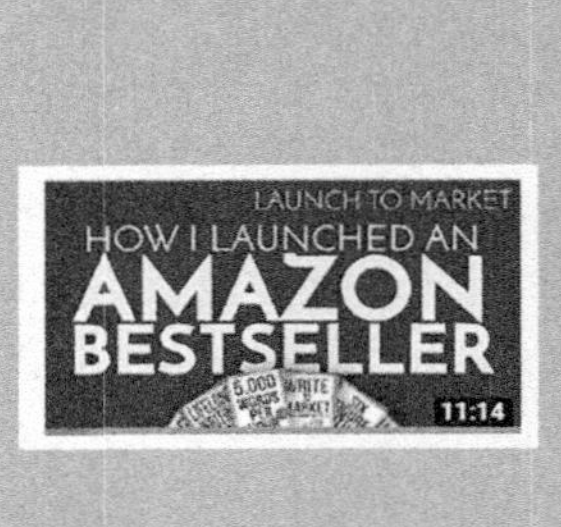

Example: Chris Fox

Learn directly from author Chris Fox how he launched an Amazon Bestseller in 2017.

Thumbnail (February 10, 2020): YouTube, Chris Fox: How I Launched an Amazon Bestseller, https://www.youtube.com/watch?v=GJqom_flVtE

Application

- Enroll in Amazon's KDP Select program and reserve a free book promotion or a Countdown deal period lasting up to 5 days. During that time book 1–3 promotions with discounted ebook alert services, such as BookGorilla, Booksends, or Freebooksy.
- Be sure to monitor the Kindle bestseller list for free or paid books in your categories every couple of hours during your promotion days.
- To get the most out of this tactic, submit up to 10 categories directly to Amazon Support (including some categories that aren't super competitive but still relevant to your book; see the tutorial in "Resources") in order to increase your chances of

reaching bestseller status by ranking high on less competitive lists.

Resources

- Book Marketing 101: How to Hit #1 on Amazon's Bestseller List: https://okdork.com/hit-1-amazons-bestseller-list/
- How to Add More Amazon Book Categories to Your Book: https://www.youtube.com/watch?v=2GO-XNA0epE
- How to Get Amazon Bestseller Badge: https://www.youtube.com/watch?v=WaFkPd_J_Ss
- How to Land the Amazon Bestseller List in Your Niche: https://medium.com/better-marketing/how-to-land-the-amazon-bestseller-list-in-your-niche-4a838b19e9ae

TACTIC 14
PINTEREST TRAFFIC GENERATION

Description

Pinterest boasts an astounding 250 million users a month. For marketers, an even more interesting statistic is that 90 percent of these users frequent the platform to make purchase decisions, and 55 percent of Pinners are specifically searching for products.[1] So not only is Pinterest a great channel for reaching your target audience, but it is also ripe for attracting buyers. Even better, Pinterest allows you to create a pin related to your book, which will drive traffic to your personal website or Amazon page.

But there is an even smarter way to market your books through Pinterest. When you use Pinterest in combination with a third-party service called Tailwind Tribes, you can team up with other authors and content creators in your niche who have a comparable number of followers to cross-promote each other's content. I will share more in the "Application" section. Tactic 14 is about turbocharging your book selling through the synergy of these two powerful tools.

1 https://blog.hootsuite.com/pinterest-statistics-for-business/.

Examples of Success

Example: Brit Poe

Adult Fantasy author Brit Poe's channel is getting 170K viewers per month by leveraging Pinterest and Tailwind Tribes.

Thumbnail (February 5, 2020): https://www.pinterest.co.uk/britpoeandco/

Example: Susan Earlham

Novelist Susan Earlham's pins get 65K viewers monthly.

Thumbnail (February 5, 2020): https://www.pinterest.co.uk/susanlearlam/

Example: Jenn Beach PA

Jenn Beach PA manages to get more than 15K viewers to her pins every month.

Thumbnail (February 5, 2020): https://www.pinterest.com/jennbeachpa/

Application

- First, set up your Pinterest business account (not a personal account) on business.pinterest.com. The business account gives you access to precious analytics on repins, clicks, and views. Fill out your profile and include your book funnel.
- Next, showcase your personality and build your author identity by creating engaging boards. Create lots of boards on the subtopics within your niche. For instance, you could create boards for all the books you have written and are going to write, for your favorite authors, and for the top 10 books you've read this year. Pin 10–20 images per board. Use relevant keywords for your niche and brand, and make sure the pins are relevant too. Images should be high-quality, descriptions should be engaging, and your pinning should be consistent and regular. However, keep in mind that you do not want to overwhelm your audience with too many pins.
- Create pins for your own content and add a watermark. Create a Pinterest-sized image (W: 1,000 px; H: 1,500 px) for each post that you want to promote to your site from Pinterest. Canva.com and other free programs offer an easy way to create images. When your pins are ready, upload them and target the relevant post on your website. Upload each of your pins to a separate board.
- If you are thinking of using Tailwind Tribes, first sign up for the free trial version. This gives you access to 5 Tribes and 30 shares per month, so you can learn the ropes and see if you want to invest in a paid subscription. A paid membership costs $7.50 per month and gives you Tribes PowerUps, boosting your exposure.

- To get started on Tailwind, fill out your profile and link to your Pinterest account. To become a member of a Tribe, click the "Tribes" feature and identify your Tribe (i.e., your niche). Use "Find a Tribe" to search for more Tribes; select one that looks like a good fit and request to join. Once accepted, you will be able to nominate which of the Tribe's content you want to share. It is reciprocal: the more you share, the more they'll share of yours. To use Tailwind effectively, aim to post 30–50 pins per day. That sounds like a lot, but Tailwind makes it easy by giving you the option to post your pins days, weeks, or even months in advance.
- Finally, to get the most out of Tailwind, you will want to track and measure. Measure the number of reins, reshapes, and pieces of content you have shared. Double down on the high-performing Tribes, and do not be afraid to leave (or stop contributing to) Tribes that are not performing. Ideally, you will want to post 50% your own content and 50% from other pinners.

Resources

- How to Skyrocket your Pinterest Traffic with Tailwind Tribes: https://www.youtube.com/watch?v=B6pJgGNxe_g&feature=emb_title
- How to Get Traffic To Your Website (Fast!) 2019: https://www.youtube.com/watch?v=Vi1RyAN8nFw
- Tailwind Tribes: A Step-by-Step Guide to Exploding Your Pinterest Traffic Fast: https://conversionminded.com/tailwind-tribes/
- Pinterest for Authors: https://jennbeachpa.com/2018/02/13/pinterest-for-authors/

TACTIC 15
BUILDING AN AUTHOR PLATFORM WITH EMAIL MARKETING

Description

Authors sometimes think that email marketing as a tactic for platform building has gone the way of the dinosaurs—if it is not already extinct, it will be soon. Nothing could be further from the truth.

Yes, email marketing has become a highly competitive, super crowded arena. But done right, it can be a tremendous way of building your platform. How do you do that? By focusing on building a platform of engaged subscribers. The rule here is that it is better to have 1,000 dedicated fans than 10,000 casual subscribers with low open rates and little interaction.

When you are building your platform with email marketing, start small and think personally. It is easy to feel intimidated by the big-name influencers and brand-name authors who have upward of 10,000 subscribers, but do not be. Getting to your first 1,000 dedicated subscribers—even to your first 100—is already a huge achievement. It is a mark many authors and marketers don't hit.

Simply put, platform building with an email list of true fans is still one of the best author tactics for 2020 and beyond.

Examples of Success

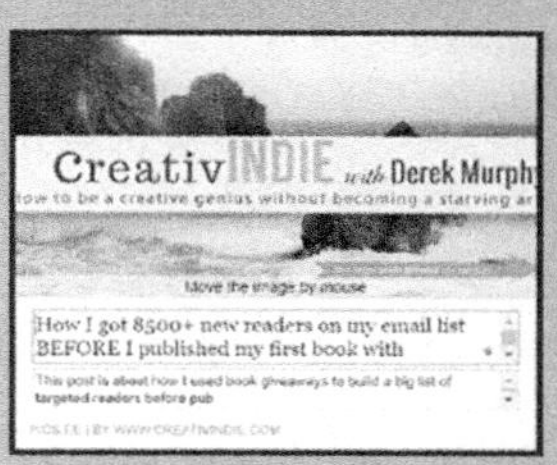

Example: Derek Murphy

Derek Murphy was able to get 8,500+ new readers on his email list BEFORE publishing his first book with giveaways.

Learn more about how he did it by visiting https://www.creativindie.com/how-to-use-kingsumo-and-rafflecopter-to-build-your-email-list-likes-and-follows-quickly-with-giveaways/.

Thumbnail (February 10, 2020): Created on PicsSee

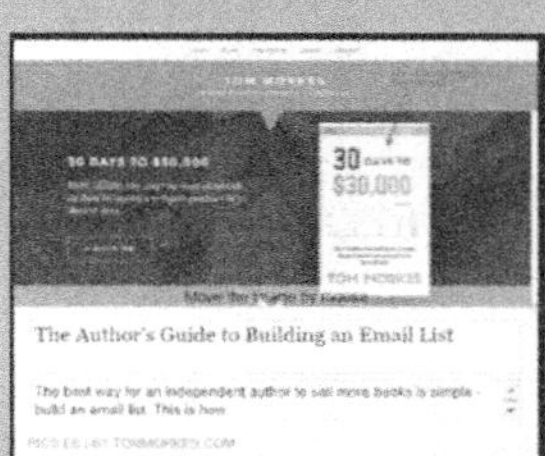

Example: Tom Morkes

Author Tom Morkes shares how he was able to build an impressive email list that helped him make sales from his books.

Learn more about how he did it by visiting https://tommorkes.com/author-email-list/.

Thumbnail (February 10, 2020): Created on PicsSee

Application

- Focus on building an author platform where you have engaged, loyal fans (ideally as email subscribers) as opposed to occasional or casual fans.
- Remember, it is more valuable to have 100–1,000 true connections, subscribers who you know personally, than 1,000–10,000 subscribers who are barely involved and where you struggle with open rates.
- Invest in an email marketing software and set up an autoresponder.
- Use viral marketing tactics like giveaways and challenges to grow your fan base more quickly and pass 1,000 subscribers.

Resources

- How to Build an Author Platform: Free Course: https://www.ingramspark.com/author-platform-course-description
- Q&A: ESTABLISHING YOUR AUTHOR PLATFORM: https://www.authorsguild.org/whats-new/seminars-member-events/business-webinars-writers/qa-establishing-author-platform/
- 0 to 1000 Email Subscribers in 30 Days: How to Grow Your Email List Fast: https://www.youtube.com/watch?v=UNvGIch-u74

TACTIC 16
COLLABORATIVE BOOK PROMOTION

Description

Being an author can feel a bit lonely sometimes, especially when it comes to book marketing. We are often fighting alone for book sales, publicity, shares, and mentions. Wouldn't it be great if we could team up with somebody? That is where Tactic 16 comes in.

Two factors make the tactic of collaborative book promotions effective:

(1) Reaching a wider, more relevant audience more quickly; and

(2) Getting recommended by a voice that people trust. Number 2 is especially important, because recommendations count heavily for authors, just like reviews.

This tactic is about tapping into the power of recommendations by engaging in various forms of collaborative book promotion, such as newsletter swaps, joint giveaways, and cross-promotion on social media.

Examples of Success

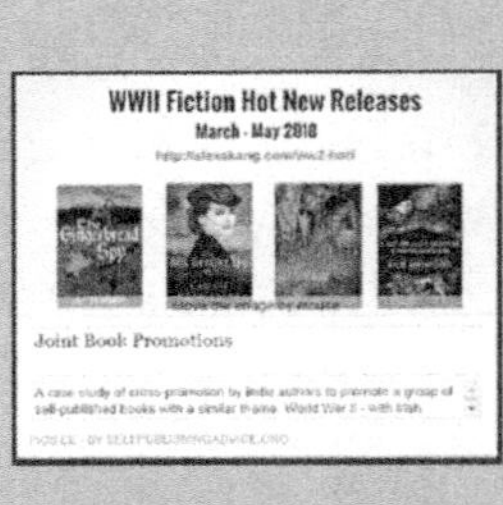

Example: JJ Toner

Irish novelist JJ Toner describes how a carefully orchestrated collaboration between indie authors of books about the Second World War truly engaged readers, with marketing benefits for all involved. The campaign helped sell 542 copies of his own book on pre-order.

Learn more about how he did it by visiting https://selfpublishingadvice.org/jj-toner-author-collaboration/.

Thumbnail (February 10, 2020): Created on PicsSee

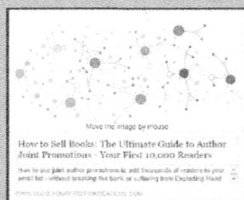

Example: Nick Stephenson

Nick Stephenson shares many examples of successful joint promotions, among them his Mystery / Thriller boxed set. He teamed up with 7 other authors to put together an anthology of short stories called Eight the Hard Way. With more than 50,000 downloads and hundreds of great reviews, this book is still getting hundreds of downloads every week, years since its release.

Learn more about how he did it by visiting https://www.blog.yourfirst10kreaders.com/how-to-sell-books-the-ultimate-guide-to-author-joint-promotions/.

Thumbnail (February 10, 2020): Created on PicsSee

Application

- Reach out to other authors in your genre to cross-promote via email (i.e., newsletter swaps) and social media.
- Boost each other's publicity by guest blogging and making guest appearances on each other's YouTube channels.
- Organize a joint giveaway to benefit each author's audience and gain exposure to a new crowd.
- Create boxed sets.

Resources

- 13 AUTHORS' STORIES: THE ULTIMATE GUIDE TO JOINT PROMOTIONS: https://www.blog.yourfirst10kreaders.com/how-to-sell-books-the-ultimate-guide-to-author-joint-promotions/
- How to Promote Your Book with Newsletter Swaps: https://www.youtube.com/watch?v=-pKnhZc9VCI
- 10 WAYS AUTHORS COLLABORATE TO PROMOTE THEIR BOOKS: https://theempoweredauthor.com/lounge-blog/how-authors-collaborate-book-marketing

TACTIC 17
VIDEO MARKETING ON YOUTUBE, AMAZON & BEYOND

Description

As authors, our medium is text, but we cannot ignore the massive influence of video on consumers' experience today. Consider these statistics:[2]

- By 2021, 82% of all internet traffic will be video traffic.
- 96% of consumers watch explainer videos to learn more about products and services.
- Adding a video to a landing page can increase conversion by as much as 80%.
- YouTube is the second largest search engine in the world, with a whopping 2 billion logged-in users per month.
- 70% of what YouTubers watch is determined by the platform's recommendation algorithm.

In other words, video is huge. Authors who embrace video to reach their audience have a big advantage in the marketplace, as many have already demonstrated by running popular YouTube channels. In the end we are all storytellers, and video is a phenomenal means of telling a story.

Tactic 17 shows you how to use video through your website, Amazon account, or YouTube channel to

2 See https://www.techsmith.com/blog/increase-conversion-rates-video/; https://www.searchenginejournal.com/seo-101/meet-search-engines/; and https://blog.hootsuite.com/youtube-stats-marketers/.

powerfully tell your story, grow your audience, and increase conversion rates.

Examples of Success

Kristen Martin, Joanna Penn, and Jeff Goins are examples of authors leveraging YouTube to promote their books—with great success. Check out their YouTube channels for inspiration on how to build your own.

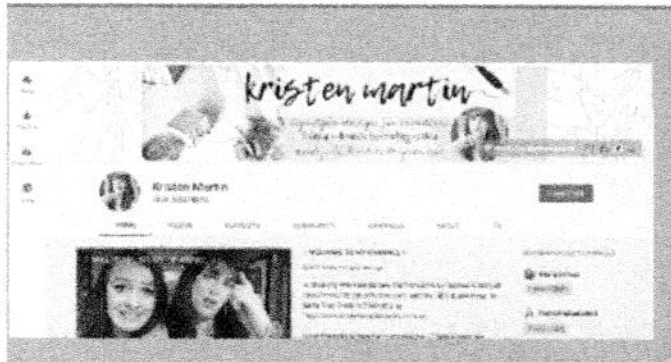

Example: Kristen Martin

Thumbnail (February 20, 2020): https://www.youtube.com/channel/UCYyy_hiZRaSLGLOn62Nc4AA

Example: Joanna Penn

Thumbnail (February 20, 2020): https://www.youtube.com/user/thecreativepenn

Example: Jeff Goins

Thumbnail (February 20, 2020): https://www.youtube.com/channel/UCXsSdIE-hbv-BwP1epYWzXg

Another great strategy for authors and publishers is to promote their books through video shorts on Amazon. See the examples below.[3]

3 Note: Brand Registry is required at the time of writing, but I suspect KDP will soon allow authors to upload videos to their sales pages.

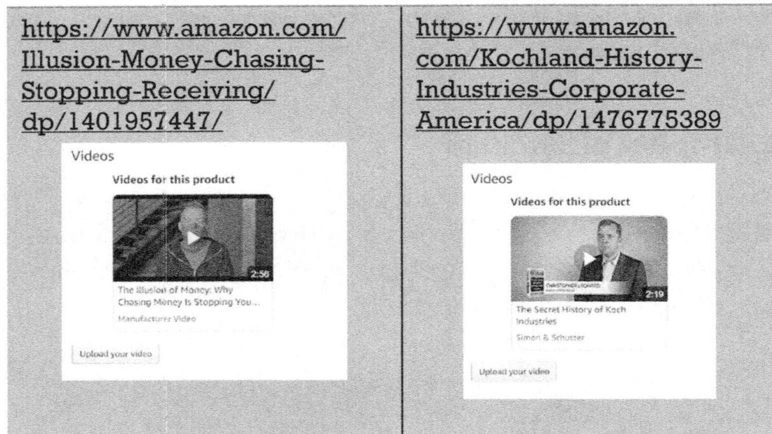

https://www.amazon.com/Illusion-Money-Chasing-Stopping-Receiving/dp/1401957447/	https://www.amazon.com/Kochland-History-Industries-Corporate-America/dp/1476775389

You can also use video on Amazon Author Central to show your audience that you have authority by sharing interviews or sequences of training sessions, as author Patrick McKeown does (see the screenshot below).

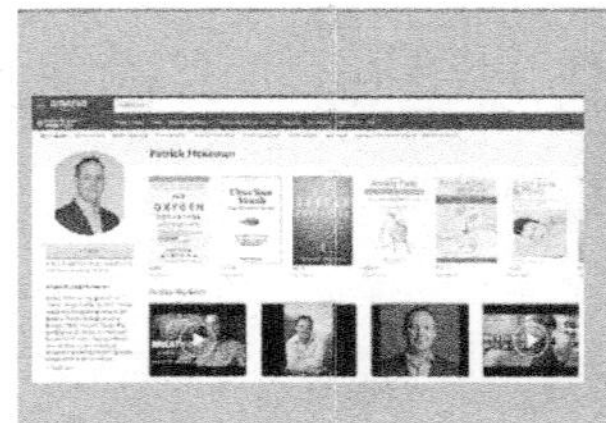

Example: Patrick McKeown

Thumbnail (February 20, 2020): https://www.amazon.com/Patrick-McKeown/e/B006X1OD3U?ref=sr_ntt_srch_lnk_1&qid=1580733651&sr=8-1

Application

Follow the lead of the authors above by creating videos for your own YouTube channel, Amazon page, or Author Central account. Video multiplies the possibilities for communication. You can tell your story in an appealing format, make a personal connection with your audience, promote products and special offers, share behind-the-scenes information (e.g., why you wrote your book), and impart special knowledge to your viewers (especially if you write nonfiction).

Many people hate seeing themselves on camera or feel awkward talking to a device. Get past that fear by starting a private YouTube channel so only you can see your performance! Record a short video of yourself talking about a random topic every day or once a week. Keep it simple, and don't worry about whether it's great. Upload it to your channel. As you do this regularly, you'll get faster, more polished, and more confident in front of the camera.

There are a few things to keep in mind if you want to put time and energy into YouTube. First, do a little market research and plan a long-term strategy. Video is competitive, and you want to be seen. Second, remember that YouTube is a search engine—that means optimizing your keywords to show up in search results. Third, make sure you upload high-quality videos in good lighting. Your phone camera is probably sufficient for your YouTube needs, but you will want to buy a microphone for better audio.

Finally, do not overthink it, and do not worry about perfection! If you put it off, you will never get to it. Just try to strike a balance between spontaneity and preparedness on camera so you come across as confident, natural, and relaxed.

Resources

- 10 Tips for Starting a YouTube Channel: https://www.adorama.com/alc/10-tips-for-starting-a-youtube-channel
- Promote Your Book with Video — Author Marketing Tips: https://www.youtube.com/watch?v=B-NwMnZxnfM
- 4 Strategies of Video Marketing for Self-Published Books: https://www.youtube.com/watch?v=U1aXDBcAP7k
- How To Use Video Marketing Like A Hollywood Director: https://www.thecreativepenn.com/2018/04/20/video-marketing/
- An Epic Guide to YouTube Video Marketing for Authors: https://booklaunchers.com/youtube-video-marketing-authors/

TACTIC 18
AMAZON SELECT PRICE PROMO + DISCOUNTED BOOK SERVICE

Description

Tactic 18 might not sound very cutting-edge if you are an experienced book marketer in 2020. However, although it is true that results today aren't quite what they were in 2013, 2014, or 2015, this tactic is still a great way of getting attention at an affordable price.

The concept is simple: You use discounted ebook alert services with a price promotion through Amazon KDP Select. See the Application section of this chapter for details.

Depending on the scale of the promotion (based on audience size and quality of the third-party service), you can easily reach 100,000 targeted readers, getting hundreds or thousands of downloads for a free book and sales for a discounted book.

This tactic can jumpstart your book sales, bring you bestseller status (as shown in a different tactic), but most importantly, boost your audience. That's why it's vital to have marketing systems—like email signup on your webpage—already in place and to ensure that your book is error-free and already has some reviews. If you have not created a way of connecting with your readers down the line, a "cold promotion" can backfire in the form of bad reviews or a wasted effort.

Examples of Success

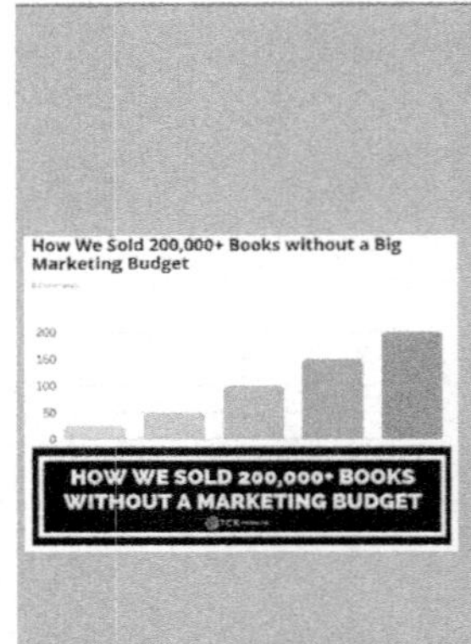

Example: Tom Corson

Tom Corson Knowles shares how his team managed to share 200,000+ copies of *Unlimited Memory*, by Kevin Horsley, through KDP Select and featured deals on BookBub. (Note: Sales started in 2014. This strategy isn't quite as dynamic today.)

Thumbnail (February 10, 2020): https://www.tckpublishing.com/how-we-sold-200000-books-without-a-marketing-budget/

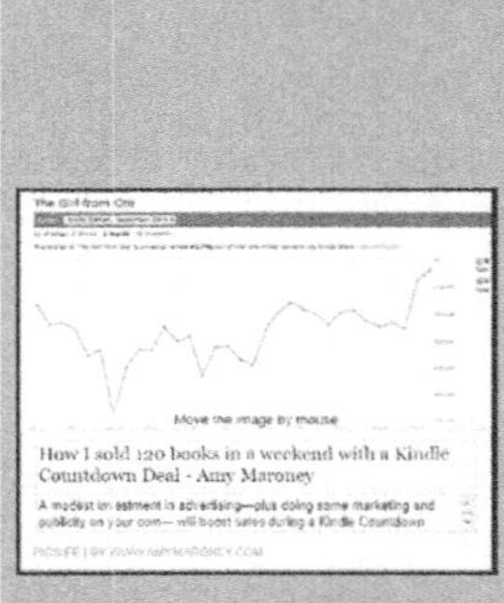

Example: Amy Maroney

Author Amy Maroney sold 120 books in a single weekend with a Kindle Countdown Deal.

Learn more about how she did it by visiting:

https://www.amymaroney.com/2017/02/25/how-i-sold-120-books-in-a-weekend-with-a-kindle-countdown-deal/.

Thumbnail (February 10, 2020): Created on PicsSee

Application

- Enroll your book in KDP Select. Make sure it's available exclusively on Amazon and nowhere else.
- Choose a price promotion (either free or countdown deal).

- Secure promotions with third-party discounted ebook alert services (list of services) during the days your book is on promo on Amazon.

Resources

- Kindle Countdown Deals: https://kdp.amazon.com/en_US/help/topic/G201293780
- Free Book Promotions: https://kdp.amazon.com/en_US/help/topic/G201298240
- KDP Select and BookBub Promotions: An Indie Author Experience: https://theseatedview.com/2019/03/kdp-select-and-bookbub-promotions-an-indie-author-experience.html
- How to Use KDP Countdown Deals — Kindle Publishing in 2020: https://www.youtube.com/watch?v=SmXRfqRAMEA

TACTIC 19
AUTHORITY BOOK PUBLISHING

Description

"Authority Book Publishing" is not directly about increasing sales. This unique tactic has to do with establishing credibility and influence and helping you reach higher-level business or career goals. Rather than merely aiming at more sales—something every author wants—you will be aiming to show your expertise in a way that enhances your image and ultimately your career.

Having a goal like this can help you straighten out your priorities and save you a lot of headache in terms of publishing and sales. Your focus will be on launching a strong book with solid content, which will appear on your webpage or social media profiles in ways that add value for readers. You might even distribute it for free in your business marketing activities.

What makes this tactic so powerful? It is that we as humans are born to follow leaders. We are conditioned to recognize authorities and pay attention to what they have to say, whether they are doctors, scholars, employers, or others in a position of superior knowledge and influence. Authors belong in that category too. Being an author still carries weight in our society. It shows that you have insight, that you are qualified to speak on a certain subject.

So, find your niche—the area where you have something special or unique to offer—and start writing. If you are still doubtful that your skills or knowledge can make you a successful author, take this little test: Would you rather buy a service from a business owner who has published a book on their industry area or one who has not? Who you go with the first? Do not underestimate the power of writing a book to establish authority!

Examples of Success

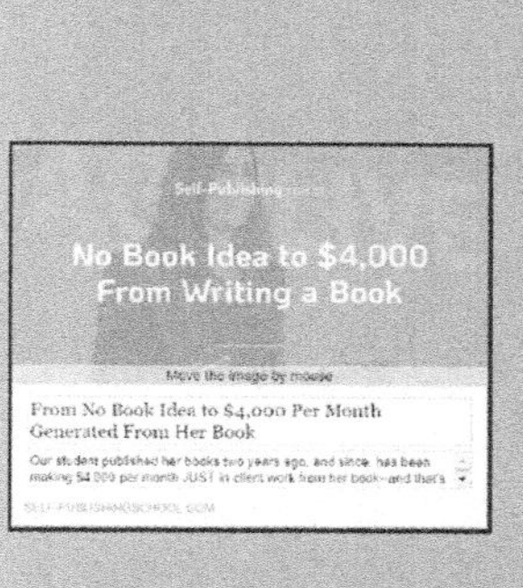

Example: Brianna Ruelas

Brianna Ruelas had no idea what to write about. But when she wrote a book about her area of expertise—navigating the music industry—she started raking in $4,000 per month from new clients who came to her for career consulting.

Learn more about how she did it by visiting:

https://self-publishingschool.com/from-no-book-idea-to-4000-per-month/.

Thumbnail (February 10, 2020): Created on PicsSee

Example: Russell Brunson

Successful entrepreneur Russell Brunson hit gold when he started the company ClickFunnels. What some people don't know is that his books played a huge part in this journey.

Learn more by watching https://www.youtube.com/watch?v=oqyIAaNkFhA.

Thumbnail (February 10, 2020): Created on PicsSee

Example: Rob Moore

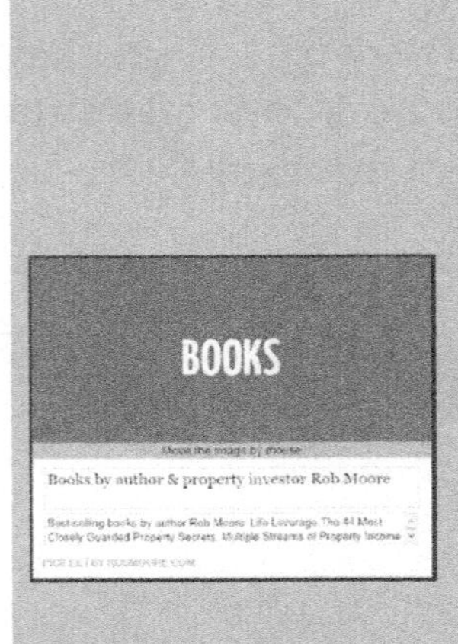

Rob Moore, an expert on property investing, built the training company Progressive Success. He's also one of the UK's leading nonfiction authors. His books feed directly into his business by attracting readers to his free weekend workshops, where, after having already invested time reading his £10 book and attended his seminar, they're more likely to commit to one of his £2,000 courses.

Find out more at https://robmoore.com/books/.

Thumbnail (February 10, 2020): Created on PicsSee

Application

Remember, this tactic is not about making quick money but about proving yourself an authority in a specific niche to "qualify leads" (i.e., attract likely customers)—leads who will buy more from you at a later stage. You invest in building your credibility now so that it pays off down the road.

At this point, you need to consider what it is you will be offering people in the end. What is your most expensive package? Personal consulting? An online course? Now, work backwards from that point. Think of the journey you're taking your audience on and map it out in reverse: start with your most valuable offer and trace your way back to your initial offering—your book.

In real time, you are going to present the book to prospective buyers (a micro-commitment on their part) and then gradually lead them to more and more expensive offers (bigger commitments). It must be a gradual process; that is the only way it will work. Imagine if we had just met and I asked you for a million dollars. You would laugh and say I was crazy. Or imagine asking someone to marry you on the first date—they would probably walk away. Similarly, you need to earn your readers' trust and commitment over time. Start with a small offer and then lead them to the more valuable offers.

That is how it works. Now you can get to writing! In Book Marketing Secrets, I talk about how your book is the star. You want to write a quality book, something people will enjoy reading and get value from. Writing can be a challenging process, but if you have built up expertise in your field, it will be much easier. You will be speaking from what you know. If you do not already have the knowledge to write a book on your subject, it is time to start learning.

Finally, some practical pointers: Your book will sit at the beginning of your book funnel at a low price, or even for free. Pitch it to people who are likely to be interested using Google ads, Facebook ads, SEO, podcasts, blogs, etc. The book funnel will act as a tripwire to qualify your leads. They are "qualified" because they've shown interest by clicking on the download button or, if the book costs something, by pulling out their credit card to purchase.

As a rule of thumb, out of a thousand people who view the book, fifty will buy. By the time those fifty have finished reading your book, you will have convinced them that you know what you are talking about. They have started to trust you, and they are now more likely to buy your more expensive offers.

Resources

- How to Write a Book to Grow Your Business: https://self-publishingschool.com/write-a-book-about-your-business/
- Do I Need a Book for My Business?: http://blog.raybrehm.com/do-i-need-a-book-for-my-business/
- 45 Marketing Experts Share Their Authority Building Strategies: https://www.authoritycontent.com/marketing/how-to-become-an-expert/
- Here's What Every Entrepreneur Should Know about Becoming an Author: https://www.forbes.com/sites/bryancollinseurope/2019/06/20/heres-what-every-entrepreneur-should-know-about-becoming-an-author

TACTIC 20
SIMPLE BUT POWERFUL AMAZON SEO

Description

Search engine optimization, or SEO, is not something we authors normally think about when publishing and marketing books. However, it is one of the most important skills an online marketer can have. SEO is critical for high keyword rankings and subsequent visibility of books online.

SEO is a vast subject, certainly too big to cover in depth in a book like this one, but I have distilled it into a basic blueprint that I share in this chapter.

Tactic 20 gives you three concrete steps for doing effective SEO on Amazon: (1) using 1–3 main keywords that have solid research volume, (2) adding those keywords to the title/subtitle/description, and (3) monitoring rankings over time to take further action.

The game plan in this chapter is simple enough for anyone to follow. It leaves out the more intricate SEO tools in the domain of pro marketers but still gives you a handle on top SEO activities.

Examples of Success

The following examples demonstrate just how big a difference good SEO can make in a book's prospects of showing up in search results. Clearly, it is important to include main keywords in the title and subtitle. By using even one keyword with search volume in your title, you already ensure success for your book due to organic traffic.

1. Results for the keywords "Oxygen" (left) and "Keto Diet" (right). It is worth noting that a novel appears in the first 10 results for "Oxygen," a highly search keyword, and the top two results for "Keto Diet" have "Keto Diet" as the first words in the title.

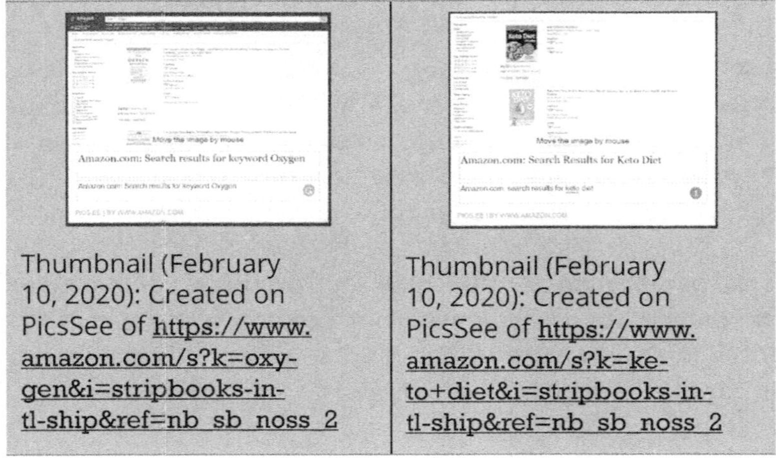

Thumbnail (February 10, 2020): Created on PicsSee of https://www.amazon.com/s?k=oxygen&i=stripbooks-intl-ship&ref=nb_sb_noss_2

Thumbnail (February 10, 2020): Created on PicsSee of https://www.amazon.com/s?k=keto+diet&i=stripbooks-intl-ship&ref=nb_sb_noss_2

2. Results for the keyword "self-publishing." There are many good books on self-publishing, but if you enter it as a keyword, you will only get results that use this word in the title.

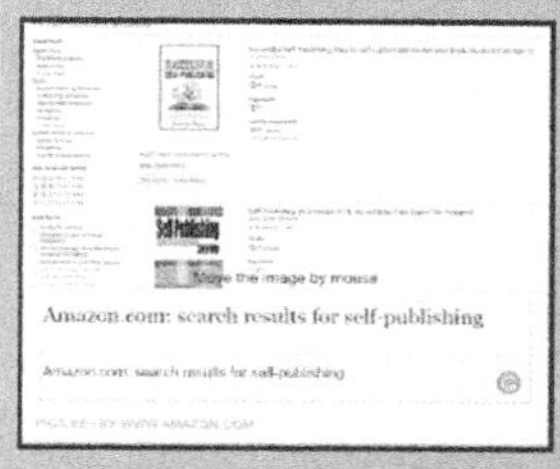

Thumbnail (February 10, 2020): Created on PicsSee of https://www.amazon.com/s?k=self-publishing&ref=nb_sb_noss_2

Application

- Use 1-3 keywords that have good search volume. Use the Google Keyword Tool and the Chrome Browser Extension of Keywords Everywhere (or the paid version of keywordtool.io) to get free information on search volume on Amazon and Google. Alternatively, you can use the paid product KDP Rocket, which also gives you estimates of Amazon search volume.

- Add those keywords to your title/subtitle/description. Title is, of course, the biggest ranking factor, followed by subtitle and then description. If you use Amazon KDP, make sure to also include your most relevant search terms in KDP's backend keywords/search terms. Please also note that each book format has a separate landing page, so make sure to fill out both and to use little variations to increase your reach.

- Monitor your book's rankings over time and take further action. Use egrow.io (free plan) to follow your rankings. Egrow allows you to monitor up to 5 keywords for free, so you can see if you rank. If your book is not showing up in searches, try using less competitive keywords.

Resources

- Amazon Ranking Hacks: https://startupbros.com/amazon-ranking-hacks/
- 21 Ways to Rank Your Products Higher on Amazon: https://www.repricerexpress.com/rank-your-products-higher-on-amazon/
- Get up to 10 Amazon Categories for Your Book: https://www.youtube.com/watch?v=2GO-XNA0epE

TACTIC 21
RUNNING AMAZON AMS ADS

Description

There are a few features that set apart Amazon Marketing Services (AMS) ads and make them superior to other advertising channels, such as Facebook, Google, or smaller ad promotions:

- They appear directly at the point of sale, targeting users with buy intent.
- They offer very transparent and simple data, making it easy for authors to assess profitability.
- They are easy to set up and less risky than, for instance, Facebook ads.

Examples of Success

Two Reedsy Case Studies (both from 2017): https://blog.reedsy.com/amazon-ads-for-authors-case-studies/

Application

- Set up a simple AMS ad campaign (sponsored product) with automated targeting, with a low daily budget.
- Set up a simple AMS ad campaign (sponsored product) with manual targeting, going for keywords and book categories.
- Check results on an ongoing basis. Assess your real profitability by only calculating your royalties (net profit) instead of total sales.
- If you run keyword-driven campaigns, remove the keywords that are not performing over time and

work on individual cost-per-click (CPC) prices for each keyword based on its performance.

Resources

- How to Double Your Book Sales with AMS Ads: https://www.youtube.com/watch?v=5TSj-GiGd2M
- Free Course for AMS ads by Kindlepreneur: https://kindlepreneur.com/ams-book-advertising-course/
- How to Find 1000's of Profitable Keywords for Your Amazon Ads in Less Than 10 Minutes: https://www.youtube.com/watch?v=b4psDxMFjbc
- Amazon Marketing Services: 20 Creative & Unique Ways to Use AMS Ads: https://self-publishingschool.com/amazon-marketing-services/

TACTIC 22
AUDIOBOOK CREATION AND AUDIOBOOK GIVEAWAYS

Description

Audiobooks are the fastest-growing content medium for publishers today. While many publishers have jumped on the bandwagon, the ratio of books (including ebooks) to audiobooks for most subjects—e.g., the Keto Diet on Amazon—is still only about 20 to 1. So, while audiobooks are a hot market, there's still truly little competition in some categories. It is a prime field for enterprising authors and publishers to get in on.

While I highly recommend publishing audiobooks, it is equally important to promote them using the right tactics. That is why this chapter deals with running Audiobook Giveaways through Audiobook Boom and garnering reviews by using dedicated services.[4]

---

4 See www.audiobookboom.com/authors and https://katetilton.com/25-ways-market-audiobook-quick-guide/.

Examples of Success

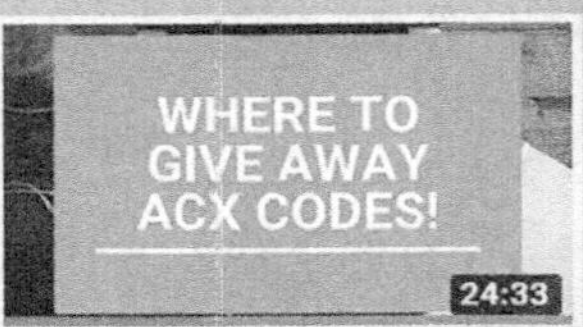

Example: Ashton Cartwright

Ashton Cartwright of Paidauthor shared his results using Audiobook promo codes and giveaways for one of his biggest clients in the contemporary romance/erotica genre in 2019 on his website. His efforts resulted in around $6,000 in extra royalties.

Thumbnail (February 10, 2020): https://youtu.be/WMhU3bWf-YI

Example: Wiley Brooks

Author Wiley Brooks ran a promotion with Audiobook Boom (January 1, 2020) and secured 3+ fresh reviews on Audible within the next 28 days.

Thumbnail (February 10, 2020): https://www.paidauthor.com/audible-or-acx-codes-and-where-to-give-them-away/

Thumbnail: Audiobook Boom Newsletter, https://mailchi.mp/audiobookboom/your-free-audiobook-boom-for-123119

Thumbnail: Audible Audiobook page, https://www.audible.com/pd/The-Next-Best-Thing-Audiobook/B0831CL9M4

Application

- Make your book available as an audiobook. I recommend using Amazon's Audiobook Creation Exchange (ACX) or Findaway Voices.
- When you publish, think "audiobook first." Do not just pass on a print/ebook manuscript to a narrator—adapt the original text or create a dedicated manuscript for an audio version.
- Get promo codes from ACX (25 in the US, 25 in the UK) or Findaway Voices (100 with Voices Plus) and run audiobook giveaways through sites like audiobookboom.com, which will share your giveaway with as many as 10K people. If you're especially tech-savvy, you can also organize your own giveaway on Facebook using Gleam.io.[5] Currently Audible even pays royalties when readers listen to your audiobook by redeeming a free code—an amazing deal!
- Get reviews by making your audiobook accessible through dedicated audiobook review submission services.
- Submit your audiobook for consideration as part of a featured deal on Chirp Books (run by Bookbub). See www.chirpbooks.com.

5 How to Run a Viral Giveaway on Facebook: https://www.youtube.com/watch?v=5tJDt5yw-z4

Resources

- 25 Ways to Market Your Audiobook: A Quick Guide: https://katetilton.com/25-ways-market-audiobook-quick-guide/
- How to Market an Audiobook: https://www.thecreativepenn.com/how-to-market-an-audiobook/
- Audible or ACX Codes and Where to Give Them Away: https://www.paidauthor.com/audible-or-acx-codes-and-where-to-give-them-away/
- Get Cookin' with New and Improved Promo Codes: https://blog.acx.com/2019/05/09/get-cookin-with-new-and-improved-promo-codes/

TACTIC 23
RETARGETING WITH FACEBOOK ADVERTISING + MESSENGER MARKETING

Description

Facebook ads have been a favorite tool of online marketers for years. Their great advantage lies in their ability to target users very specifically. However, please do not read Tactic 23 as an all-out recommendation to run Facebook ads. Without some marketing savvy, newbies can do more damage than good and end up wasting a lot of money.

Still, there are two powerful Facebook advertising tactics that I do recommend based on the results they have had for my clients. One is Facebook retargeting. The other is Facebook Messenger marketing.

To understand retargeting, it helps to realize that there are three basic types of audiences: cold, warm, and hot. Cold audiences are those seeing your content for the first time. They do not know you, do not know if they can trust you, and will not buy from you without further proof. They are still in evaluation mode. Hot audiences, on the other hand, are those who have seen your ads, purchased your products, and know your brand. They are committed.

If you are starting out as a Facebook marketer, the people you want to target (or retarget) are "warm": they are already aware of your existence and just need to be brought in. The reality is that your target readers need to see your offer—i.e., your book—many times before they will purchase.

So how do you retarget a warm audience? Fortunately, Facebook allows you to send ads to users who have previously interacted with your content in some way, even if they haven't shared their information. You can do this by installing a Facebook Pixel, an embedded code in your funnel that lets you retarget anyone who visited your website.

The second part of this tactic is using Facebook Messenger as a strategic marketing tool. Marketing on Messenger yields 10–80 times better engagement than email marketing, reporting astonishing 88% open rates and 56% clickthrough rates for certain campaigns. Facebook Messenger marketing is still new terrain, but if you can get in on it with a smart campaign (see examples below) and set up simple autoresponders through ManyChat.

Examples of Success

Example: Albert Griesmayr

I use my Facebook page as a hub for Messenger marketing. Visitors get a reward for connecting via Messenger (i.e., by sending a message), and responses are automated through ManyChat.

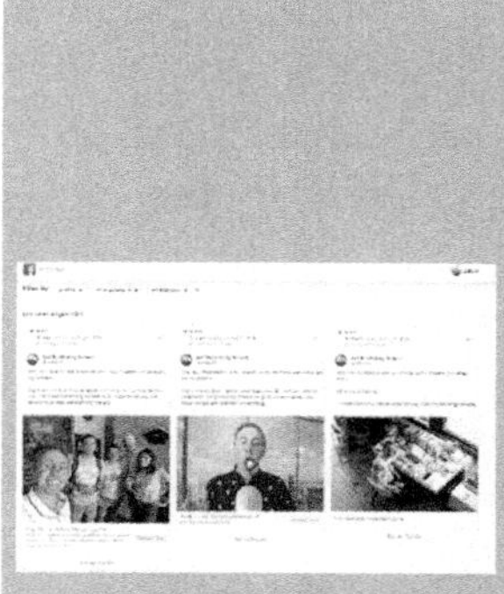

Example: Chandler Bolt

Chandler Bolt of Self Publishing School demonstrates how to retarget ads, directly addressing audiences in a way that shows they've previously visited his webpage.

Thumbnail (February 3, 2020): https://www.facebook.com/ads/library/?active_status=all&ad_type=all&country=AT&impression_search_field=has_impressions_lifetime&view_all_page_id=751114201604736

Application

- Collect data for creating a warm audience. To get started, install Facebook Pixel on your website. This is a lot easier than it sounds; you do not need a tech background or any IT experience at all. YouTube and Facebook make it simple for you to create and activate the Pixel, which will track visitors and collect essential information for building an audience profile. Once you understand who is viewing your content, you can design retargeting campaigns aimed at those users or "Lookalike Audiences."
- Learn more about Facebook Messenger marketing and ManyChat. Brainstorm creative ways to boost your audience outreach with these tools.
- There are two types of ads to be aware of: (1) Video ads are great for talking to your readers about a new book or about your writing process. You can create them simply, with minimal equipment and no

professional crew required. (See also the YouTube tactic for more information.) (2) Carousel ads feature multiple images for viewers to swipe through. You might want to showcase artwork from inside your book, or maybe you are looking to promote multiple books in a single ad. You can also make each image in the sequence a different type of ad.

- The main thing is to find what works for your genre and your specific kind of readers. Always think from the reader's perspective!

Resources

- Facebook Retargeting Ads: A Step-by-Step Guide to Sending Website Visitors on a Facebook Retargeting Journey: https://www.abetterlemonadestand.com/facebook-retargeting-ads/
- What's Working Right Now: Facebook Ads: https://selfpublishingformula.com/episode-175/
- Create and Install a Facebook Pixel: https://www.facebook.com/business/help/952192354843755?id=1205376682832142
- Facebook Messenger Chatbot Marketing: The Definitive Guide (Updated for 2020): https://www.crowdspring.com/blog/facebook-messenger-marketing-guide/

TACTIC 24
KOBO PUBLISHING

Description

Tactic 24 is a bit out-of-the-box, and that is a good thing. Since the market is so competitive, sometimes it is smart not to copy what everyone else is doing.

We all know that Amazon towers over the industry with its insanely large market share, but other retailers—like Barnes & Noble, Apple Books, and Kobo—have big audiences too. If you can dominate keywords or categories on those platforms, you can generate healthy sales there as well. In this chapter I'm focusing on the opportunity for authors on Kobo.

The Kobo Publishing Tactic can be quite beneficial for authors who aren't exclusively enrolled in KDP Select and are looking to run promotions with less competition. At the time of writing, Kobo has special promotions for books in the Romance, Science Fiction, and Mysteries & Thrillers departments.

Examples of Success

The screenshot below (circle added) gives you an overview of the different promotions you can run on Kobo. If you publish directly through the service, you have access to Kobo Promotions. It is possible you might have to contact Support to get it (as I did), but that is even better, because it means the promotions aren't a high-demand service and you won't face too much competition.

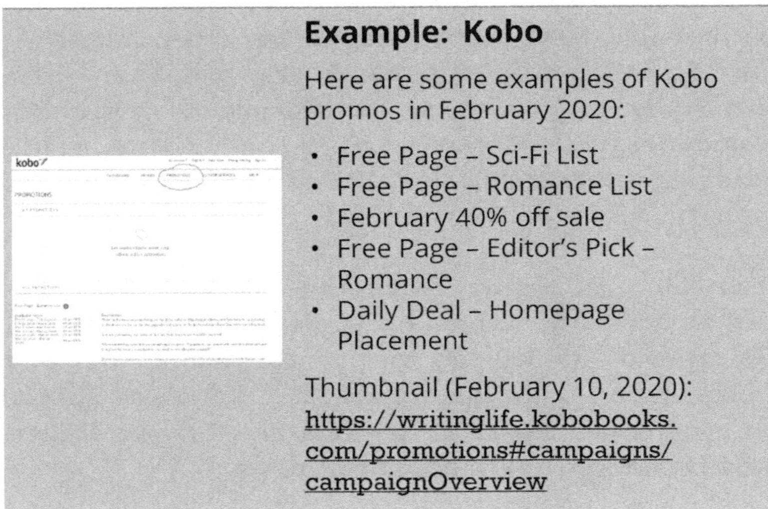

Example: Kobo
Here are some examples of Kobo promos in February 2020:
• Free Page – Sci-Fi List
• Free Page – Romance List
• February 40% off sale
• Free Page – Editor's Pick – Romance
• Daily Deal – Homepage Placement
Thumbnail (February 10, 2020):
https://writinglife.kobobooks.com/promotions#campaigns/campaignOverview
kobo
PROMOTIONS

Application

- Publish your ebook directly through https://writinglife.kobobooks.com/.
- Make sure you have the promotions tab available (if not, request access through Support).
- Pick one of the promotions, ideally within the categories where promotions are offered and can be applied for your book.

Resources

- Using Promotions to Sell More Books on Kobo: https://kobowritinglife.zendesk.com/hc/en-us/articles/360002502933-Using-Promotions-to-Sell-More-Books-on-Kobo
- Dashboard Promotions Tab: How the Money Works: https://kobowritinglife.zendesk.com/hc/en-us/articles/115002501414-Dashboard-Promotions-Tab-How-the-Money-Works

TACTIC 25
THE UPSELL PRODUCT TACTIC (INFINITE SELLING LOOPS)

Description

Here's a fact that may surprise you: in 2006, Amazon was already reporting that 35% of its revenue came directly from cross sales and upsells.

Cross sales and upsells are a crucial channel for getting profitable, especially in markets with low profit margins like the book industry. Think about the uphill battle you face trying to make a profit: you only earn a few dollars per book on royalties, then you have ad costs and truly little room for investing to make sales—and that is all apart from the costs of labor and other expenses. I am constantly working to help authors and publishers increase their profits.

Competition in the book world is growing every day, favoring marketers who already have top-ranking books, outstanding content, or the deepest pockets. Speaking of deep pockets, this is where upsells come into play. Picture marketer A, who has a profit margin of $50 from selling a paid course at the back end. Now picture marketer B, who has no upsell product and a profit margin of only, say, $2. From a raw economic standpoint, marketer A can easily outspend marketer B on paid advertising while continuing to invest more in improving his product and marketing. Of the two, marketer A clearly has the advantage.

That is why I encourage all my authors and publishers to offer upsell products, like related books, companion courses, or affiliate products. You can dramatically increase your profit margins and your room for investing and advertising.

Examples of Success

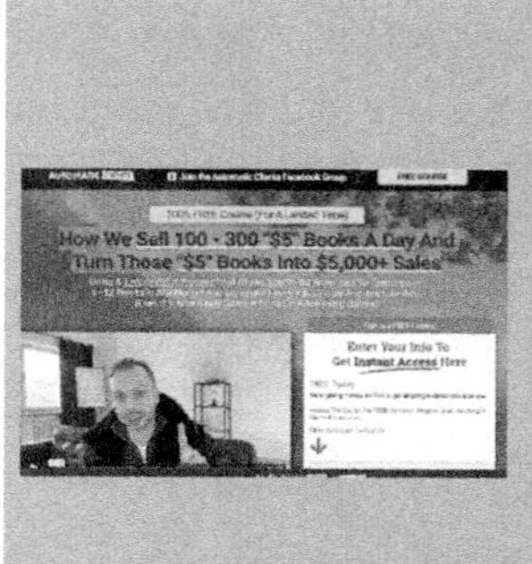

Example: Robert Neckelius

In this free course (free at the time of writing), Robert Neckelius, author of the 4-hour agency, describes how his team can sell a few hundred $5 books a day and turn over a massive profit through upsell products.

Thumbnail (February 10, 2020): https://get.automaticclients.com/access

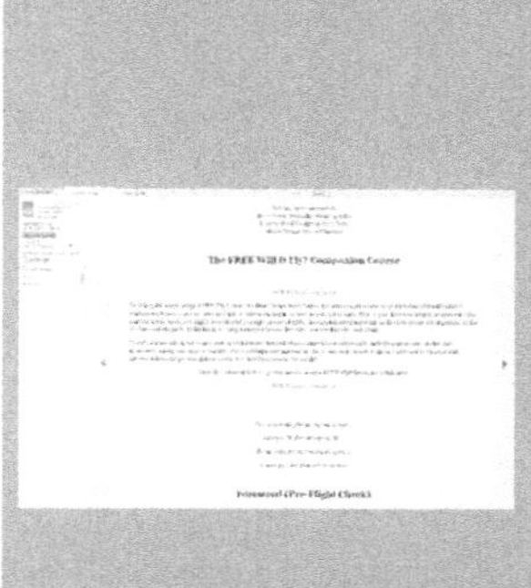

Example: Pat Flynn

Like business author Pat Flynn, you can use the first few pages of your Amazon book (visible to readers using the "Look Inside" feature) to get people to your webpage. You can also list other books at the end of your book to give readers an offer to buy more from you.

Thumbnail (February 10, 2020): https://www.amazon.com/Will-Test-Business-Waste-Money/dp/0997082305

Application

- Make a list of potential upsells relevant to your book that you would be able to deliver.

- Start with simple upsells, like affiliate links to related books or products on Amazon.
- Create your own upsell products, such as other books, companion video courses, book bundles, or coaching offers.
- Remember, you do not need to have your upsell products ready yet to start leading readers down the trail. It is just like taking pre-orders: you can create a pre-order for an upcoming book on Amazon, generating buzz and sales even if you will not be publishing it for another 12 months.
- Have the mindset of never closing the loop. Ideally, you will always have another offer for readers at stages where they would normally assume the process is closed—for example, when they've finished the book, subscribed to your email list, or sent you an email. Always give them something else. Keep the loop going.

Resources

- 15 Upselling Tips & Examples Proven to Boost Average Order: Value: https://optinmonster.com/upselling-tips-and-examples/
- 7 Best Examples of Upsells to Help You Maximize Your Sales: https://www.autogrow.co/best-upsell-examples/
- How To Boost Ecommerce Sales With Upselling: https://cxl.com/blog/upselling-techniques/

TACTIC 26
BOOK REVIEW AUTOMATION [BONUS I]

Description

As I wrote in Book Marketing Secrets, "Reviews are the lifeblood of books in the digital age." That is why this bonus tactic might be the most powerful of them all. Without reviews you will not be selling many books—maybe none!

And yet, anyone who has tried to promote their books online knows how hard it is to get reviews. Book sales largely depend on the quantity and quality of reviews, but most buyers just will not take the time to write one. They might if they got something in return—but unfortunately, Amazon forbids incentivizing reviews in its Terms of Service (ToS).

That is where Tactic 26 comes in with a nifty little workaround—one that is compliant with Amazon's rules. Here is the secret: instead of asking for a review, you ask customers for personal feedback by email. In exchange you offer a bonus, such as a free short story or a piece of advice. And when you give them the gift, you ask if they would be so kind as to copy-paste the feedback they have already written into a review post. Clever, right? It is easy for the customer—and perfectly within the bounds of the ToS.

Think of everything you accomplish by using this one simple tactic:

- You get feedback from readers on how to improve your work.

- You establish personal contact with your readers/ reviewers.
- You get to thank your engaged readers with a gift.
- You set up a sure-fire mechanism for getting reviews that doesn't violate Amazon's ToS.
- Most importantly, you get more book reviews!

And you do all of this without having to invest in another service or technology. All it takes is your email account and a ready gift that will make your most loyal readers happy. Try it. You will be amazed by the results.

If you are working with a bigger audience, I recommend setting up a dedicated email address (e.g., feedback@ author.com) and creating automated responses. Alternatively, send your readers to a landing page where they can submit their feedback and email address to receive the bonus. This has the added benefit of building an email list of your reviewers.

Examples of Success

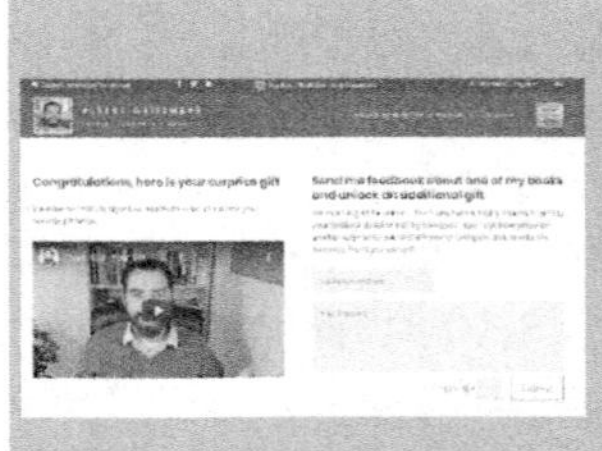

Example: Thank-You Gift on my own webpage at albertgriesmayr. com: https://www. albertgriesmayr.com/ thank-you

Application

- Prepare a bonus for readers who give you feedback on your book.

- Clearly communicate to your readers that there is a bonus for feedback available by including a "Call to Action" in your book's back or front matter. Add your contact details so readers can get in touch and take advantage of the offer.
- If you have a bigger audience than you can manage through personal communications, simplify the process by sending your readers to a landing page and setting up automated emails.
- Offer a variety of ways (besides Amazon reviews) for people to share publicly the feedback they sent you—they can post it on Audible, Goodreads, your website, or other forums.
- It is good to ask your readers for reviews, but don't push them. Remember, the personal feedback itself is already valuable! If you apply this tactic, be OK with not getting a post from everybody.

Resources

- How to get Book Reviews in 2020: https://www.slideshare.net/griesmayr/how-to-get-book-reviews-2020-edition

TACTIC 27
GETTING BOOK REVIEWS WITH PUBBY.CO [BONUS II]

Description

It is no secret that getting reviews is one of the most challenging activities for self-published authors. For new authors and authors who are not comfortable engaging with their network, promoting their books actively, or being physically located in the United States with a reliable system to tap, this can be especially challenging.

However, we all know that a book with zero reviews will likely make zero sales. So, for years, the focus was on investing in having book launch teams, engaging review generation services like Booksirens or Hiddengemsbooks, and compiling lists of power reviewers to contact.

Those activities often resulted in a good launch in which 5-10 reviews were gathered that helped the book to grow from that base. However, this process often turned out to be time-consuming and difficult.

In 2019, a new service emerged, called Pubby.co. Pubby helps authors get reviews by supporting other authors and earning snaps. Snaps are Pubby's currency that you can use to post your books and to get them reviewed by others.

The advantages of Pubby are as follows:

- You have full control of when and how often to get reviewed.

- You can support other authors and earn snaps to have your books read and reviewed by peers.
- You can get reviews for books within 5-10 days, making book launches or preparations for book promotions far easier.
- You save time and money by reducing efforts to contact book reviewers by email or via social media.

I tested Pubby extensively, and I have been part of publishing groups who have done the same. So, in today's market, it is safe to say that Pubby is a truly helpful service for getting book reviews. It might even be the secret weapon for book authors in 2020.

You can learn more about how Pubby works and get a 15% discount by clicking the following link: https://pubby.co/?invite=5101

Examples of Success

Example: Book Launch of Kids Activity Book "Get This Book Wet" | Getting review count to 5 in a matter of days.

In 2020, I published a kids activity book on Amazon, and solely relied on Pubby for getting the first reviews. It worked well, and within a matter of days I had 5 reviews, that allowed me to start Amazon ads and to look for further promotion opportunities. https://www.amazon.com/Get-This-Book-Wet-Experimenting/dp/B08CJNYJY8

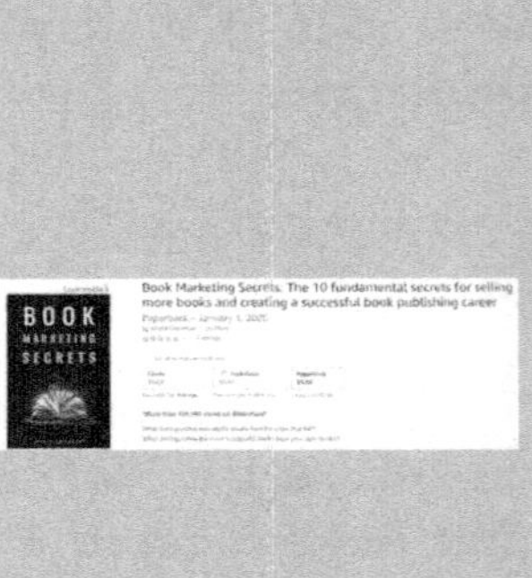

Example: Getting Reviews for Book Marketing Secrets [Backlist Book Project]

Earlier in 2020 I had published Book Marketing Secrets, but never really started promoting it on Amazon. The results were little sales and little reviews on Amazon. By posting the book, I quickly added a couple of reviews as well.

https://www.amazon.com/Book-Marketing-Secrets-fundamental-self-publishing-ebook/dp/B083CVHGV9

Application

- Start reviewing books on Amazon yourself and start earning snaps on Pubby.
- Launch a new book with the help of Pubby, and get your first 5 reviews quickly, when reviewing books of other authors and earning snaps.
- Use Pubby to grow review count for previously published books (both successful books and books that might need a new push).
- Prepare for the ultimate book launch, by earning lots of snaps before your book launches, to have lots of snaps to invest.
- Help fellow authors by sharing Pubby with them and helping them growing review count more quickly.

Resources

- Get Reviewers [Pubby.co] http://tarrantsmith.com/2020/02/11/get-reviewers/
- The new way to get book reviews: A look at 'Pubby' https://deviancepress.com/2019/05/21/the-new-way-to-get-book-reviews-a-look-at-pubby/
- Pubby Review [2020] – Video https://www.youtube.com/watch?v=cGyd-_F8AAw

TACTIC 28
USING LIBRARYBUB [BONUS III]

Description

2020 has been a year for libraries. When you look at the numbers [include them], 2020 has brought a big increase in readership for libraries. LibraryBub is a service that enables authors to reach all important libraries throughout the United States by one single email.

I have successfully used this with my own clients in 2020 so it is a fantastic tactic to choose. However, not all books are suitable. Make sure that you fulfill the following characteristics:

- It must be interesting for libraries.
- The book should have been on the market for some time.
- The book needs to have a strong level of credibility (especially in the form of reviews).
- It should be an established book that libraries can confidently offer to their patrons.

Examples of Success

***S.L. Morgan**, Best-selling, award-winning author*

To gain exposure like this, is what every self-published author dreams of! Having our books considered by libraries only expands our opportunities to reach new readers everywhere! LibraryBub's plan to reach them is an invaluable service and every author who is considering this service should jump on board without reservations! Thank you, LibraryBub! This service exceeded my expectations!

S.L Morgan reporting on Librarybub: Screenshot taken on 1/14/2021 from: http://librarybub.com/librarybub-authors-feature/

***Dina Colman**, Best-selling, award-winning author*

When the email was sent out to librarians, my book ("Four Quadrant Living: Making Healthy Living Your New Way of Life") had an 18% click rate. That's extraordinary in email marketing. My book received over 400 clicks, which means that hundreds of librarians were interested in my book. I thought it was a big win to get my book into my local library. I'm very excited about the possibility of my book being in even more libraries across the country. LibraryBub helped make this happen for me!

Dina Colman reporting on Librarybub, Screenshot taken on 1/14/2021 from: http://librarybub.com/librarybub-authors-feature/

Application

- LibraryBub encourages libraries to "join 10,000 happy libraries" since they work with all major libraries and are the industry's first service connecting indie and small press authors with libraries. http://librarybub.com/
- Authors can apply for a featured deal in LibraryBub's targeted weekly email that reaches over 10,000 librarians every week. http://librarybub.com/authors/

Resources

- Getting Your Book into Libraries by Eric Otis Simmons https://www.amazon.com/gp/product/1671459954
- How I Sold 80,000 Books: Book Marketing for Authors (Self-Publishing Through Amazon and Other Retailers) by Alinka Rutkowska https://www.amazon.com/HOW-SOLD-000-BOOKS-Publishing-ebook/dp/B00WWUR1O4
- Self-Publishers Toolkit: Includes Self-Publishing in the 2020s and Marketing Your Book to Libraries https://www.amazon.com/gp/product/B08C97TFXP
- Video Interview of Alinka Rutkowska, Founder of Library Bub and #1 bestselling author of more than 20 books https://www.topbusinessleaders.com/alinka-rutkowska-outsource-your-book/

TACTIC 29
USING PATREON [BONUS IV]

Description

Patreon is a platform where creative people can be found and supported. For authors, this is an excellent way to share book projects. The amazing thing is that you can build a monthly subscription system with basically zero technical skills. Patreon is focused on authors and creative projects in general.

Examples of Success

Zach Weinersmith
is creating SMBC Comics and Books

Example: Zack Weinersmith

Zach Weinersmith lists five different levels of giving in the amounts of $1, $3, $5, $10, and $100. Authors offer things like early access to their work. For instance, since Zach is also a comic illustrator, at the $5 and above level, Zach takes drawing requests in a half-hour live webcast. At the time of this writing, he has over 3200 supporters and is receiving over $6800 per month. That is impressive.

https://www.patreon.com/ZachWeinersmith

© Thumbnail/Screenshot, January 2021

Example: Nicolas Lietzau

Nicolas Lietzau named his different levels of support all with memorable names (that may have to do with the Enderal Trilogy he is requesting financial support to write): 1) Nefarious Nihilist ($2/month), 2) Cantankerous Cynic ($5/month), 3) Passionate Pragmatist ($10/month), 4) Hard-boiled Hedonist ($25/month), 5) Inebriated Idealist ($45/month), 6) Uncouth Utopist ($90/month), and 7) Vociferous Visionary ($250/month). At the highest level of support, Nicolas includes a personal call with him to discuss the novel, writing, or anything that comes to mind. This is a great offer for his fans. At this writing, he has over 125 supporters and receives over $1100 in support. Nicolas is a published author who is continuing to write fiction books.

https://www.patreon.com/niseam

© Thumbnail/Screenshot, January 2021

Application

- Describe in detail what it is you write about. Be creative. Remember, you are trying to motivate others to financially support you. It also helps to share a few personal details about yourself. For example, you could mention the name of your loyal pet companion and a short description about their personality and what it is they do while you write.
- Share a professional picture of yourself as well as any images (that you have permission to share) which are related to your writing project. This helps others connect to what you are doing.
- Think about your writing goals as well as the level of support you want and the level you would like to have. Decide how many giving levels you would like to offer and what you can include as a gift back to them.

Resources

- The Crowdfunding Guide for Authors and Writers by Judith Briles (Winner of the USA Best Book Award)
https://www.amazon.com/CrowdFunding-Guide-Authors-Writers/dp/1885331576
- The Poet and Writer's Complete Guide to Being A Writer: Everything You Need to Know About Craft, Inspiration, Agents, Editors, Publishing, and the Business of Building a Sustainable Writing Career by Kevin Larimer and Mary Gannon
https://www.amazon.com/Poets-Writers-Complete-Guide-Writer/dp/1982123079

TACTIC 30
BUILDING TRAFFIC, CREDIBILITY AND YOUR NETWORK THROUGH THE MAGIC 100 [BONUS V]

Description

Russell Brunson originally coined the term, "Dream 100". For Russell Brunson, the Dream 100 is coming up with a list of 100 influencers with whom you would love to collaborate. The idea is to carefully research influential bloggers, business owners, or anyone with a strong following or shared mindset. Then you should build a relationship with each of these 100 people so that you have access to them before you need it.

The concept is great, as it allows to jumpstart your audience and make powerful shortcuts to the top. In today's digital landscape, it does take a lot of time, to go from 0 to the top. Thus, it is much smarter using aggregators or influencers to build an audience and to attract attention quicker.

The concept of the MAGIC 100 is like Russell Brunson's Dream 100; however, it has one major tweak. It contains to not only look for people with an audience of influence, but you also look for channels, websites, and articles with existing traffic, where you potentially could be featured.

So, with the MAGIC 100, we are not only looking for influencers, but also popular sources on the web (such as Quora posts, blog articles, and Google snippets) that might provide an opportunity for us to be recommended.

Examples of Success

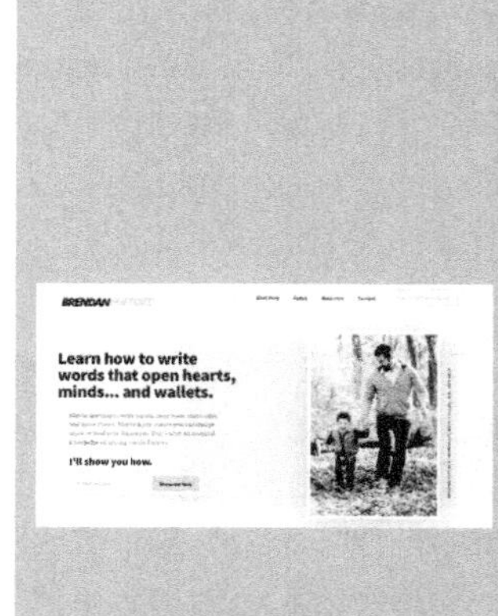

Example: Brendon Hufford

Brendon Hufford is an expert in SEO and states that Russell Brunson's Dream 100 have been pivotal, in building his business. Check out the video below, to learn about his experiences and applications for applying the Dream 100 (with a focus on link building, like suggested in the Magic 100).

https://youtu.be/MvhqG7gNs7Y

Example: Novelify | Albert Griesmayr

When re-launching Novelify in early 2021, I decided to build upon my previous contacts from my Magic 500, as well as adding new traffic targets with success

https://www.novelify.com

Application

- Research at least 50 influencers (within your niche) with whom you would love to work. Choose those who have a strong following and who would be a true gamer changer if they decide to support you.
- Research 50 channels and/or unique articles/videos/websites within your niche, that have strong existing traffic (e.g., come up at rank 1-3 for your main keywords via a Google search, have the most subscribers on YouTube, come up on top of a YouTube search, etc.). They might be blog articles, Wikipedia pages, social media sources, videos, etc.
- Reach out to the 50 influencers on one hand, and on the other hand, try to be featured on your 50 target sites.
- Focus on the long game. Seek to build a relationship with your Magic 100 first, before asking them for favors or bluntly promoting your content.

Resources

- The Dream 100 by Russell Brunson — Podcast https://marketingsecrets.com/the-dream-100-part-1-of-3/
- The Concept of the Dream 100 https://medium.com/@donaldlee50/the-concept-of-the-dream-100-af471e76afee
- Dream 100 — The Ultimate Tactic for Exploding Your Business https://brendanhufford.com/dream-100/
- The Ultimate White Hat Link Building Technique NOBODY Tells You — Video https://www.youtube.com/watch?v=MvhqG7gNs7Y

TACTIC 31
INCREASE BOOK RANKINGS WITH A CASHBACK CAMPAIGN [BONUS VI]

Description

Book launches can be doomed to fail without proper preparation. Failing to get into Amazon's SEO rankings can mean your work fades into obscurity very quickly.

This is why we suggest having a marketing tactic which gives you control over your initial book sales and grabs your readers' attention.

Cashback services is one of these tactics. Cashback services allow you to give potential readers a discount of your choice on your book, providing them an offer they can't possibly refuse.

Competition is getting fiercer and fiercer on Amazon and there are already quite a few examples of cashback services out there. Most of them do not apply to Kindle eBooks. Fortunately, we've managed to find one that does and which has proven itself to be successful: Massview by Snagshout.

Examples of Success

Example: The Love Hex [Book Launch]

The book launch of The Love Hex, was supported by a small Snagshout campaign, distributing 10 ebooks for free, making sure to get initial sales in the first couple of days.

https://www.snagshout.com/offers/the-love-hex-or-nicest-flings-in-mexico-eb/3b20220

© Thumbnail/Screenshot from snagshout.com, January 2021

Example: The Photographer's Field Guide [Ranking Campaign]

We needed the ebook for the Photographer's field guide to sell initially, in order to get results from an AMS ad campaign. By running a snagshout campaign, we helped Amazon to notice the book, and subsequently ads started to show up and produce results.

https://www.snagshout.com/offers/ebook-the-landscape-photographer-s-field/2be4be4

© Thumbnail/Screenshot from snagshout.com, January 2021

Application

- Firstly, support your book launch by setting it up on Massview, offer readers a discount or even offer your book for free.
- It is recommended to run this campaign on a month where your book is already discounted (e.g. its launch month)
- Some services offer to add custom URLs with rankings, do not choose this option though as it is against Amazon's TOS.
- Some services offer to ask purchasers for posting reviews later. This can be a very useful additional feature. Make sure that this process is not incentivized though, in order to comply with Amazon TOS.

Resources

- Myth Busters: Are Amazon Product Launch Websites Bad for FBA Sellers?
  https://www.junglescout.com/blog/amazon-product-launch-websites-bad-for-fba/
- Paul Johnson of Massview: Five Strategies I Used To Grow My Business To Reach Seven Figures In Revenue
  https://medium.com/authority-magazine/paul-johnson-of-massview-five-strategies-i-used-to-grow-my-business-to-reach-seven-figures-in-42df4b58aef2

TACTIC 32
USE GOOGLE PLAY BOOKS PROMO CODE CAMPAIGNS TO GENERATE BUZZ

Description

Google Play Books recently launched promo code campaigns, which can be used to offer select customers a discounted print book, ebook or audiobook without lowering the list price.

As an author or publisher offering books through Google Play Books, you can create up to 5,000 codes per campaign and up to 3 promo code campaigns per month.

Nate Hoffelder of the Digital Reader described this new feature and a "good development" and "another reason to set up an author/publisher account in their bookstore."

Google Books recently updated their terms of service and have increased their royalty split to 70% in 60+ countries from 52%, showing that they are serious players in the publishing game.

Recommendations

Recommendation: How To Sell Books In 2020

PublishDrive highly recommends using Google Play Books in 2020 going into 2021 with this very informative video.

https://www.youtube.com/watch?v=2rT0GyrgY3w

Recommendation: Google Play Books, Is It Worth It?

In this video by Self Publishing With Dale, he covers Google Play Books and the benefits of choosing it over rival services such as Amazon Publishing or Kobo books.

https://www.youtube.com/watch?v=HXQMra_qwbo&ab_channel=Self-PublishingwithDale

Application

- Firstly, sign up to Google Books if you haven't done so already. Click here to do so
- Upload titles and start a promo code campaign.
- Choose which discount you would like to offer readers: Offer your book for FREE, for a DISCOUNTED PERCENTAGE or a DISCOUNTED FIXED PRICE.
- You can use up to 5,000 promo codes and up to 3 campaigns per month.

Resources

- The Digital Reader: Google Play Books now pays a 70% Royalty in 60+ Countries. https://the-digital-reader.com/2020/10/13/google-play-books-now-pays-a-70-royalty-in-60-countries/
- Google Play Books Unveils Promo Code Campaigns. https://goodereader.com/blog/digital-publishing/google-play-books-unveils-promo-code-campaigns

4

CHEATSHEET

BOOK SALES EXPLOSION CHEATSHEET

DISCOVER ALL 32 BOOK MARKETING TACTICS AT A GLANCE

1) BOOK SALES FUNNELS
2) LOOK INSIDE BONUS
3) FREE PRINT BOOK
4) ALEXA SKILLS
5) AFFILIATE MARKETING
6) NEW FORMATS & TRANSL.
7) KICKSTARTER FUNDING
8) CIALDINIFY YOUR BOOK
9) PERMAFREE EBOOK
10) MATCHING COVERS
11) IRRESISTIBLE BONUSES
12) PRE-ORDER TACTIC
13) AMAZON BESTSELLER
14) PINTEREST TRAFFIC
15) EMAIL MARKETING
16) COLLABORATION
17) VIDEO MARKETING
18) AMAZON SELECT +
19) AUTHORITY PUBLISHING
20) SIMPLE AMAZON SEO
21) AMAZON AMS ADS
22) AUDIOBOOK CREATION
23) RETARGETING
24) KOBO PUBLISHING
25) UPSELL PRODUCTS
26) BOOK REVIEW AUTOM.
27) REVIEWS VIA PUBBY
28) USING LIBRARYBUB
29) USING PATREON
30) THE MAGIC 100
31) CASHBACK CAMPAIGNS
32) GOOGLE PLAY

www.albertgriesmayr.com

5

EPILOGUE
LOOKING BEYOND 2020

"The biggest room in the world is the room for improvement."
Harvey Mackay

Dear Writer,

I want to finish this book with a quote by one of my former clients, 7-time New York Times bestselling author Harvey Mackay. He hit the nail on the head when he said, "The biggest room in the world is the room for improvement." This quote became one of his most memorable and has been re-shared by thousands of people around the world.[6]

I absolutely love this quote because it always reminds me of the road ahead. Even good products should never be seen as completely finished; otherwise, they'll become obsolete faster than you can blink.

6 Source: Google the quote and you get tens of thousands of search results. Some sources also cite German statesman Helmut Schmidt as the original source, others share the quote with source anonymous.

That is why I will certainly be updating this book over time and creating new editions if better tactics and strategies emerge.[7] Furthermore, I recommend you do the same with your own books.

Do not see them as finished, but keep on improving, make them masterpieces, and all your marketing efforts will be easier as well.

I truly hope that this book was of high value to you and that you have learned tactics you'll be able to apply in your marketing—and more importantly, that these tactics will help you multiply your book sales.

In case you haven't taken a look at Scribando (www.scribando.com) yet, I highly recommend doing so. My service will help you stay not only up to date on what is happening in the market but also informed about the latest success strategies for how to sell books.

In the end, to hit the jackpot as an author, you need to master both areas: timeless book marketing knowledge + the latest success strategies. With this book + Scribando, you have the perfect knowledge setup for selling lots of books.

I also invite you to look at the surprise gift that I have prepared for you. It will also help you grow your career as an author. In addition, when you sign up on my webpage, you will be in touch with me and will not miss any new releases or book marketing insights.

---

7 If you know of a book promotion tactic that should be in this book, don't be shy! Reach out to me. I'll certainly reward contributions that find their way into updated book editions.

CLAIM YOUR SURPRISE GIFT

Thanks for purchasing this book. To express my appreciation, I've prepared a special gift for you that will help you sell more books. Access it by visiting www.albertgriesmayr.com/thank-you.

As a writer, you'll also gain insight into how important it is to get reviews. I like to say that "reviews are the lifeblood of books in the digital age."

That's why I would also be super happy to receive a review of this book from you.

HOW DID YOU LIKE THIS BOOK?
LEAVE A REVIEW

I would love to hear your thoughts on your journey through this book. I always value and appreciate your feedback.
Leve a review for this book on Amazon:
https://www.amazon.com/review/create-review?asin=B087KWKL7K

THANK YOU!

Finally, let me close this book by sharing one last insight with you that has been quite valuable to me in recent years. It comes from the German saying "Der stete Tropfen höhlt den Stein," which means "Constant dripping wears the stone."

When I started following this simple principle and applying it to my business in various areas, my performance began to improve significantly. It is important to be involved in something for the long run, to put continuous and concentrated effort into fewer things and to create routines and realistic plans for achieving what is profoundly important to you.

That is a core principle that I follow and apply in my own business, and I am sure that if you apply it, you will improve your results as well. You do not always need to create new books, new projects, offers, or features. Nor do you need to change careers or whole businesses to become—and stay—successful.

Instead, focus on what you already have, polish it, and develop it until it shines like a diamond—a product that you are proud of and that your customers will want to have.

Writing this book was a pleasure to me, because I did what I love to do: share my knowledge on book marketing with you. With that, I wish you all the best in your publishing career.

Best Wishes,

Albert Griesmayr
Vienna, January 1, 2021

FINAL WORDS [ONE FOCUS]

Dear author,

First of all, congratulations for reading SELF PUBLISHING BLUEPRINTS. You are now equipped with proven knowledge on how to market books successfully. I've acquired this knowledge through working personally for almost a decade with more than a hundred authors and publishers, with the result that they've achieved more than two million copies sold worldwide, and I'm delighted to share the secrets with you!

In this final chapter I want to answer one important question: What do you do when things go wrong? What do you do when, even after you've gained all this knowledge and done your best, you haven't quite reached success?

It's time to introduce you to a concept I've developed over the last few years. The concept is called: ONE FOCUS.

ONE FOCUS is all about reducing all distractions, unnecessaries, and side projects to a minimum, and instead truly focusing on one thing over a sustained period of time. The focus might be on a book, a concept, an activity, a skill, a product, or a business.

ONE FOCUS is based on the understanding that if you do something for a very long time – and I mean years or even decades – with the right knowledge, passion, and skillset, the probability for going the distance is high, and much higher than what people usually believe.

This is especially true today, when there are so many opportunities out there and so many distractions at the same time. We can easily jump from project to project, from opportunity to opportunity, from technique to technique, without sticking to one activity long enough to truly master it.

I want to invite you to resist the urge to jump to the next thing when something goes wrong. Instead, stick to what you believe in. Improve over time. Make your effort into something valuable. From my experience, people who follow through are usually more successful than those who just jump to the next thing.

But let me be more specific. Let me guide you through the process.

Let's assume for a moment that your book did not hit its sales target for the first year. You sit down at your desk and ask yourself what to do next. Most importantly, you will ask yourself the following questions:

Has something fundamental changed in regards to your goals? Has your passion faded? Do you really still believe in your current book? Are your publishing goals still important to you? Did your priorities change?

If some of your answers are YES, then this is perfectly fine. You can accept that and move on. It's not wise to stick with something that you just don't believe in anymore, or something for which the market has disappeared.

However, if you answer NO, and you still have no idea how to make it work, it's no time to quit. Instead, it's time to keep going, time to dive deeper, time to create a gameplan. Come back to the trilogy at a later date, especially Bestseller, and go through the exercises again. Update your answers and use them to construct your gameplan for getting to the next level. In my experience, this approach is much more promising than starting from scratch with something else.

Focus on that one thing for a long period of time, until you excel in it. That's what the concept of "ONE FOCUS" is about.

Cut out distractions, don't jump to new projects, say no to fresh opportunities, and be married to your current project.

In my professional career, applying the ONE FOCUS method has certainly paid off. When I was fresh out of university, I found myself caught up in the extremes of entrepreneurial drive, afflicted with Shiny Object Syndrome. I started about ten different business projects in less than two years. I hired a developer, sketched out prototypes, registered domains, and flung alpha versions into the ether.

Not surprisingly, the projects failed. Not because the ideas or prototypes were nonsense, but because of a lack of focus and persistence. Excellent execution is hard, but it's necessary for winning in today's market. And this is absolutely true for books.

It took me a couple of years to realize that, though most of my ideas had brilliance in them, I would have to focus on a single idea at a time, ignoring the others, if I wanted to find success.

And it took me many more years to finally put my epiphany to work and to say NO to new opportunities. I committed to my company Scribando | Novelify and to my work in book marketing with authors and publishers. I have found my niche at last, and I'm not planning to change it. Rather, my approach is to hone what I do, to improve my company, to work on my platforms and products, ideally reducing them further into the simplest and most promising directives. The same is true of the books I write. I'm done with writing in the field of book marketing, since I have completed the title I've been working towards, Self-Publishing Blueprints. Now, my aim is to improve the trilogy over time, and to add to its excellence. I want it to be the best book on successful publishing of all time.

Less is more, simplicity is beauty, ONE FOCUS is all you need.

Don't stop, focus on what you believe in, and make your book the best book in the world.

All the best for your publishing career,

Albert Griesmayr
Vienna, August, 25 2021

BONUS MATERIAL

BOOK REVIEWS ON AUTOPILOT: THE SURPRISE GIFT SYSTEM

Core activity: **Include a "surprise reveal" of bonus material available via your website to drive traffic and increase value and engagement. Make sure to include the link!**

ON YOUR WEBSITE, CREATE AN EMAIL SIGNUP FOR ACCESSING THE SURPRISE GIFT.

After email signup, readers get the "digital surprise gift," such as a bonus ebook, a video message from you, etc.

IMPORTANT: MAKE SURE TO ASK FOR FEEDBACK! ONCE YOU'VE RECEIVED THAT, FOLLOW UP WITH A POLITE REQUEST FOR A REVIEW. (BOTH VIA WEBSITE AND IN AUTOMATED EMAIL SEQUENCES.)

Your advantages:
-> growing an email list of your readers
-> without being salesy or pushy
-> learning from feedback and pre-qualifying reviews

SEE THE SYSTEM IN ACTION: BROWSE THIS BOOK AND VISIT: HTTPS://ALBERTGRIESMAYR.COM/THANK-YOU

Download: https://bit.ly/3yk0BRo

SEO FOR BOOKS ON STEROIDS

Core insight: Modern Amazon SEO focuses on conversion rates and customer satisfaction.

VISIT YOUR AMAZON BOOK SALES PAGE AND CHECK THE FOLLOWING:

- ☐ Main keywords (1-3) used throughout the title, description, A+content and editorial reviews
- ☐ Up to 10 relevant book categories submitted to Amazon via Author Central
- ☐ Author profile optimized: Good Author Image, Bio with lots of credibility
- ☐ Bestseller Status, Awards and Accolades Received in Bio, Description, A+ Content
- ☐ Ratings Count: At least 25+, better 100+ Average Score: At least 4+ better 4.5+
- ☐ Irresistible Book Offer Communicated and Cialdini Principles (Scarcity, Liking, etc.) applied

SEE GOOD CONVERSION IN ACTION: VISIT THIS BOOK ON AMAZON: HTTPS://WWW.AMAZON.COM/GP/PRODUCT/B09927CR71

Download: https://bit.ly/3BedcY5

GET YOUR BOOK TO # 1

THE IRRESISTIBLE BOOK OFFER FORMULA AND CHECKLIST

THE IRRESISTIBLE BOOK OFFER FORMULA AND CHECKLIST

1) CREATE A FANTASTIC BOOK

- [ ] great manuscript
- [ ] great layout
- [ ] great cover
- [ ] great author profile
- [ ] great title/subtitle
- [ ] great reviews/ratings
- [ ] great description
- [ ] product/market fit

2) BASED ON TRUE DEMAND

- [ ] clarity on main search term(s)
- [ ] clarity on USP and problem solved
- [ ] existing traffic + obtainable share for search term(s)

3) SUPPORTED BY A FANTASTIC OFFER PACKAGE

- [ ] USP, selling points and bonuses communicated
- [ ] Cialdini Principles applied (eg. scarcity, social proof,,.)
- [ ] Built-In Virality Applied (eg. collaborative elements)
- [ ] Reviews, Awards, Bestseller status communicated

Download: https://bit.ly/3sNW2NQ

HOW DID YOU LIKE THIS BOOK?

As an author, you know that reviews are the lifeblood of books in the digital age. That's why I would be extremely appreciative if you'd send me your feedback to **hello@scribando.com** and/or share a rating or post a written review of this book online on Amazon, my website, and/or any other retailer. Let me – and other readers – know what you learned from the book, what was especially useful, and what you would like to see improved.

I highly appreciate your feedback. Thank you!

-Albert

Printed in Great Britain
by Amazon

65885368R00254